Acquaintances

Acquaintances

ARNOLD J. TOYNBEE

London
OXFORD UNIVERSITY PRESS
NEW YORK   TORONTO
1967

PRINTED IN THE UNITED STATES OF AMERICA

Preface

THE sketches of acquaintances of mine that are included in this book are, of course, only a selection. I have picked out, for publication, recollections of personalities that seemed to me as if they might be of some general interest. The degree of interestingness will be different in different cases; but I have aimed at excluding recollections that have significance and value for me alone. On the other hand, I have also deliberately excluded some recollections that would, I believe, be of no less general interest than those that appear in the present selection.

My reason for not dealing with these excluded topics is that I have felt that I could not deal with them consistently with *pietas*. This expressive Latin word has no concise equivalent in English; but the feeling which the Latin word denotes is one of which most human beings are aware. In most people's experience there are persons whom they love or revere too much for them to be willing to risk wounding those persons, if they are still alive, or to risk calling their reputation in question if they are already dead. We therefore forbear from publishing our recollections of such persons, and this not only for their sake but for our own sake too. We know that, if we were to stifle our compunction and were to violate this self-imposed tabu, we should feel remorse. This feeling has been my touchstone in deciding what to put into this book and what to leave out of it. All the people dealt with in the book, except for one or two whom I have mentioned incidentally, are now dead, and I have aimed at publishing nothing about the dead that might have wounded them if they had been still alive or that might still wound living people who loved or revered these dead friends of theirs and mine in their lifetime and who cherish the memory of them. My relations with the dead people about whom

I have written in this book were of different degrees of intimacy, ranging from mere acquaintance to close friendship. What is common to them all is that it has seemed to me possible, without offence, to give an account of them that is true in itself and is also of some general interest. I have also been acquainted with other personalities who are not less interesting but who could not, without offence, have been dealt with by me at all, or at least could not without my having to avoid mentioning so many things that were characteristic and important that the resulting account would have been incomplete to the point of being perhaps misleading. These are the acquaintances that I have deliberately refrained from including in the series of sketches in this book.

October 1966   Arnold Toynbee

Contents

Illustrations

Plates 9(a) and (b) and the drawing of Barbara Hammond are reproduced by courtesy of Miss L. Chitty, plate 12 by courtesy of Professor Agnes Headlam-Morley, and plates 8, 10, 11 by courtesy of the Radio Times Hulton Picture Library.

Acquaintances

I

Uncle Harry

I WAS standing by Uncle Harry's long cane chair, and he was telling me that we were not brought into the world in order to be happy. Though this is now seventy-four years ago, I remember my reaction clearly. 'I am not disputing it, but I am only three; it is rather early to have been told.' This was my silent comment (I prudently kept it to myself), though, of course, I did not put it to myself in those grown-up words.

My memory of the cane chair is clear too. It looked rakish, for each of its arms had a cavity in it that could have held a very long tumbler; but its looks were incongruous with its owner. Uncle Harry was an evangelical teetotaller, non-smoker, and non-swearer, in spite of his having been the master of an Eastindiaman before he retired from the sea.

At the time when he told me that we were not brought into the world in order to be happy, he was four years younger than I am now. He was born in 1819, and I was born in 1889. (I suppose I could make myself look, and feel, as old as he did then if I were to dress the part by growing a white beard and putting a black skull-cap on my head and a black woollen shawl round my shoulders.)

Born in 1819, Uncle Harry died in 1909, so he managed to live just short of ninety years without being involved in either Waterloo or the First World War. The century that his life so nearly spanned saw the face of Britain transformed by immense economic and social changes; but, for Britain, this was a century of external peace; and, though, for 'the working class', both agricultural and industrial, it was an age of insecurity and tribulation, for anyone who could clamber up into the middle-class minority it was a century of certitude and affluence.

Uncle Harry's father, my great-grandfather, farmed a six-hundred-acre farm between Swineshead (Sven's hide ?) and Heckington, within sight of 'Boston Stump', the gracefully tapering tower of St. Botolph's church that can be seen for miles across the Lincolnshire fens. The 'Stump' stands up dark against the summer sunset if you are looking at it from the Norfolk coast of the Wash. George Toynbee's farm was large—as it needed to be, since he had fifteen children by two marriages, and only one of them died in infancy. Uncle Harry was the seventh and youngest child and my grandfather the fourth in the first family. The first family and their descendants have produced brains, but have not made much money, though they were given just as good a start by farmer George as the second family, which did make money and, no doubt, has good brains as well.

Their father started them all off by turning one of his barns into a schoolroom and hiring a schoolmaster to teach them. They used to shoot at their schoolmaster with arrows humanely tipped with willow-wood—humanely, because willow is comparatively soft. (Uncle Harry whittled a set for me once, one summer holiday; my mother was slightly alarmed.) Some of the boys went on to a boarding-school in King's Lynn ('Beloe's Bulldogs'). Farmer George must have made enough money during the Napoleonic Wars to give all his fourteen children who grew up a chance of entering the liberal professions, and only two sons and one daughter, out of the fourteen, stayed on the land—and one of these not in England but in Jamaica. The daughter who became a farmer's wife, Aunt Burbidge (her Christian name was Ann; Uncle Harry used often to reel off the fourteen names to me), used, every Christmas, to send Uncle Harry two golden guineas sewn up in a piece of red flannel. I remember the excitement of watching the coins being extricated.

Uncle Harry himself went to sea. My grandfather became a doctor in London. My grandfather was the first to specialize there in ears and throat, and also the first to charge two guineas, instead of one guinea, for a consultation. His consulting room was in Savile Row (now occupied, not by doctors, but by tailors). He lived in a house called Beech Holme on Wimbledon Parkside, and he used to come home by underground as far as Putney station, at the foot of the hill. Here his children (there were nine of them) used to meet him on horseback, with a groom leading a horse for him to mount; and then they would all ride up home together. Apart from his special practice, my grandfather was a pioneer in public health and in anaesthetics. In experimenting on himself with anaesthetics (then in an early experimental stage) he killed himself accidentally. I have said that my great-grandfather's first family did not make much money. Yet my grandfather, in a prematurely terminated professional career, made enough money for his nine children or their widows to receive £200 a year each after my grandmother's death; and £200 a year, before 1914, was the equivalent of something more like £2,000 a year in 1966 values.

Like my grandfather Joseph Toynbee, my other grandfather, Edwin Marshall, paid for being a pioneer by having his life prematurely cut short. He was a manufacturer of railway rolling-stock in Birmingham, and his business was financed by cousins of his who had set up as bankers on capital which their forebears had accumulated as iron-founders. One day, my grandfather announced to his banker-cousins that he had decided to use iron henceforth, instead of wood, as his material for building his vehicles. One might have expected this forward-looking design to have commended itself to bankers whose family had once been in the iron-founding business. So far from that, they jumped to the conclusion that my grandfather had gone out of his mind. Falling into a panic, they withdrew their capital from my grandfather's business, and thereby ruined him. Worry can be as lethal as gas, and my grandfather died of his undeserved disaster. He had paid a grievous penalty for having been before his time; but the purchasers of his derelict business—which, no doubt, they bought up cheap—were able, eventually, to profit by the foresight that had been fatal for him.

When, as my train reaches the outskirts of Birmingham, my eye catches the title 'Marshall and Co., Railway Rolling-Stock

Builders', placarded on an imposing range of factory buildings, my thoughts start running on the difference that it might have made to my sisters' lives and my life if our two grandfathers had each lived his own life out to its normal term. Between them, our grandfathers might have left enough money to endow their grandchildren with ample unearned incomes. This is a fate from which we have been saved at our grandfathers' cost. Human nature, even when it has a natural bent towards some art or craft, is usually disinclined to exert itself if it knows that it has been endowed with the means for living comfortably without effort. Among my school-fellows, I can think of only one, Sir John Stainton, who started life well-to-do yet, nevertheless, showed the strength of character to put himself to work for conscience sake, as strenuously as if necessity had been driving him. (John Stainton was called to the Bar, and, from his practice there, he went on to become a parliamentary draftsman, which is also a most exacting occupation.) Both conscience and ambition are capable of serving as alternative spurs; but, to be effective for this, they must be raised to a high power, and this is rare. For most of us, the prick of necessity is an indispensable stimulus.

Among my farmer great-grandfather's children, perhaps the ablest in the first family was the eldest, George, who went in 1833 from the fen-farm to the University of Bonn (reorganized by the Prussian Government after the peace-settlement of 1815). George Toynbee afterwards settled in London and became, so my Aunt Gertrude was told, a contributor to the *Westminster Gazette*. He would, I guess, have made his name as a writer if he had not died at the age of twenty-nine—a year younger than his also short-lived nephew Arnold.

Another brother became a missionary in India, another became a lawyer in Lincoln, another became a horse-dealer there. During one summer holiday in Norfolk when I was a child, we made a tourist trip to Sandringham, and I remember, in the stables, being startled by a brass plate with 'Toynbee' engraved on it. Edward VII must have bought that horse from my horse-dealer great-uncle or his successors, and have called the horse by the dealer's name because the name had struck him as being quaint. It would look less odd if, instead of being spelled like Ashbee, it were spelled like Ashby, Whitby, Selby, and dozens of other East-English place-names ending in 'by'. In Danish, 'by' means 'place', while 'toyn' looks as if it were the equivalent of 'tuin', which means 'garden' in Dutch. Since a garden is an enclosure (is in fact a 'tun', 'town', or 'zaun'), my surname might mean 'a fortified village'. (The earliest Toynbees whom my sister Margaret Toynbee has traced lived at Coleby and Waddington, not in the fens but on the wolds.) In Lincolnshire there are at least five villages called Toynton, in two clusters, to the east and south-east of Horncastle. To the south of Horncastle there is a Tumby, and this must have been the place from which my forebears took their name.

In the fens, when Uncle Harry was a child, everyone carried a leaping-pole in his hand for crossing the dykes. Yet, though, by that time, the fens had been pretty well drained, the fen-people were still being afflicted by quartern ague (i.e. malaria). Though, from the age of about fourteen onwards, Uncle Harry spent his working life far from the fens, first at sea and then in the Meteorological Office in London, he remained a fenman at heart. On summer holidays he was always on the look-out for flowering rush, and he was overjoyed when he found it.

Living under the same roof with Uncle Harry, as I did, I did not get away with being told, once for all, that we were not brought into the world in order to be happy. Later on, I was once made painfully unhappy, by Uncle Harry himself, over a mishap that had overtaken his chronometers. As a navigator, he had been famous for the accuracy of his reckonings and observations; and he had brought his chronometers on shore with him when he had retired from the sea to join the staff of the newly-founded Meteorological Office. Naturally he prized these delicate instruments, and he kept them on the top of a chest-of-drawers in his bedroom. One day they were knocked over, and he insisted that I was the culprit. I was not, but my parents could not persuade him of my innocence, till eventually they convicted the cat. I do not know what their evidence was. Perhaps they found tell-tale paw-marks. Anyway, the evidence was so cogent that

Uncle Harry had to accept it; but he found a way out of admitting that he had been in the wrong. A child, he said, could not learn too early in life that it would often be accused unjustly.

In treating a child severely, Uncle Harry was doing as he had been done by in his own childhood. He was severe with a good conscience, because he was convinced that severe treatment had been the making of him, and that it was therefore his bounden duty to see to it that the latest generation should be not less well brought up.

He used to drive this point home for me by telling me the story of an early experience of his own. In his childhood on the farm, he was sitting, one day, reading a book, when his father came in and gave him an errand. Harry thought he would go on reading to the end of the sentence before obeying, but he had not reached the next full stop before his father brought down his stick on beguiling book and delinquent hand. The farmer struck with such force that the stick drove right through the book and cut open the child's hand that was holding it. Farmer George was a just man, so he paid for a new copy of the ruined book; only the hand, not the book, had been the offender; and the wounded hand could not be made good so quickly. The combination of instant severity with scrupulous justice produced its intended effect on the victim's imagination. This early lesson stayed with Uncle Harry for the rest of his long life. Instant obedience, or else . . . . When Uncle Harry became master of a ship, he practised his father's lesson on his crews before practising it on me.

He used to reinforce the story of the cut-open hand by a story of a bitten-off ear which was more sensational, but was not first-hand. A young man, condemned to death for a capital offence, asked permission for his mother to visit him in prison before he went to the gallows. When she entered the cell, he said that he had a secret to tell her, and, putting his mouth to her ear, he bit the ear off. At this, even the hard-boiled warders were shocked. 'First you murder a man, and now you bite off your poor mother's ear. What possessed you to do that?' 'Can't you see?' was the answer. 'Why, it is all my mother's fault that I am now a convicted murderer under sentence of death. When I was a child, she never taught me to obey. She did not do her duty by me; and this is what she has brought me to. Having her ear bitten off is a light punishment for having done her son to death.'

Uncle Harry missed a passage on the *Mayflower* besides missing the Battle of Waterloo. If he had been alive at the time, he would surely have been on board, but he would just as surely have been disappointed in the theological tenets of his fellow-pilgrims. After entering into theological discussions with them, he would almost certainly have found them culpably contaminated with the leaven of Archbishop Laud. This is probable because, on summer holidays, Uncle Harry would always call on the local clergyman (Uncle Harry was an Anglican himself); would always force him into a theological discussion; and would always quarrel with him eventually, in spite of the clergyman's desperate efforts to avoid controversy and to keep the peace. One of the merits of the Church of England is its capacity for accommodating a wide range of altitudes; but Uncle Harry's low-churchness was at rock-bottom, and there was only one Anglican church in all London whose parson's position was low enough to satisfy him. This was the Lock Hospital chapel. Uncle Harry was anxious to take me there on Sundays for my good, and he did once succeed, though my parents usually parried these pressing invitations. If I am right, the Lock Hospital was one for venereal disease, and the patients were locked in, to prevent the spread of infection. I do not know for certain whether this is really what the Lock Hospital was, for, even at the tail-end of the Victorian Age, such subjects were mentioned only by circumlocution. My guess is founded on my parents' evident embarrassment. Uncle Harry was not embarrassed. The Lock Hospital chapel's theology was uniquely satisfactory from his point of view, and this was what mattered.

Uncle Harry was a militant anti-papist. His hero was Mr. Kensit—a martyr in Uncle Harry's eyes, since, like Pyrrhus in Argos, Mr. Kensit in Liverpool had been killed, in street fighting, by an improvised missile. Uncle Harry had a seal that was fascinating for a child. One way up it showed the Pope's head; the other way up it showed the Devil's.

Uncle Harry had an invincible proof that the Pope was Antichrist. He was a member of the Trinity Brotherhood, the fraternity that looks, or used to look, after lighthouses in the British Isles. As a Trinity Brother, it had once fallen to him to inspect lighthouses in Ireland, and one day he had found himself crossing an estuary in a ferry-boat with a Catholic priest as his fellow-passenger. The priest was reading his office with a shot-gun across his knees. Suddenly he dropped his breviary, snatched up his gun, shot a bird that was flying overhead, collected it, and then started reading his office again. Uncle Harry had taken note, with a fearful joy, of this Catholic wickedness running so incriminatingly true to type; and, when they reached the jetty, he had found fishermen there, presumably Catholics too, cutting fish up alive for bait. Together, the two incidents gave him his take-off into the stratosphere. What further proof was needed? The Pope was convicted of being Antichrist without question.

Such proofs were retailed by Uncle Harry frequently and circumstantially at meal-times. My parents were Protestants too; but they were not fanatics; and, as far as they could without flagrant disloyalty to Uncle Harry, they used to warn me to take his anti-Catholic tirades *cum grano salis*. Uncle Harry, like the notorious Byzantine Greek grandee in the last days of Orthodox Christian Constantinople, preferred the Prophet's turban to the Cardinal's hat. For my parents, this was too much. I eventually solved the problem for myself by learning to feel kindly towards both Roman Catholicism and Islam.

My parents' dislike of intolerance was, I should say, characteristic of the attitude of a majority of the English people, at any rate since our experience of our civil war and its sequel. The moderate-minded majority's policy had been to export as many as possible of the fanatics in their midst to the plantations in North America. If they had succeeded in exporting rather more of them rather earlier, perhaps England might have escaped her seventeenth-century civil war; and, if America had received rather fewer of them, perhaps she might have escaped her nineteenth-century civil war. As it turned out, there were enough of them in each country at the time to generate a civil war; and, of

1   The author already at work on a book

2 Captain Henry Toynbee ('Uncle Harry'), as the author knew him

course, in both civil wars, there were fanatics on either side. It takes that to divide a house against itself.

Religion was not the only subject on which Uncle Harry displayed prejudice. One of his entertaining tall stories (he had an apparently inexhaustible store of these) was that the bows of American ships were so bluff that one could only conclude that the American shipwrights' technique was to build a long continuous stick of ship and then chop the completed stick, crosswise, into so many ship's-length sections. Now, just at the time when Uncle Harry was at sea, the shipwrights of Baltimore and New England had been designing a new build of full-rigged ship —the clipper—which surpassed all previous builds in the gracefulness of its lines and consequently also in the speed with which it could cut its way through the water. Was Uncle Harry's bluff-bowed American ship the clumsy predecessor of the elegant clipper? Had the clipper been designed in a revulsion against the antecedent American type? Or was the bluff-bowed American ship a myth? Was it a British response, in the realm of make-believe, to a challenge that was defeating British shipwrights in real life? Had the slicing technique story been thought up by British seamen as balm for their chagrin at finding their own ships outpaced by a new American type which they could not emulate? I suspect that the second of these two alternative hypotheses may be the one that hits the truth. I do not know, but I expect Admiral Samuel Eliot Morison could tell us.[1]

The evangelical ship's captain was perhaps a rarity, but he was not a novelty in Uncle Harry's day. Before the abolition of the slave-trade, there had been evangelical captains of slavers. (One of these, John Newton, had taken Anglican orders after his retirement, and had then impinged on the poet Cowper's life.) However, the type was still rare enough to cause surprise when encountered; and Uncle Harry used to tell with gusto the comment of a lady who had brought her child on board, to place it in

---

[1] Admiral Morison has now given the answer in a letter to me of 12 February 1966. 'Your great-uncle's joke is recognizable as a form of the joke of American merchant mariners about whaling ships: "Built by the mile and cut off in lengths to suit." They really were chunky and bluff-bowed—they had to be; but the merchant vessels, even before the clippers, had very graceful lines.'

the captain's care, when his ship was just going to sail from Calcutta. When the lady came on board, Uncle Harry was busy, giving a spate of orders for getting under weigh. As soon as he had finished, he walked over to the lady and introduced himself. 'What, you the captain?' she exclaimed. 'Why, I have been listening to you for a quarter of an hour and I haven't heard you swear once.' Uncle Harry was justly proud of this testimonial.

Being puritanical was, of course, compatible with being authoritarian. Uncle Harry used to boast that his crew had voluntarily attended even the second of the two Sunday services that he regularly held on board. When he repeated this boast, one asked him, if one was sly, what he did to a sailor who took the liberty of absenting himself. 'Why, I put him in irons,' he would reply. He remained convinced that the attendance had always been voluntary.

After retirement from the sea, Uncle Harry could no longer resort to coercion; so, if he caught a boy smoking in the street, he would stop him and ask him what a penny a day added up to in a year. If the boy could not do the sum, Uncle Harry would do it for him, in the fond hope that, in default of irons, a latent thriftiness would henceforth deter the boy from vice.

There had been one occasion at sea on which Uncle Harry had shown humour as well as resourcefulness. Passengers and officers were boxed up together at close quarters on a voyage from Sydney to London that might last for three months; so a single tartar could be a torment to the whole company. On one voyage there was a lady-passenger who was a shrew, and everyone had been suffering from her tantrums. At the height of one of these, the lady rushed towards the gunwale, shrieking 'I am going to throw myself overboard.' There was a moment of general consternation, but Uncle Harry (by now second mate) did not lose his head. From the quarter-deck he shouted 'Let her go.' This stopped her dead, as he had reckoned that it would. For the rest of the voyage, she behaved rather less outrageously.

Captain Henry Toynbee was a first-rate weather-forecaster and navigator. My sisters and I have inherited, between us, a massive set of Victorian silver—tea-pot, coffee-pot, milk-jug, sugar-basin. On the coffee-pot there are engraved the names of the donors: officers in the King's and the Company's armies, and Company civil servants. These passengers of Uncle Harry's had been on their way from England to India, but, at the southern approaches to Madras, Uncle Harry, in clear weather, had scented a cyclone ahead and had hove-to till this had passed. The passengers, who had chafed at the delay, changed their minds when they learnt what had happened to other ships whose captains had not been so weather-wise as Uncle Harry. The silver service is a memorial of the salvaged passengers' gratitude. The navigational feat of which Uncle Harry was the most proud was his success in saving his ship from being driven by a gale on to the French coast in the very last lap of a voyage back to England from India. In telling this story, Uncle Harry used to declare that the gale was so violent that it blew the brass buttons off his pea-jacket.

Uncle Harry went to sea at the age of fourteen, and retired early, in 1866 (a century ago today), to take up a post on shore in the newly-established Meteorological Office. His second voyage was in a barque; but, except for that, he never sailed in anything but a full-rigged ship. His last command was the Eastindiaman *Hotspur*. He never boarded a steamer except as a passenger. His life was thus bound up with the classical sailing-ship that had been invented by the Portuguese in the fifteenth century and, since then, had given the Western peoples the dominion over all the navigable waters of the globe.

In 1892 and 1893 we spent our summer-holidays at St. Margaret's Bay, on the English shore of the Straits of Dover. Small though I then still was, I used to stand on the brow of the cliff with Uncle Harry for hours on end, while he taught me to identify and distinguish the rigs of the passing ships. I became as good at this as children are, nowadays, at identifying the makes of cars. If there were any barquentines and three-masted topsail schooners now still afloat, I should be able still to tell you correctly which was which, and I should also be able to distinguish correctly between a two-masted topsail schooner and a brigantine. The procession of ships through the Straits was as animated as the contemporary procession of carriages and riders in Hyde Park. My recollection is that, in the early eighteen-nineties, about two-thirds of the craft were still sailing-ships, not steamers. By then, full-rigged ships were already becoming rare; but those that were still in commission were big. Some of them were four-masters, with their yards and sails worked by donkey engines. These were mostly grain-ships or timber-ships. Smallish topsail schooners were the commonest sailing craft. At St. Margaret's Bay in a later year, I was thrilled to see Nansen's *Fram* on her way to the North Pole. On her top-mast she carried a huge crow's-nest, from which a look-out man would be able to give warning of approaching icebergs.

I was never tired of Uncle Harry's stories of his early life at sea. His stepmother had brought the child on board his first ship, dressed, like Jackanapes, in a frilly collar. The ship's carpenter had received the new member of the crew boisterously. 'Pick him up by the gills', he had shouted, and he had heaved the boy up by the collar till he had ripped the collar off his neck. This was the last that the poor lady was to see of the little boy for a year or so.

On one voyage to the China Seas, they had been warned to be on the watch for Chinese pirates, and they had been practising a drill for repelling hostile boarding-parties. They half feared but also half hoped that the pirates would materialize; so when, one day, during drill, the captain, to test them, suddenly shouted 'Boarders on the port bow!', the crew—Uncle Harry among them —all rushed to the forecastle, weapons in hand, in wild excitement, and, though the alarm was a fake, there was a casualty. One sailor had risen to such a pitch of martial exaltation that, before he knew what he was doing, he had jabbed the chief mate in the back.

On arrival off Ceylon on another voyage, the self-willed captain of the ship insisted, though the surf was heavy, on going on shore forthwith in his own boat, without waiting to signal for a native surf-boat. More than that, he insisted on wearing his full-dress uniform. The chief officer, watching the captain's progress through his spy-glass, saw the boat capsized on the beach by a huge roller. Later, he spied a catamaran making for the ship from the shore through the surf, which was still as heavy as ever. The captain was perched in the stern, and the tails of his full-dress coat were streaming out over the frothing water behind him. As he stepped on board, drenched and crestfallen, the ship's band, at the chief officer's word of command, struck up: 'Oh dear, what can the matter be? Johnny's so late from the fair.' The captain had given the chief officer a fair opening for teasing him.

The most fascinating story of all, which I must have heard Uncle Harry tell at least a dozen times without its ever palling, was the story of the pet monkey who had saved his life on his first voyage. In port, one day, Uncle Harry, then still a boy, had been sent up aloft on some job, and had slipped and fallen. Fortunately, his fall had been interrupted by some rigging. If he had fallen to the deck, he would have been killed. As it was, he had fallen far enough to be knocked senseless. Nobody was about—nobody except the monkey, who had remained on deck, following her master's every movement with her eyes. When Uncle Harry fell, the monkey screamed and went on screaming till somebody took notice, and Uncle Harry's life was saved.

Naturally, on his next spell of shore-leave, Uncle Harry took his life-saving monkey with him to Six-Hundred-Acre Farm; but, from this point, the monkey's story takes a sad turn. Uncle Harry's stepmother had just acquired a polished mahogany dining-room table, by which she set great store; so she took a poker to the monkey when the monkey invaded the dining-room; but the monkey dodged behind one of the table-legs, and the poker inflicted the injury that it had been wielded to ward off. Already, before landing, the monkey had opened a cage in which Uncle Harry was bringing home two doves as a present for his sister and had started to pluck one of the birds. Finally she nearly killed a calf. Shore life in a cool climate had demoralized her. She had to be sent to the Zoo.

By the time when I knew Uncle Harry, he was living in the past. A retired artillery officer, General Crofton, whom Uncle Harry had taken out to the Mutiny, was our neighbour. (General Crofton lived in Westbourne Square, and we lived at No. 12, Upper Westbourne Terrace. Some cousins of ours, belonging to my great-grandfather's second family, lived in Westbourne Terrace proper, with a carriage and pair and a coachman and a footman.) Every Sunday afternoon, General Crofton used to come to tea, and then he and Uncle Harry would submerge into the eighteen-fifties to exchange reminiscences about old times. By this time I was already enough of an historian to enjoy being carried back nearly half a century in time.

One Sunday afternoon, when the two old men were well submerged, Baden-Powell, back from the South African War, turned up to call on his uncle-in-law. Uncle Harry had married one of the daughters of Admiral Smyth, who had conducted the Admiralty's Mediterranean Survey after the end of the Napoleonic Wars, and Baden-Powell's mother and Uncle Harry's wife, Aunt Ellen anow dead), were sisters. Baden-Powell joined my parents and me in listening demurely while the two old men talked on, till at last they re-emerged for a moment into the present. 'Am I right in thinking that you have been in some war somewhere lately?' said Uncle Harry to his nephew politely. Thereupon, Baden-Powell told them about his defence of Mafeking. He spoke simply and modestly, without showing a trace of being ruffled, though he was a man who enjoyed fame. In fact, he behaved extremely well. As for my parents and me, we could hardly contain our inward laughter from bursting out; for, by this time, Baden-Powell had been in the headlines for months past. He was famous—all too famous for this to be to his sovereign's liking. When Baden-Powell had printed postage-stamps in beleaguered Mafeking, had he not placed his own image and superscription on them, instead of Queen Victoria's? This had been a gross infringement of royal prerogative, and it was said that the old lady never forgave him. However, though he may have blotted his copy-book with the Queen, he came out of his trying call on Uncle Harry most creditably.

Admiral Smyth—Baden-Powell's grandfather and Uncle Harry's father-in-law—had spent many years on making his magnificent survey of Mediterranean coasts and waters. Since the task had been long and pacific, the Admiral had been able to have his family on board with him. To put it more accurately, he had been able to beget his family on board. The professional task being long, the children were many, and he christened at least one of them by the name of the place that he happened to be surveying at the time of that child's birth. In this case the name was felicitous. The child got the name Rosetta, which did quite well for a girl. (I knew her as Lady Flower, the wife of Sir William Flower, the Keeper of the Natural History Museum.) The Admiral must have finished surveying the Delta coast before his next daughter was born; for there was not a Damietta in the family. There was, however, a Pennsylvania (this was Aunt Ellen's second Christian name), and there was a son whose name was as exotic as 'Pennsylvania' was, and as 'Damietta' would have been. Since this son was born at Naples he could have been named Napoleone, but in fact he was named Piazzi, after a Sicilian astronomer.

In Charles Piazzi Smyth Uncle Harry had a brother-in-law who was as exotic as his name. He was already a legendary figure by the time when Uncle Harry passed the legend on to me. Piazzi Smyth wrote the first of that long series of books that read the signs of the times in the measurements of the Pyramids. Piazzi's book was so heavily charged with madness that it sent one reader insane just through reading it. It is no wonder that the author himself, poor fellow, went mad too eventually. The first symptom was that, in the tropics, he forbore from killing mosquitos. People shook their heads gloomily over this, but on insufficient evidence. These pessimists had forgotten the Jains—the Indian sect whose adherents not only spare the lives of insects but provide them with lovely fretwork stone refuges, while they wear cloths over their own mouths for fear that they might kill an insect inadvertently by swallowing it. These Jain insectophils are not insane. So far from that, they are successful business men, with their feet planted firmly on the ground. However, Piazzi Smyth did go mad after all, though his tenderness towards mosquitos was no valid indication that he was going to. The end came when, after starting to say family prayers one morning, he never stopped. He was still carrying on with that morning's prayers on his death-bed, years afterwards—at least, so Uncle Harry used to declare.

Uncle Harry was spartan—one had to be, if one was going

to be at sea, out of reach of both green vegetables and doctors, for perhaps three months at a stretch. Mid-nineteenth-century seamen's fare was as unpalatable as the Spartiates' black broth or as the bitter herbs with which the monks of the Ethiopian convent at Debra Libános season their one meal in the day in order to take the carnal pleasure out of it. Uncle Harry used to recall how bitter the taste of a weevil had been when he had bitten through one in chewing a ship's biscuit. The weevil had the merit of momentarily overpowering the nastier taste of the mouldy hard-tack itself. When the ship's rats unwisely made themselves too annoying to the crew, there would be a rat-hunt; and then, for the next few days, the seamen could regale themselves on rat-pie, to vary the monotony of their staple plum-duff. If one could learn to do without fresh food, one could learn, too, to do without medical aid. To the end of his life, Uncle Harry was his own dentist. When a tooth decayed, he would dip a match in carbolic and would scrape out the cavity with it. If the decayed tooth then persisted in giving him trouble, he would tie one end of a piece of string round it, tie the other end to a door-handle, and slam the door—an operation that usually extracted the tooth, though not always with all its roots. At 5.00 a.m., summer and winter, he used to take a cold bath, practising total immersion and making a point of keeping his eyes open under water. This bracing habit was his undoing; for, one day, he had a fall and cut his face; next morning, before the family could intercept him, he had taken his cold bath as usual; and, as a result, he contracted erysipelas. After that, he was never his old self again.

Uncle Harry's was the first personality (except for my parents' personalities, of course) that made a memorable impact on me. Uncle Harry's personality was a powerful one, as the reader will have realized. It is still making its effect on me today, fifty-seven years after the date of his death. For me, however, Uncle Harry was not only a personality; he was also one of the forces of Nature—part of the universe in which I awoke to consciousness. He could have counted as one of my experiences, and, in that context, too, he would have come first in the series.

The picture of Uncle Harry that lingers in my mind is of his setting out, as he did, every Saturday morning, after family prayers, to buy oranges from his favourite barrow-man in the Harrow Road. He used to take with him a huge bandana handkerchief, and come back with it full of oranges. He was pleased to have bought them at four a penny. Even in the eighteen-nineties, this was cheap. When he had counted them, he would say 'O.K.', which he explained as meaning 'All correct'. I had supposed that this was an archaic joke from before the mast or from the fens, and that Uncle Harry's lips were the last on which I should hear it. I was the more surprised when, years later, 'O.K.' suddenly became half the vocabulary of half the human race.

By the time when I had become conscious of Uncle Harry's presence, his range had shrunk to the distance between Upper Westbourne Terrace and the Harrow Road; but in his heyday his range had been ocean-wide, and this wide world of his was opened up for me, not only by his stories, but by the curios that he had brought back from his voyages. At No. 12, Upper Westbourne Terrace, these orientalia were part of the furniture of the dining-room and of my mind. There was the section, two joints long, of a giant bamboo-stem that stood in a corner of the back part of the room near Uncle Harry's writing-desk. In the front part, in a glass-bookcase and, inside that, under a glass dome, there was an Indian procession of miniature ivory soldiery, horse and foot, escorting a miniature ivory grandee mounted on a miniature ivory elephant. On the mantlepiece there was a Chinese symmetrical pair of bronze long-beards mounted on buffaloes; and round the dining-room walls, frame touching frame, there was a continuous frieze of Aunt Ellen's water-colours.

My mother used to tell me that these works of Aunt Ellen's were not great works of art. They may not have been, but, for me, that was not the point. I valued them because they had the look of being conscientiously documentary; and, when, years afterwards, I saw India with my own eyes, I recognized that Aunt Ellen's pictures had given me a faithful pre-view of the reality. That frieze of pictures has vanished long ago, but one picture still stands out clear in my visual memory. It was a picture of an apparently endless line of full-rigged ships moored stern to bow, as close to each other as Aunt Ellen's pictures were. I expect Aunt Ellen's and Uncle Harry's Eastindiaman *Gloriana*, or their last ship, *Hotspur*, was in that painted row of ships, for the anchorage in the picture was at Calcutta, on the River Hoogly. Uncle Harry used to make fun of the grand airs that the Hoogly pilot assumed when, at the mouth of the Ganges Delta, the captain of an incoming ship handed over to him the tricky task of bringing the ship up to Calcutta through the treacherous maze of waterways.

I have called the ship Aunt Ellen's ship as well as Uncle Harry's; and this is correct; for the captain of an Eastindiaman had the right to take his wife with him on his voyages. At No. 12, Upper Westbourne Terrace, Aunt Ellen's and Uncle Harry's cabin dining-table had found its way up to my nursery. The table-top opened like a lid to reveal a chest in which I used to keep my toys. Round the table-top's edges were the tooth-marks left in it by the clamps with which the cabin-lamp had been affixed to it (a necessary precaution; for a loose lamp in a high sea might have set the ship on fire). Aunt Ellen, as well as Uncle Harry, made her contribution to the advancement of science. While her husband was distinguishing himself by the accuracy of his observations, Aunt Ellen was busy making accurate drawings of marine animals. An Eastindiaman ploughed through the water slow enough for that! If she had been a clipper, she would, I suppose, have slid through the water too fast to allow Aunt Ellen to observe and portray the marine fauna *en passage*. Speed has its price, as anyone who has travelled in a jet-plane knows. The price is that one's pace is in inverse ratio to one's opportunity for seeing, *en route*, something of the fascinating world that we have been given for our habitat.

I knew Aunt Ellen only from her works. She herself had died some years before I was born. In fact, the reason why I grew up in Uncle Harry's house was because my father and mother, after their marriage, had come there to keep house for him now that he was a widower. Uncle Harry had been devoted to Aunt Ellen, and he cherished his memory of her so long as his memory lasted. But, in his last phase, Nature played on him her cruel trick of killing the mind before the body. One day, after he had become pathetically senile, he asked my mother 'Who was Ellen?' when my mother had mentioned Aunt Ellen's name. 'Why, you know, she was your dear wife,' my mother answered gently. 'And where is she now?' 'Why, you know, she is dead; she died quite a long time ago.' 'Well, we get on very well without her, don't we?' The voice that paid this innocent tribute to my mother at poor Aunt Ellen's expense was Uncle Harry's voice only nominally. Uncle Harry was now spiritually extinct, though he was still in being physically.

A relative whom, unlike Aunt Ellen, I did meet in the flesh, and who made a vivid impression on me, was Cousin Fred, a nephew of Uncle Harry's in my father's generation. Cousin Fred operated a plantation in Malaya. (I do not know whether he was the manager only, or whether he was the owner; and I cannot remember what the crop was that he raised; in the early eighteen-nineties it can hardly have been rubber yet; the cultivation of rubber in Malaya, to supplement, and eventually supersede, the collection of wild rubber in the Amazonian forests, had hardly begun before the year 1900.) Uncle Harry was Fred Toynbee's chief living link with the family, so, when Cousin Fred was on leave at home, he used to be a frequent visitor at No. 12, Upper Westbourne Terrace. I used to look forward to these visits; for Cousin Fred was good-natured, and he used to go out of his way to be kind to me. I was an eager listener to his talk about a European planter's life in the tropics. It put another Asian country, besides India and China, on my mental map.

Cousin Fred's talk, together with Aunt Ellen's pictures and Uncle Harry's oriental curios, had given No. 12, Upper Westbourne Terrace, for me, a perceptible aroma of Southern and Eastern Asia. My pre-view of this great world had been enlarged by the array of Asian trees, labelled with their Latin names, and with a note of where they came from, along the Flower Walk in Kensington Gardens; and I was soon enlarging my Asian panorama still further, for myself, by paying frequent visits to the Indian Museum in South Kensington—a collection of oriental curios that, of course, far outshone Uncle Harry's modest one. In the Indian Museum, as one entered, one's eyes met the model of an

Indian village. Farther on, there were two exquisite Chinese models of mountain landscapes that had been shipped off by the Emperor as a present for Napoleon but had been intercepted, and deflected to George III, by a predatory British frigate. (Probably the Imperial Court did not much care which of those two tributary barbarian princes acquired these tokens of its favour; such works of art were, anyway, more than any barbarian deserved to receive.) As one walked along the gallery, one passed case after case of Mogul illuminated manuscripts (animated scenes of cavalry engagements, tranquil scenes of formal gardens, and vindictive scenes of elephants executing prisoners by trampling them to death). The climax of fascinating gruesomeness was Tipoo Sahib's wooden tiger trampling on a prostrate wooden Frank. This is a mechanical toy in the Frankish style. It has a handle, and, when the handle is turned, the tiger roars. Turning that handle used to relieve Tipoo's feelings. This one-time solace of Tipoo's was an unconsidered trifle that had been salvaged from the loot of Seringapatanam. (It was not till 1957 that I saw the island fortress itself, with its triple ramparts embraced in the arms of a rushing river.)

My first sight of India and China was in 1929, and by then I had turned forty; but, thanks to Aunt Ellen, whom I never saw, I had been preparing myself for this longed-for visit for at least thirty-seven years by the time when, at last, I was able to make this long journey to the far side of the globe.

2
Auntie Charlie

Where my head will go, my body will go;
My Auntie Charlie told me so.

I WAS chanting this extempore couplet lustily in my nursery,
with my head tightly wedged between two of the bars of the
end-piece of an iron bedstead. Down below, in the drawing-
room, I had been listening eagerly to Auntie Charlie[1] giving
an exciting account of a cross-country walk that she had taken
somewhere near Oxford. The climax had been her successfully
forcing her way through a rather small hole in a very thickset
hedge. I had run upstairs to test whether her anatomical thesis
was correct. No doubt it was for her. She was tiny and indomit-
able. Till she was over eighty, she had not ever, even for a single
day, been laid up in bed. So when, at last, her body betrayed her,
she was indignant.

Auntie Charlie (Charlotte Toynbee) was the widow of my
Uncle Arnold, after whom I had been named, because I was
the first male child to be born in our branch of the family after
my uncle's sudden early death. He had died, dramatically, of
'brain fever' (? meningitis) in the middle of a series of debates, in
the Lincoln-Douglas style, with the American economist 'single-
tax' Henry George. Auntie Charlie had been more than eleven
years older than Uncle Arnold, but she outlived him by nearly
forty-eight years.[2]

---

[1] The 'Ch' in 'Charlie' was pronounced as it is in 'Charlotte', which was my
aunt's real name.

[2] Charlotte Maria Atwood was born on 30 March 1841, and died on 8 January
1931; Arnold Toynbee was born on 23 August 1852, and died on 9 March 1883.

Though Arnold Toynbee was only thirty when he died, he was already a famous man, and the tragedy of his sudden death at that age made him more famous still. Under his father's inspiration, he had been one of the pioneers in the attempt to bridge the shocking gulf, enlarged by the Industrial Revolution, between the 'working class' and the middle class in Britain. In Victorian Britain, these two classes had indeed become 'two nations'. If they were ever to be brought together again, social justice must be done by state intervention. 'The welfare state', which Uncle Arnold did not live to see, has been partially achieved in my life-time—only partially, so far; for, in 1966, the British 'welfare state' is still far from being what it should be and what it might be. Moreover, it needed, and needs, something more than even the most benign and comprehensive social legislation to bring the two sundered 'nations' together. It needed, and needs, the renewal of human social relations; and this was the field in which Arnold Toynbee had played his part. Canon Barnett, a Church of England clergyman with a parish in the East End of London, had suggested to my uncle that he should go to live in the East End, and should get to know some of Canon Barnett's parishioners personally. My uncle followed this advice; and, after his death, the first university settlement in East London, Toynbee Hall, was founded in his memory, with Canon Barnett as its first Warden.

The idea was to plant in the East End a community that would bring to 'under-privileged' people there the best things that an Oxford College had to give. Young men who had just come down from Oxford to enter on professional careers in London were to live at Toynbee Hall, as they had been living in their Oxford colleges, and were to give their evenings to organizing various social and cultural amenities for Whitechapel: debating societies, boys' clubs, art clubs, a library, a travellers' club, and so on. In this way the residents at Toynbee Hall would be able to pass on to a wider circle some, at least, of the good things that they themselves had been privileged to receive—and in England (though not in Scotland), till after the First World War, a university education was the privilege of a very small minority of the population. One of the early residents at Toynbee Hall was Lord Attlee; and his experience there may have played some part in determining his subsequent career.

After his marriage, Uncle Arnold had been living in Oxford. He was a fellow of Balliol, much approved of by the Master of the College, Benjamin Jowett. My aunt and uncle had first met at Wimbledon. Her parents, too, had lived there. Her father had been in some secret organization connected with the Foreign Office. She and my uncle had made friends, riding on Wimbledon Common together. After my uncle's death, my aunt went on living in Oxford, first with her mother and aunt, and then, after their deaths, alone—no, not alone, for she had two inseparable life-long Oxford friends.

One of the two was Mrs. T. H. Green, the widow of another fellow of Balliol, the philosopher, who had been my uncle's senior contemporary there, had shared his philanthropical interests, and, like him, had died young. Mrs. Green was the sister of a well-known Victorian man of letters, John Addington Symonds. My aunt's and Mrs. Green's personalities were complementary to each other. Mrs. Green was usually gentle; my aunt could be incisive. Auntie Charlie had something of David Copperfield's aunt in her. Every Sunday, for years and years on end, the two ladies used to go to mattins together at St. Giles's Church. They also shared a pony-trap, pony, and groom with each other and with the third member of the trio, Mrs. Arthur Johnson, whose husband was alive (he was a fellow of All Souls). Each lady had the use of the trap for two days in the week. The bond between them was close, and they were highly esteemed friends of many of the Oxford grandees—Phelps of Oriel, for instance; Spooner, whose 'spooner-isms' have made his name a household word throughout the English-speaking world; and others of the same stature.

Dr. Spooner was the Warden of New College. He was an albino, he was short, and his voice had a high pitch. He looked like a rabbit, but he was as brave as a lion. He was prepared at any moment to stand up to anybody, however formidable. He gave evidence of this bravery during the First World War. At New College the names of members of the college who had been killed were posted, in an ever lengthening list, on the chapel door. The names of four fellows of the college—Guy Leonard Chees-man, Leslie Whitaker Hunter, Arthur George Heath, Geoffrey Smith—were there before the war was over. The college had some German members—Rhodes scholars and others as well—and, when the news reached Oxford that one of these German members of New College had also lost his life, Warden Spooner would post his name on the chapel door with the rest. Among some narrow-hearted Oxford people there were murmurs; but Spooner was a man who could not be deterred from doing what he knew to be right. 'They, too, are members of the College,' was his reply; 'and they, too, have given their lives for their country.' So the German and the English names remained on the chapel door together.

An amusing exhibition of Dr. Spooner's hardihood in less tragic circumstances was once witnessed by my aunt, at a time when she and Dr. Spooner were both serving on the Oxford Board of Guardians. At one of its meetings, the Board had to deal with an Irish applicant for outdoor relief. The Irishman's demands were high, and his manner was truculent. When he saw the Board hesitate, he rounded on them. 'Do you want to see me die on the carpet?' he asked, with a melodramatic gesture. There was a moment of embarrassed silence. The Irishman's preposterous rhetoric had done its job. It had made all the Guardians feel un-comfortable—all except one. The silence was broken by Dr. Spooner's lisping, in a voice that was all his own: 'Yes, we should like to see you die on the carpet—like to very much.' The situation was saved; the Irishman fell back deflated, and, after that, he took like a lamb the amount of relief that the Board voted for him.

A 'spoonerism', in the broadest sense of the word, means 'getting something the wrong way round'. Most of the 'spooner-isms' that are in circulation are verbal ones, since these are concise and portable. 'Boil your icicle' for 'oil your bicycle' is an example of the 'spoonerisms' of this verbal type. A collection of them might fill a volume as big as this; and most of them are spurious; for, when Dr. Spooner himself had spontaneously generated a few, many ingenious Oxford minds—well prepared by a long

3   George Toynbee, the author's great-grandfather, a
    farmer in the Lincolnshire fens

4 Mrs. Arnold Toynbee ('Auntie Charlie') sitting on the right of the picture, Miss Wordsworth sitting on the left, Mrs. Arthur Johnson standing. To those who know, the dresses give the date

training in the composition of Greek and Latin verse—set to work
to improve on nature by art. So, the wittier or more elegant the
specimen, the less likely it is to be authentic. Genuine 'spooner-
isms', however, were not confined to transpositions of words;
they sometimes took the form of *non sequiturs*; and at least one of
them was performed, not in words, but in action. I will mention
here one example of each of these two less familiar kinds.

When my school-fellow Reginald Coupland was a scholar of
New College, he was coming out of chapel one day when Dr.
Spooner stopped him, to say: 'Mr. Coupland, you read the lessons
very badly in chapel this morning.'—'But, Warden, it wasn't I
who was reading them this morning.'—'Oh, I thought it wasn't,'
said Dr. Spooner, and left Coupland to disentangle the train of
the Warden's thought.

The acted 'spoonerism' was witnessed by my mother's old
friend Eleanor Jourdain. At a dinner-party in Oxford, she saw
Dr. Spooner upset a salt-cellar and then reach for a decanter of
claret. He then poured claret on the salt, drop by drop, till he had
produced the little purple mound which would have been the
end-product if he had spilled claret on the table-cloth and had
then cast a heap of salt on the pool to absorb it.

Transpositions were Dr. Spooner's individual contribution
to 'Oxford English' (in the literal meaning of the term). Arch-
aisms had a wider currency in the Oxford academic world. My
tutor, and afterwards colleague, at Balliol, A. W. Pickard-Cambridge, was once out for a walk along the grassy track on the
top of Shotover Hill when he caught sight of some strange phen-
omenon ahead of him. On approaching it, he found that it was
a combination of a man, a horse, and a gate. The rider's hand
was clutching the top of the gate; the horse was sidling away
from the gate; and the rider himself was falling off his saddle
by inches. The effect was like a slow-motion movie picture.
Running up, Pickard-Cambridge released the hand from the gate,
righted the body's seat in the saddle, and saw that the rider
whom he had rescued was Tommy Case, the President of Corpus.
All that the President said was: 'Young man, I do not know your
name, and 'twere best that you should not inquire mine.' This

request was evidence of modesty, since, for years, Tommy Case
had been one of the best-known cranks in all Oxford. The point
about the language is that it was not affected; it was Tommy
Case's natural idiom.

I once ran up against this archaic Oxford English myself. I had
been giving a course of lantern-lectures on Greek historical geography in the Ashmolean, and the attendant who had been operating the lantern had been obliging. My course was under the
auspices of Percy Gardner, the Professor of Classical Archaeology;
so, meeting him in the corridor when I was coming out from the
last of my lectures, I asked him: 'Should I give the lantern-man a
tip?' If I had put my question in Greek or Latin, communication
would, no doubt, have been established instantly; but I had addressed Percy in the vernacular, and I had even used a colloquial
word. For a few seconds Percy stood silent, looking perplexed,
and I realized that he was searching for the equivalent of my
vulgarism in his own language. Finally he got it. 'Oh . . . you
mean "tender him a gratuity"? Certainly not.' Percy began life
on the stock exchange. *Credo quia absurdum*, for it is not made
credible just by happening to be the truth.

An amiable practice of Percy's was to burst into song when,
at last, he was showing to the front door an undergraduate who
had been calling on him and Mrs. Gardner on a Sunday afternoon.
We realized that his song was an expression of his joy that he
was now going to be free to get back to Greek art or perhaps to
Pauline theology. (This was his side-line.) We also realized that his
song was unconscious and therefore inoffensive. (Percy was kind
and courteous, and he would have been devastated if he had caught
himself being rude. His nature shone out through his kind, candid,
guileless blue eyes.)

Sunday-afternoon calls on married dons and their wives who
had previously invited one to lunch were part of an undergraduate's education; and, on our hosts' part, it was a highly disinterested act to lend themselves for us to practise on. What a shy undergraduate had to learn by practice on dons' wives was the art of
taking his leave; so his calls were sometimes long-drawn-out,
and the convention was that his hostess should endure this without

giving him a hint that his departure was long overdue. The undergraduate would be unhappily aware of this already; his problem was how to extricate himself; and his don's wife would rightly act on the principle that a child never learns to swim if it is given a helping hand.

At the time when I was an undergraduate, the institution of Sunday-afternoon calls was firmly established; and, if one failed to pay a call after a lunch-party, this was likely to be taken note of, with disapproval. Yet at that time (1907-11) the institution can hardly have been more than half a century old; for, till at least half way through the nineteenth century, one of the conditions for holding an Oxford college fellowship had been celibacy. Inverting the Roman Catholic Church's rule, post-Reformation Oxford ruled that, if a fellow wanted to marry, he must take holy orders. The colleges had a number of Church of England 'livings' in their gift; and, if one of these happened to be vacant, and if the fellow who wanted to marry was on good terms with his brethren, his induction into a college 'living' would be the penalty for his breach of a fellow's lay celibacy. The waiver of the rule of celibacy for fellows of colleges revolutionized Oxford's social life. A suburban North Oxford now opened up to meet the demand of married dons and their wives for housing. The first don's wife had made history; and there is a monument to her in New College cloisters, recording how she had been the first woman to civilize the donnish way of life by importing into it the sweetness of the home.

Percy Gardner's philosophy of life was a gentle pessimism. I once met someone, whom I cannot now identify, who had been riding with Percy on mule-back through Central Greece when the news reached Percy, by some grape-vine telegraph, that his brother Ernest had just been appointed to a chair in the University of London. As the mule journey continued, my informant heard Percy murmuring 'Poor Ernest! Poor Ernest!'—'But surely he is not to be pitied,' said Percy's companion. 'Becoming a professor is not a misfortune.'—'Oh, it is, it is,' was Percy's reply. 'In accepting this distinguished post, Ernest has exposed himself to the risk of making conspicuous mistakes. Poor, poor Ernest.'

Percy's anxiety was uncalled for. His brother Ernest was a most capable man, and his performance of his professional duties was *musterhaft*. Ernest Gardner survived, with equal credit, his term of service in the exacting job of being the University of London's Vice-Chancellor. Percy's doleful exclamations had been no reflection on Ernest; they had just been an expression of Percy's own temperament.

Percy broke off his uncongenial adventure in the City of London by doing what Dick Whittington set out to do. He turned his back on the City for good, and made his way to Oxford via Cambridge. It is more usual for undergraduates, after taking their final examinations, to go off to London and not to return. A contemporary at Oxford of my Uncle Arnold's who had kept up his friendship with my aunt after my uncle's death and after his own departure from Oxford was Lord Milner. He was faithful in his friendships. He used, for example, to find time, in a busy life, to pay an annual visit to his stepmother in Hamburg as long as she lived. Milner's decision to seek a career outside Oxford had distressed an old Oxford acquaintance of his. Milner had, of course, already distinguished himself intellectually while he was an undergraduate, and, just after he had passed his final examination with high honours, he met this elderly don in the street. 'Well,' said the don, as Milner told the story to my aunt, 'we look forward to having you with us in Oxford permanently now.' 'No, I shall not be staying up,' Milner replied. 'Oh! what a pity. But why?' 'Well I do not see anything for me to do in Oxford after this.' 'Oh, my dear friend, there is any amount of work to be done here on Greek accents.'

Action, not accents, had been Milner's choice, and a distinguished career in the public service had culminated in his appointment to be British High Commissioner at Cape Town when the prospect of war between Britain and the two South African republics was becoming threatening. Just before sailing for Africa, Milner, characteristically, found time to run down (or, in Oxford parlance, up) to Oxford to see my aunt and say goodbye to her. When she congratulated him on his appointment to so responsible a post, he said: 'Yes, some people believe that there is going to be a war in South Africa, but I am sure that I shall be able to prevent that.' Within a few weeks of the date of this conversation, the South African War had broken out, and, rightly or wrongly, it was widely believed that Milner had had a major responsibility for this. By the time when he left South Africa and came home to England, the counter-tide of anti-imperialist feeling in England was running strong, and Milner found himself under a cloud. In his hitherto brilliant career this was his first experience of a serious reverse, and it was one that was particularly painful for him. It put him out of action at the height of his powers, and he was an ambitious man—ambitious, not for wealth or fame, but for opportunities of exercising his great abilities in an adequate field. The stoicism that was a prominent trait in his character now came out strong. He took his eclipse with patience and dignity.

> Quo magis in dubiis hominem spectare periclis
> convenit, adversisque in rebus noscere qui sit;
> nam verae voces tum demum pectore ab imo
> eiciuntur et eripitur persona, manet res.

Lucretius's observation is exemplified in this chapter of Milner's life. The man of action's character never showed to better advantage than during his period of involuntary inaction and comparative obscurity.

After having heard so much about Lord Milner from my aunt, I met him once while I was still at Oxford as an undergraduate. Coming back to my rooms in Balliol one evening, I found his visiting-card on my table, and, before he went back to London, I was able to call on him to thank him. His feeling for my uncle and aunt had led him, characteristically again, to go out of his way to show this courtesy to me. Towards the end of the First World War it came my way to do some job of work for him after he had come back to public life—now, right at the top—as one of the four members of the newly instituted War Cabinet. I found him good to work for. He was considerate as well as businesslike. Above all, his character won one's respect without regard to one's political views. (I was, and am, a Liberal of the Campbell-Bannerman school.) Lord Halifax's personality had the same effect on me

when, in the Second World War, it came my way to do some
jobs of work for him. (In the nineteen-thirties, I had been strongly
opposed to the United Kingdom Government's policy of 'appeasement'.)

The distinguished Oxford men of my uncle's and aunt's generation who, unlike Lord Milner, had stayed in Oxford and had
become grandees there showed their regard for my aunt by the
way in which they rallied to her on the occasion of a sad mishap
that she had suffered. My aunt was no feminist. Indeed, she and
Mrs. Humphry Ward once tried to found a women's anti-suffrage
society. It is surprising that the militants did not burn the two
traitoresses' houses down. Nevertheless, my aunt was, for many
years, treasurer of Lady Margaret Hall, and there is a building
there called 'Toynbee' after her. Her treasurership was the cause
of the mishap. One day, at the beginning of term, she had
collected the students' fees in cash. She had then put all this money
in a trunk, together with a gold watch and other valuables of her
own, had taken the trunk by train from Oxford to Paddington
Station, had left it, unguarded, on the platform, and, coming
back for it, had been surprised to find that it had disappeared. All
Oxford was deeply moved by her distressing loss. Distinguished
heads were put together; a generous subscription was raised; a
party was arranged; and a presentation was made. The gold watch
and the other valuables were handsomely replaced. But what
about the lost fees? 'Well,' my aunt used to say, when she was
telling the story, 'I couldn't have afforded to refund those, so I
just told the students that they must pay again.' What is more,
they did—and this, apparently, without a murmur. They wouldn't
today. But at that date, sixty years and more ago, my aunt (as was
evident when she told the story) had no notion that she had committed an enormity, and the students of the period were too
lady-like to make a fuss. Perhaps they were also too much in awe
of the College's treasurer. Anyway, they preferred to pay their
fees twice over.

The students would, indeed, have needed courage to refuse
the preposterous demand when it was my Aunt Charlotte who
was telling them to stand and once more deliver. I have mentioned

that Auntie Charlie reminded me of David Copperfield's aunt. Her heart was always kind, but her personality was commanding, and her manner was sometimes imperious. An impressive testimony to her potency was her subjugation of Miss Rogers.

On principle, Miss Rogers ought to have broken with Auntie Charlie when my aunt got together with Mrs. Humphry Ward with an eye to starting an anti-women's suffrage movement. Miss Rogers was a woman of principle, if ever there was one. She was what nowadays is called a freedom-fighter, and her cause was just. She fought a lifelong fight to get the women students at Oxford integrated into the University. Miss Rogers's contention was that women students who passed the University's intellectual tests ought to be rewarded with the same recognition, carrying with it the same status, as was automatically conferred, by the same achievements, on the women's fellow-students who happened to be of the opposite sex. Today, the justice of this demand seems so manifest that it is hard for us to imagine how there can have been men—and highly educated men at that—who had the face to oppose it. Yet, in both Congregation and Convocation in Miss Rogers's day, the anti-integrationists were in a large majority, and the pro-integrationist minority could do little, as yet, to help Miss Rogers's cause. Well, *Italia farà da se*. Miss Rogers helped herself. Among her weapons there was one that had proved its efficiency in Florence Nightingale's hands. This weapon was the mastery of all the relevant facts—especially the juridical facts and their implications. Miss Rogers was better versed in the University's statutes and regulations than the proctors were, better versed, even, than was the Registrar himself. This made Miss Rogers a redoubtable antagonist for them; and, when she did compel them to join battle with her reluctantly on what should have been their own territory, she gained ground from them as often as not. In this battle the movement was as slow and as stiffly contested as it is in trench-warfare or in American football; yet, in the course of years, Miss Rogers succeeded in gradually pushing her freedom-front forward, inch by inch.

Miss Rogers was a formidable woman for any man to encounter—even for those few who were on Miss Rogers's side. Gilbert

Murray was one of the minority of Oxford dons that sympathized with the women's cause; and he wanted to express his sympathy in terms of practical support; so one day he offered to Miss Rogers to give personal tuition to women students of hers who were reading for the classical Honour Moderations and Literae Humaniores. After accepting G.M.'s offer, Miss Rogers asked him what his fee would be. G.M. had not thought about that. Like Hitler,[1] he was not doing it for money. He now quickly thought up a figure that was well below the standard scale. 'Oh, we only pay our best tutors that amount,' was Miss Rogers's quick reply. G.M. was slightly disconcerted and embarrassed. 'Oh, well,' he said, 'a fee is not the point. You know my concern for women's education. I shall be very happy to give this tuition gratis.' This time Miss Rogers pounced even more swiftly and more sternly than before. 'We don't take charity,' she said. Checkmate! She had left this male sympathizer with her cause no line open for retreat. She had him cornered. He might be *bien-pensant*, but he was a man; so, instinctively she had gone into action against him, as a dog goes into action when it spies a cat.

With this incident in mind, I was astonished when Auntie Charlie told me casually, one day, that she had chosen 'Annie Rogers' for her companion on a holiday trip to the Continent. When Miss Rogers had laid a right-thinking man low with her flail, what ought she not to have done to a woman traitor to the women's cause—a traitor who was the more damaging because she was conspicuous? On principle, Miss Rogers ought to have ostracized Auntie Charlie, at the very least; and here she was, going out of her way to be friends with her. I was still more astonished when, later on, I saw the two of them together, planning their tour. Auntie Charlie was treating Miss Rogers as unceremoniously as if she had been a silly girl, and Miss Rogers was taking this cavalier treatment lying down. Her manner was meek and even deprecatory. This *malleus maleficorum virilis sexûs* had never equipped herself for meeting her match in a woman. Miss Rogers's capitulation to Auntie Charlie revealed to me what my aunt's potency must be.

[1] See p. 285.

Being called after a famous man has its disadvantages. One's name is not completely one's own. Yet human beings, like dogs and horses, do need names that are distinctive. This was brought home to me when my first book was published. The printer had put 'by Arnold Toynbee' on the title-page, and I had passed the proofs without its having occurred to me that there was anything wrong with this. 'Arnold Toynbee' was, after all, my name. All the same, within a few days of the book's appearance, every live Toynbee uncle and aunt that I had, with one exception—and there were nine of them still living—all these nine, save one, wrote to me, saying 'What business had you to call yourself "Arnold Toynbee" on the title-page of that book of yours? That is not *your* name; it is your uncle's.'

This seemed to me inconsequent, since I had been given the name, in infancy, at their wish. It wasn't as if I had impertinently assumed the name myself. However, for the sake of family peace, I took, after that, to signing myself 'Arnold J. Toynbee', American-fashion. The 'J' stands for Joseph, my grandfather's name, and I am glad to bear his name as well as Uncle Arnold's. The tabu that my aunts and uncles had put on the name 'Arnold' for me was strong. It was not till after the death of the last survivor of them, my Aunt Grace, that I ventured to start signing myself 'Arnold Toynbee' again. I can do this now with an easy mind, because I feel sure that Uncle Arnold would not grudge me the use of our common name if he were alive to say his say.

Why do I feel sure of this? Partly because of my impression of what Uncle Arnold was like. This impression is, of course, a second-hand one. Born, as I was, six years after his death, I never had the happiness of knowing him in the intimate personal way in which, as a child, I knew his and my Uncle Harry. I believe, though, that my second-hand picture of Uncle Arnold is substantially true to life; and it is the picture of a lively, sociable, genial personality, so keenly interested in the human world around him—so idealistic in his eagerness to make life better for his less fortunate fellow creatures—that he can have had no time or attention to spare for standing on his dignity or for fancying himself affronted.

Uncle Arnold, in fact, was one of the representatives of the jollier of the two groups between which my Toynbee uncles and aunts were divided. This genial group took, I imagine, after my grandfather, whom, also, I never knew in the flesh. The other group certainly took after his widow, my grandmother, whom I did know. Like many other mothers of large Victorian families, my grandmother was a minor replica of Queen Victoria herself; and one had to be careful to treat her with the deference that she expected of one, as of right (though what right these uncrowned queens had to grandeur I do not know). The contrast between the conventional and the unconventional half of the family was typified in the persons of my Aunt Mary and my Aunt Gertrude (Auntie Geddy).

One of the most pathetic things, in a minor way, that I have ever heard anyone say was Auntie May's once remarking, half to herself: 'If I dressed as badly as Geddy does, people would never ask me to their houses. But Geddy dresses like that, and she is asked out everywhere.' It was true, she was. She was welcome because her exuberance was seasoned with a spice of genius. One day, in her forties, she rushed into the National Gallery and began to copy the Turner water-colours there. She had had no training whatever in painting, yet her copies (I possess several of them) are remarkably good. On principle, Auntie Geddy lived in squalor. She thought it wrong to employ a fellow human being on menial labour, and also wrong to waste any time of her own on that. As she lived in London in the age when the Underground—not yet electrified—was belching clouds of coal-smoke up into the streets, night and day, there was an unspeakable cumulative effect, in her flat, of this doctrinaire refusal of hers to do any housework herself or to have any done for her. There were exciting books on her shelves, but I still shudder at the memory of the filth that cascaded over one's hand if one took a book out. As for the final state of the things that, year by year, she had thrown away under her bed, no member of the family ever had the courage to pry into that. In the cottage that she once had at Chiddingfold, the régime was like the Mad Hatter's tea-party. There were seven sets of cups, plates, knives, spoons, and forks, and dirty sets were left to wait festering for a grand collective washing-up at the end of the week.

In spite of the warmness of her heart, Auntie Geddy was not the aunt who refrained from writing me a reproachful letter about my usurpation of Uncle Arnold's name. She, too, did write to reprove me, and I do not hold this against her. She was moved to it by loyalty. Uncle Arnold and my grandfather and John Ruskin were her gods. The aunt who did *not* write to reproach me on this occasion was the one who had the best right of all to do so, had she chosen. It was Auntie Charlie, Arnold Toynbee's widow.

When the author's copies of my book arrived, I brought one of them to her house to give to her. Taking it in her hands and looking at it, she said: 'Your uncle could never have written as big a book as that, poor young fellow.' Poor young fellow! I was struck dumb with amazement and compassion. At that moment —it was in 1915—I myself was already only four years younger than Uncle Arnold's age at the time of his death. Auntie Charlie, who was his senior, was by now nearly two and a half times as old as he had been at the moment at which they had suddenly and tragically parted. Till I heard these amazing words issue from Auntie Charlie's mouth, Uncle Arnold had been, for me, a time-less demigod on a pedestal; for, since early childhood, I had been indoctrinated in the family cult. I now realized that, for Auntie Charlie, he was not a demigod at all; he was a lovable human being who had suffered an unkind fate. Ever since that day, Arnold Toynbee has been 'poor young fellow' for me too. A few months later, half my contemporaries were killed on battlefields in France. Poor young fellows. They now keep company with Uncle Arnold in my thoughts of them—and I think of all of them often. Those whose lives are cut short prematurely have one advantage over the rest of us. They remain young eternally, while we are being carried on towards the inexorable end of life's normal trajectory.

When Auntie Charlie said that Uncle Arnold could never have written as big a book as mine, she was thinking, I suppose, of the book of his that did see the light: *The Industrial Revolution.* He did

not live actually to write the book himself; it was most skilfully
put together, after his death, from the notes, taken by two students
of his, of a course of lectures that he had given at Oxford. This
book was a pioneer work. I believe Uncle Arnold was the first
person to use the term 'Industrial Revolution' in English. (It had
already been coined in French, I have been told.) No doubt, the
passage of more than eighty years has put Arnold Toynbee's
The Industrial Revolution quite out of date from the technical
standpoint of an up-to-date economic historian. Yet a book can
'date' technically without 'dating' as a work of art or as the expression of a notable personality. Gibbon's *The Decline and Fall*
is a universally admitted case in point. I venture to make the same
claim for my uncle's book. His personality does seem to me to
inform it and to lend it a perennial vitality. I am not, I know, an
impartial judge of this. I am not detached, and, indeed, my feeling
for Uncle Arnold grows stronger with every year that I myself
go on living. Today, in 1966, I am more than two and a half
times as old as he was when he died. What might he not have done
if he had lived to my present age? I should count my own life very
well spent if, by the time of my death, people could say of me
that I had done, for the world, the half of what Arnold Toynbee
had done for it already before dying at the age of thirty.

3
Montague John Rendall

WHEN I was at school at Winchester (1902–7), Mr. Rendall was Second Master (*Ostiarius*); it was not till later that he became Head Master (*Informator*, i.e. 'character-former', not 'delator'). The Second Master was the equivalent of a house-master for College, and I was a College man; so, for five formative years, I was within very close range of Mr. Rendall. Since then, his influence on me has been powerful and permanent.

When one is in one's teens, the grown-up people under whose authority one finds oneself may fill one with awe or may move one to make fun of them. One's reactions towards them may be mixed; for making fun of them may be a form of self-defence against an awe that, uncounteracted, might be overwhelming. We did make mild fun of Mr. Rendall's foibles. His personality was colourful, but, above all, it was commanding; so, when we did caricature, say, his manner of speaking, which was staccato and pronouncedly cadenced, our mocking was no sign of disrespect; we respected Mr. Rendall to the point of admiration; and this tells one something about Mr. Rendall's character; for the admiration of College was not easy to win for someone who, like the Second Master, was always in the public eye. The spirit of College was critical, with a spice of irreverence in it; we scholars—there were seventy of us (the auspicious number of Christ's disciples)—were, after all, a brood of 'egg-heads'.

We admired Mr. Rendall because his character was noble. Its nobility was so palpable that you could not be insensitive to this, and it would have been impossible to deny it, even if one had fallen foul of him and had wished to believe that he was made of common clay. He was not. 'He nothing common did or mean.' Andrew Marvell (introduced to us by Mr. Rendall) claimed this for King Charles upon the memorable scene of his execution. But that occasion was a supreme one, and it was brief. Can any human being live without ever doing anything common or mean from the beginning to the end of his life? Perhaps, for Man, this is impossible; but it is possible for human beings to approximate towards realizing this ideal; and, of all the human beings whom I have known, Mr. Rendall came the nearest to this in my belief. This may be an optical illusion. When one is not yet grown-up oneself, a grown-up person whom one admires is likely to loom larger than life-size, and, if he does, this magnification of his stature is likely to persist in one's subsequent mental picture of him. It is impossible for me to tell whether my picture of Mr. Rendall needs scaling-down to make it true to life. But, even if its scale is too big, I am convinced that the features, as I still see them, are, nevertheless, a true likeness.

The mental affectation that underlay the touch of affectation in Mr. Rendall's speech was an inclination to see himself in the role of a Renaissance man. He had one first-class title to this role; he had the Italian passion for beauty; but, if he had been challenged to throw himself into the part unreservedly and realistically, it would have been morally impossible for him to go to that length; for, unfortunately, Renaissance Italy had a seamy side that was the obverse of its cult for beauty. There was a depravity in Renaissance Italian life that shocked the Spanish puritanism of St. Ignatius Loyola. Mr. Rendall was a puritan too. It was not for nothing that he was a child of the parsonage. He would, no doubt, have been thrilled if, with the aid of H. G. Wells's time-machine, he could have stepped into Benvenuto Cellini's workshop and watched the artist at work. But, if Benvenuto, flattered by this visit from a queer stranger, had then taken Mr. Rendall by the arm and invited him to accompany him on an evening out, Mr. Rendall could not have walked a yard with Benvenuto before he would have recoiled in disgust at the great master's uninhibited way of spending his leisure hours.

Mr. Rendall admired the Ancient Greeks as much as he admired the Renaissance Italians, but he did not approve the Greek practice, which he pointed out to us, of using the word καλός, which means beautiful, as a synonym and substitute for the word ἀγαθός, meaning good. Though beauty meant as much to Mr. Rendall as it did to his Greek and Italian exemplars, he could never have borne to reduce morals to terms of aesthetics. For him, beauty was much, but it was not everything. Virtue was distinct from it. What was remarkable and unusual in Mr. Rendall was that he was both an aesthete and a puritan, and that each of these two antithetical veins was developed in him so strongly.

You became aware of Mr. Rendall's sense of beauty as soon as you entered his house. If you had not known that he was a bachelor, and a confirmed one, you would have sworn that the house had been decorated by a woman's hand. Mr. Rendall had an eye for colour-schemes and a feel for textures that is rare in men. He was sensitive and perceptive in a field in which most men are out of their element. Yet, for Mr. Rendall, women were virtually non-existent. When he had to deal with a woman, he showed her an exaggerated courtesy that could not completely mask his quizzical aloofness from this strange incomprehensible being. A woman, for Mr. Rendall, was like some mythical creature in a medieval bestiary. I believe there had been only one woman whom Mr. Rendall had taken quite seriously—but he had taken this one very seriously indeed. She was his mother, and she had a right to command his allegiance. Mr. Rendall's mother had been a solitary queen. In Great Rollright Rectory, she had reigned over a husband and nine sons single-handed, with no other woman in the family to give her countenance and support.

I have known only one other man who was as aloof from women as Mr. Rendall was, and that was R. M. Dawkins, a Director of the British School of Archaeology at Athens who afterwards held the chair of Byzantine and Modern Greek Studies in Oxford. After the outbreak of the Second World War, I persuaded Dawkins to join the Foreign Research and Press Department of Chatham House which eventually turned into the Research Department of the Foreign Office. But when, in the normal course of my duties, I found for him a suitable assistant in the person of Kitty Leatham (afterwards Mrs. M. A. Thomson), Dawkins was panic-stricken. He might have put up with her Greek being Ancient, not Modern, but he could not get over her sex. The idea of having to work with a woman was, for him, quite novel and most alarming. In fact, he could not face this ordeal; and Mr. Rendall, I guess, would have been equally unadaptable if he had ever been required to come to terms with the Shorthand Typist Age on which the world had entered in his lifetime.

Mr. Rendall's passion for beauty was matched by his missionary zeal for communicating this to everyone within his range; and this was his *forte*. His passion was infectious; for he had a remarkable power **of** making the beauty, latent in things, come alive. This made Rendall a most stimulating, and indeed exciting, 'div don' (the antithesis of the 'dug-out' who was to make the Classics odious to my son Tony). Our textbook of Ancient Greek history (still being used at Winchester in Tony's time) was repulsively arid. I will not mention the author's name. In this book, he did not do himself justice; for there is another book of his that is everything that a book should be. Anyway, for the div don, this unfortunate textbook was a challenge, but Rendall found an answer. He used to enliven our Greek history hour by producing snapshots, taken by himself on a visit to Greece, of the historic Greek landscapes and buildings and works of art that our textbook dealt with so uninspiringly, and he would illustrate the photographs by telling us something of what travel in present-day Greece was like. This imaginative treatment was more than an antidote to the textbook. It made the Greek history hour a treat to which we looked forward. This was a brilliant *tour de force*. Mr. Rendall was a fine photographer. The keenness of his sense of beauty made him set his sights high in photography, as in everything else into which beauty could enter. The finest of his photographs that I know are those that he took, years afterwards, in the Sinai Peninsula and in Palestine, when he made the Grand

Tour after his retirement from the headmastership. 'Grand Tour' is the right name for this journey of his. He made it in Byron's and Kinglake's lordly style, with saddle-horse, pack-horse, and servant.

Besides having to read the dreary textbook of Greek history, we had to spend much of our working time on translating pieces of English prose and poetry into Greek and Latin prose and verse. Mr. Rendall turned this exacting exercise into an opportunity for enticing us to roam at large in the field of English literature, as well as in the Greek and Latin classics. *The Oxford Book of English Verse*—published just before I entered Mr. Rendall's div— proved a marvellous instrument in Mr. Rendall's hand for widening our cultural horizon. After he had set us, as our 'task' for the week, some passage from a poem of, say, George Herbert's or Coleridge's, we would find, to our surprise, that we had become familiar with a much wider range of the poet's works. Mr. Rendall had excited our curiosity by reading aloud to us other passages, which he was not requiring us to translate. He had counted, and not in vain, on awakening the feeling for beauty which is innate in all creatures. He was, in fact, practising on us the mythical magic of Orpheus. Being in Mr. Rendall's div for a year was just what a higher education for precocious teen-agers ought to be.

Mr. Rendall's *chef d'oeuvre*, however, was performed out of school hours. Every year, he used to put on an optional course of lantern-lectures on the Italian painters. Attendance was truly voluntary (unlike the attendance at my Uncle Harry's Sunday service on his ship); yet, every year, a large contingent of the senior part of the school came to see and hear what Mr. Rendall had to give them. It is noteworthy that his voluntary audience was not confined to 'egg-heads'. These lantern-lectures were also attended by 'low-brows' who must have been surprised to find themselves impelled to turn up. What drew us all was the infectiousness of Mr. Rendall's love for the beauty that he was sharing with us. The visual memory of him that stands out most clearly in my mind's eye is a tableau. I see him entranced by the beauty of a picture that had just come on to the screen. His delight in that picture was so great that, for a few seconds, he could not find the words for telling us about it. He just stood there, silent, but with the intensity of his enjoyment revealed in the beatific smile on his countenance. It was a smile that embraced the picture, the audience, and the Universe.

4
The Margoliouths

THE poor Dean of Canterbury, Robert Payne Smith, was on his death-bed, with his life-work still unfinished. He had been compiling a definitive dictionary of the Syriac language, and he had come within sight of completion, but was still at, let us say, the letter *qoph*. He was a widower, and his unmarried daughter Jessie had been keeping house for him and had been working with him on the *Thesaurus Syriacus* at the same time. (She, too, was a Syriac scholar.) 'You must finish the dictionary when I am gone,' her father was saying to her. 'You will need help, and there are only two men in England who would be of any use to you. One of them is Mr. X (if my Aunt Charlie mentioned Mr. X's name when she was telling me the story, I have forgotten it); 'the other man', the Dean concluded, 'is Mr. Margoliouth.' Mr. X died six weeks after Dean Payne Smith himself, so now, for Miss Payne Smith, it was Mr. Margoliouth or nothing. She asked for his help; he agreed to give it; and, since Mr. Margoliouth was a don at Oxford, she came to live at Oxford with my aunt, to get on with the dictionary there. She got on with both the dictionary and Mr. Margoliouth—and with him so well that, by the time the dictionary had reached, let us say, the letter *shin*, they were husband and wife. My aunt had been watching developments with sympathetic amusement.

If the *Thesaurus Syriacus* had been finished before Dean Payne Smith's death, my guess is that Mr. Margoliouth would have remained a bachelor till the end of his days. By the time when I came to know him—he was Archbishop Laud's Professor of Arabic by then—he had become superficially domesticated; but he always looked as if he were surprised that this had happened to him. If there had not been those two successive happy incidents (if one may describe two sad deaths in this incongruous language), he would, I believe, have been another Mr. Rendall or Professor Dawkins. The combination of Miss Payne Smith's vivacity with the spell-binding effect of the Syriac language on a dedicated Semitic scholar was perhaps the only magic that could have produced the auspicious change in Professor Margoliouth's destiny.

The Margoliouths' marriage was a most happy one—perhaps partly because the contrast of temperaments was so extreme. The Syriac scholarship that had brought them together was the one point of resemblance between them. For the rest, Mrs. Margoliouth was lively and talkative, while Professor Margoliouth was grave and was sparing of his words. His wife could manage him because she was not in awe of him, though he was an awe-inspiring figure, with his snow-white hair and his piercing black eyes and his hat that was a cross between a bowler and a topper. (The Master of Balliol, too, used to wear a hat like that; it was headgear fit for Zeus himself; but on James Leigh Strachan-Davidson's head it did not have quite so majestic an effect as it had on David Samuel Margoliouth's.) Professor Margoliouth also wore a white bow tie, to signify that he had been ordained a clergyman of the Church of England. He may also have needed it as a reminder to himself, for I never heard of his having ever officiated. I can still see Mrs. Margoliouth bustling fearlessly round him—like the keeper in a zoo who is not afraid to give his elephant a tiresome wash and brush-up, because he knows that the elephant loves him too much to think of turning and rending him.

Mrs. Margoliouth was indulgent to her husband's tastes. When I was an undergraduate, Professor Margoliouth used, from time to time, to invite me to go for a walk with him; and, one afternoon, when, for this purpose, I called at the Margoliouths' house in North Oxford by appointment, I asked whether the professor was at home when Mrs. Margoliouth opened the door. 'Oh, I expect he is at the pub, as usual,' was her startling answer; and then, noticing my surprise, she explained to me that 'the pub' was her short title for the piece of work, whatever it might be, in which the professor was engrossed at the time. In his own unalcoholic way he was an addict. He was the slave of his success-ive intellectual hobbies. Mrs. Margoliouth had her hobbies too. One afternoon I found her sitting at home, surrounded by a sewing-party of other North Oxford dons' wives, all hard at work on a heap of velvets and brocades. She had mobilized her North Oxford friends to help her to make vestments for the clergy of the Nestorian Church in Kurdistan. The Nestorian Church meant much to Mrs. Margoliouth; its liturgical language is Syriac; but it can have meant little to the ladies who were working with her for the benefit of this distant enclave of Christ-endom. They were sewing for His Beatitude Mar Shimun be-cause one could not easily refuse Mrs. Margoliouth's requests.

This was difficult because she was so amiable. Indeed, she carried her benevolence to lengths at which it produced boom-erang-like effects. 'If', my aunt once advised me, 'Jessie Margol-iouth ever says to you "so and so is my *particular* friend", and if she then asks you to do something for this particular friend of hers, take warning from the word "particular" and think twice about committing yourself. When she says "particular", that is a sure sign that it is some lame dog whom she is mothering.' To be known to have been called her particular friend by Mrs. Margol-iouth came to be serious for the person so designated. His or her stock would at once fall sharply in the North Oxford gossip-market.

On another visit to the Margoliouths' house, I found the *fiches* of entries for a Syriac dictionary spread out on a very large table. I must have been watching the birth of the supplement to *A Compendious Syriac Dictionary*—the Margoliouths' joint work that had been the sequel to their completion of the *Thesaurus Syriacus*. By this date they had been partners in work and life for many years.

Professor Margoliouth's dominant passion was for Semitics. It was not the same kind of emotion as Mr. Rendall's passion for Italian painting. Mr. Rendall was drawn by love; Margoliouth was drawn by a fascination that was not less strong but was com-patible with simultaneous contempt and reprobation. Semitics had gripped Margoliouth at an early age. There was a legend that, while he was still a boy at Winchester, he had compiled an Arabic dictionary for himself because no Arabic dictionary so far published came up to his already exacting standards. He was an addict, but he was not an enthusiast. He was also a sceptical addict—a combination of contradictory attitudes which one might have thought to be psychologically impossible if one had not met it in the life in Professor Margoliouth's psychic make-up.

This queer combination was exemplified strikingly in Professor Margoliouth's attitude towards Islam, the field of Semitic study to which he gave most of his attention. He once told me that he made a practice of reading through the Qur'ân at least once a year. This must have taken a big bite out of his working time, completely at home in Arabic though he was; for the Qur'ân is appreciably longer than the Bible. In this connexion, Professor Margoliouth said—I am sure, with truth—that an Islamic scholar could not keep himself *en rapport* with the spirit of Islam unless he had the Qur'ân at his finger tips all the time. Yet he did not admire the Qur'ân, not to speak of loving it, and he did not admire or love the Prophet Muhammad either. When he undertook to write the Prophet's life for a series called *The Heroes of the Nations*, what came out was a super-Voltairean satire, rendered all the more formidable by the author's unquestionable mastery of the facts. Muhammad a hero? He? He did not look like one by the time that Professor Margoliouth had put him through his mangle and wrung him out. The book evoked cries of horror in the Islamic world. Indeed, it was so merciless that it distressed a Coptic Christian contemporary of mine at Oxford, Fanous. A Copt had no call to hold a brief for Islam; but the impression made by Professor Margoliouth's book on Fanous was that it was an attack, not merely on Islam, but also on everything 'oriental'.

Professor Margoliouth's scepticism could be paralysing on occasions. When, during the First World War, I was working in the Political Intelligence Department of the Foreign Office, I persuaded him to undertake to read, and report on, the Armenian press. He soon returned my first batch of Armenian newspapers with the dry comment that there was nothing in them worth noting. I was, and am, fairly sure that, for the purposes of political intelligence, those newspapers were full of meat, but Professor Margoliouth could not bring his mind down to the pedestrian level of the Foreign Office's needs in war-time.

His scepticism sometimes toppled over into credulity. One day, Gilbert Murray received a script from Margoliouth. (G. M. was a close friend of Margoliouth's; they had once gone travelling together in the Levant.) This script turned out to be a paper in which Margoliouth was able to tell the prospective reader all the things that we should most like to know about the poet Homer: his birth-place, his father's name, his date, and the number of lines in the poem from which all this information had been elicited. I forget whether it was the *Iliad* or the *Odyssey*. Whichever of them it was, Margoliouth had detected an acrostic, formed of the first and last letter in each of the first six lines. The sensational information had been lodged there by the poet, as a silver trowel is sometimes buried under the foundation-stone of an important building. In a covering letter, Margoliouth asked Murray to give him his opinion on the paper before he published it. He pointed out that the number of lines given to the poem by the acrostic tallied with the number in our manuscripts, and that this was presumptive evidence that the unverifiable items of the acrostic's information were likewise correct.

When Murray read this, he felt anxious about the effect of the paper, if published, on Margoliouth's reputation as a scholar. In the event, Murray's anxiety about this proved to have been excessive. Margoliouth's reputation was based on enough solid work for him to be able to squander a bit of it on a fantasia without risk of his being declared intellectually bankrupt. However, Murray did feel a concern to head Margoliouth off from his intention to put the paper into print. He must deter him, but how could he do this tactfully? After a few minutes' thought, he picked out, at random, a play by Aeschylus, a play by Sophocles, and a play by Euripides; noted the first and last letters of the first six lines of each play, and read, in each set of twelve letters, the acrostic which gave the playwright's birthplace, his father's name, his date, and the number of lines in that particular play of his.

Murray then posted Margoliouth's paper back to Margoliouth, with his own companion paper enclosed, and with no comment beyond that. Margoliouth sent Murray no comment on Murray's paper; but he quickly published his own, and his reputation survived this escapade. His urge to publish had been compulsive. Until the Homeric acrostic was off his chest, it was 'the pub', to use Mrs. Margoliouth's phrase.

As this incident indicates, Margoliouth was a Greek scholar as well as a Semitic one. A College man at Winchester in his generation could hardly have failed to be well versed in Latin and Greek. In Greek, his favourite author was Aristotle, and his Aristotelian scholarship was a useful companion to his Arabic scholarship, considering the historical importance of the Arabic translations of Aristotle's works. Greek and Arabic, however, were not the sum-total of Professor Margoliouth's learning, as I discovered on my afternoon walks with him. We usually walked on Port Meadow, within sound of the Great Western trains; and, whenever an express train rumbled by, Professor Margoliouth would look at his watch to verify whether that train was keeping time. Evidently he knew by heart at least the Oxford section of Bradshaw's Railway Guide. I should not have been surprised to learn that he was literally omniscient.

5
Sir Alfred Zimmern

ONE of my most thrilling intellectual experiences when I was an undergraduate at Oxford was a course of lectures by the Ancient History tutor at New College, A. E. Zimmern. This was an introductory course in Greek history for people who were just starting to read for Literae Humaniores. Zimmern used to give it in the summer term; and, as the attendance was large, he gave it in the college hall.

As I listened to Zimmern's course in the summer of 1909, I recognized that this was just what a course of lectures ought to be. This lecturer was bringing Ancient History alive. He was doing that by taking it for granted that the Greeks had been real people, living in a real world, not paragons, living in some holy land on a perpetual Sunday. Since the Greeks were authentically our fellow human beings, their history—their ideas, ideals, successes, failures, and fate—must have practical significance for us, who were living on the same planet in a later age. Zimmern made this capital point by throwing any number of bridges over the time-gulf between the Greeks' history and ours. Evidently his interest in the Graeco-Roman World, which was as keen as mine was, did not rule out a parallel interest in the present-day world. Zimmern's example showed me that the two interests could co-exist in the same mind, and that each of them was illuminating for the other. This course of lectures at Oxford was the prelude to a lesson that I was to finish learning, two and a half years later, in Greece itself.

Zimmern's present-day world was far-flung. One day, when, after the lecture, I had gone up to the dais to ask him something

about some point that he had been making that morning, my eye
was caught by a book that was lying on his desk beside his
lecture-notes. This was not a book about any episode of Greek
history. Its title was *Racial Problems in Hungary*; its authorship
was masked under the *nom de plume* 'Scotus Viator'; the publica-
cation date was recent—the previous year (we were now in
1909)—but Zimmern had got on to it already. This book excited
my curiosity, though, at this date, my hitherto blank map of
Eastern Europe was not yet being filled in by my fellow Balliol
undergraduate, Namier (originally Bernstein), who did not come
up to Oxford from the Sorbonne till the beginning of the next
academic year. Zimmern noticed what was holding my eye. 'Oh,
that is my friend R. W. Seton-Watson's latest book,' he said.
'We are planning to do some travelling together in Austria-Hungary this coming long vacation.' He picked the book up and put
it in my hands. 'Borrow it', he said, 'if you like.' I borrowed it
gratefully and read it eagerly. It proved to be a landmark in my
education, and it had been brought to my notice by a scholar
whose *Fach* lay in what would be a distant field, supposing that
the division of mankind's history into compartments made any
sense. It looked, however, as if, for Zimmern, these compartments
were non-existent.

Alfred Zimmern's historical horizon had been kept wide, not
only by his own wide-ranging curiosity, but also by his unusual
family history. The family had come from Frankfurt, and Alfred's
father had begun his career in business there. Some years, however,
before the conquest and annexation of Frankfurt by Prussia in
1866, Alfred's father had foreboded that the Prussians were coming, and he had decided to get out before they arrived. He had
therefore migrated to England and had there made a new start in
business—this time in the China trade (i.e. the trade, not in china,
but with China). His affairs had gone well, and Alfred had grown
up in the bosom of an English business community in a comfortable house in Surbiton. He had won a scholarship at Winchester (he had about ten years' seniority over me there) and had
then won a scholarship at New College, where he was now a
tutorial fellow. Alfred seemed just as English as the rest of us,

yet at the same time he had retained, from his family's past, a familiarity with Continental Europe which few of the rest of us ever acquired. One noticed, for instance, that he spoke German, Italian, and French as fluently as he spoke English, and also as readily as if these Continental foreign languages had as good a claim to be current as English had. If any of the rest of us could speak any Continental language at all, he was likely to speak it haltingly and with a self-consciousness that was compounded of overt shame at betraying so gross an intellectual incompetence and suppressed indignation that he had been put to shame by his lack of proficiency in a tongue that had only a questionable title to survive. There was a difference here between Alfred and the rest of us—a difference that we recognized to be wholly in Alfred's favour.

Alfred's hold on cosmopolitanism was a double one. His origin was not only Continental; it was also Jewish on his father's family's side. After I had come to know Alfred rather well, I was able to ask him, without fear of giving him offence, a personal question that had, long since, been exciting my curiosity. Did he, I asked, think that his Jewish background had had any effect on his outlook on the world or on his attitude to life? Alfred's answer was that he had many times put this question to himself, because he had felt the same curiosity about it as I had; and he had found that, as he had grown older, his answer had changed. At Winchester, and, later, as an undergraduate at Oxford, he had not been conscious of any difference between himself and his non-Jewish contemporaries. He had not, after all, been brought up as a Jew in religion. If he had been, and if his parents had been practising Jews, they could hardly have sent him to Winchester; for Winchester's tactics with non-Anglicans were like Australia's tactics with Asians. Australia has no Asian (Exclusion) Act on her statute book; but an Asian applicant for an immigration visa will be given a dictation-examination that he will be unable to pass because the dictation will be given in some language, carefully chosen by the immigration authorities, of which the applicant is certain to be ignorant. At Winchester in Alfred's time and still in mine, there was no religious test, but attendance at Chapel

was obligatory and the Winchester College chapel services are
Anglican. (Since then, non-Anglican boys in the school have been
given the option of attending their own religious denominations'
own places of worship in the city.)

As a schoolboy, then, and as an undergraduate, Alfred had
done what the other boys had done and had felt as they had felt.
Since then, though, he now told me, he had thought that he had
noticed in himself a certain detachment that he did not observe
in the people round him. I was much interested, but, in the light
of what I knew of Alfred, I concluded that this distinction that he
had noticed must be a subtle one; for he was certainly not detached
in his attitude to current human issues. He was a whole-hearted
liberal (not just in the partisan political sense, but in the broader
sense of the word), and whole-hearted liberalism is hardly compatible with detachment.

Alfred could, and did, draw subtle distinctions, for he was
sensitive and perceptive to an unusual degree. He was endowed
with some special psychic organ that served him like a seismometer
or like a butterfly's antennae. This organ of his could register the
slightest tremors in the structure of society and could foresee
things that were to come when they were still far off in the
future. Perhaps Alfred inherited this gift from his father. He certainly did, like his father, have a presentiment of what the Prussians
were going to do. Once, for instance, when I was telling him
about my impressions on my return journey from Greece to England in August 1912, I mentioned that I had felt that the mounting curve of civilization, which I had followed upwards as I had
travelled north-westward, had reached its peak in the Rhineland
and had been descending again by the time that I had reached
Folkestone. I had felt rueful about this, I said. Alfred pulled me
up short. 'What were you judging by?' he asked. 'Well, I suppose
by the state of the buildings', I answered, 'as I saw them from
the ship's deck and from the railway-carriage window. In the
Rhineland the buildings were so spick and span; at Folkestone
they looked dilapidated by comparison.' 'You must not judge by
outward appearances,' Alfred said. 'They are not the thing that
matters. What matters is something that is invisible. It is the

spirit of the people; and, if you judge by that, as you should, you will not find that Germany stands at the peak of human progress.' Within two years, I was recalling this conversation and admiring Alfred's prescience.

Towards the end of the Oxford summer term of 1909, after I had listened to Alfred's Greek history lectures, I was his guest at a small farewell supper-party that he was giving in his rooms in New College. The party was for his New College pupils of that year, but he had added me because I was a Wykehamist, as he and they were, and was also their close friend and, by this time, his too.

Alfred's undergraduate guests were sad at the thought of his leaving Oxford. We ourselves had two more years ahead of us before we should be taking our final examination in Alfred's field, and we were now feeling that, with Alfred's departure, part of the life that had meant so much to us would have gone out of Oxford. We were also puzzled by Alfred's decision. He was resigning from his fellowship after having held it for not more than about half a dozen years. Yet an Oxford tutorial fellowship was a much-sought-after prize. We undergraduates who were reading for honours all aspired to be elected to fellowships, and we were conscious that this was an ambitious hope and that we should count ourselves lucky if it were to be fulfilled. Alfred himself was sad at leaving Oxford, though he had found good reason for taking this decision and his mind was now made up. After supper he took us up to the top of New College tower. (As a fellow of the college, he had the key.) It was a fine summer evening, and the view of the heart of Oxford from that vantage-point is incomparable. If anything could have made Alfred reverse his decision, it would have been the beauty of that sight.

One of the experiences that had prised Alfred loose from his post had been a comic yet disturbing encounter with Warden Spooner. At the beginning of Alfred's third year as a fellow and tutor of New College, the Warden had sent for Alfred and had said to him: 'Now, Mr. Zimmern, that you will have finished writing your lectures, Mrs. Spooner and I think it would be a good thing if you were to write a book about the Minoans.' The delivery of this directive as a joint command in which Mrs. Spooner was implicated had not made the assignment any more palatable to Alfred. He had been more seriously dismayed by the Warden's assumption that, within the first two years of a possible forty or fifty years' tenure of his fellowship, Alfred would already have written his lectures once for all—to be delivered henceforth, year by year, as they stood, with 'no variableness, neither shadow of turning'.

Alfred's dismay had been justified, for, unlike some of the other Oxford dons of his time, Alfred was a born lecturer; so he understood what the function of a course of lectures is, and also what it is not. What a lecturer can do for his audience is to introduce them to a subject. He can stimulate their imagination and arouse their curiosity to a point at which they will feel an impulse to pursue the subject farther and to go more deeply into it on their own initiative. This will have to be done, not by listening, but by reading; for the proper medium for conveying factual information in detail is a book. If a lecturer tries to make a course of lectures do a book's work, he will be missing his own true opportunity and be wasting his audience's time. To confuse a lecture-course's function with a book's is a mistake that some Oxford lecturers of that period were making, and the unfortunate effects of the mistake were repeated annually in courses that were perennial. A lecturer ought not to repeat a course at all without, each time, revising it first; and his revision, or successive revisions, ought all to be in one direction. They should be directed towards transforming his lecture-notes into possible raw material for an eventual book, and, when this material has been brought to boiling-point, he should work on the book, or, if the book does not then take shape, he should tear his notes up. In either case he should not ever give that particular course of lectures again. He should start fresh with a course on some different subject. I have learnt all this from Alfred's practice. By the time when he resigned from his fellowship he already had on the stocks the book which he afterwards published under the title *The Greek Commonwealth*. He was now going to spend a year in Greece to write his book in the appropriate environment.

The Greek Commonwealth turned out to be all that Alfred's lecture-audiences would have expected. It has a quality that I also find in my Uncle Arnold's *The Industrial Revolution*, and, on a much grander scale, of course, in Gibbon's *The History of the Decline and Fall*. A book of this kind can come to 'date' as a record of matters of fact without losing its freshness as a work of art in which an original mind has enriched the world with a κτῆμα εἰς ἀεί. Before Alfred had sent *The Greek Commonwealth* to press, his thoughts had turned to a project for producing a counterpart of it. This was to be a companion portrait of the modern Western World; and his achievement in *The Greek Commonwealth* was sure evidence that he had the capacity to produce a second work of the same kind and quality. The difference between the two enterprises was not one of character or structure; it was merely a quantitative difference in the amount of the materials that needed to be mastered in each case.

One of the advantages of Greek and Roman history, as a field for intellectual work, is that the surviving evidence, literary and documentary and archaeological together, is scanty enough to allow a mind to do effective work on it within the span of a working lifetime. The problem for a worker in this field is not Psyche's; it is Sherlock Holmes's. He has to reconstruct an intelligible history of past events out of fragmentary traces and clues; he does not have to cope with infinity. On the other hand the infinity of the materials is the crux for a student of Western history. Even the documents and literature that have come down to us from the Western 'Middle Ages' far surpass the surviving Graeco-Roman body of historical evidence in volume; and, for the subsequent age of Western history, since the invention of printing, the volume increases, in a geometrical progression, century by century and, latterly, decade by decade. The bulk of this already accumulated and ever faster accumulating material has now become so fantastically great that the atomic weapon itself would have its work cut out to reduce it to the dimensions of those relics of the Graeco-Roman evidence that have been spared by fire and sword. So, in undertaking to write a book, in the manner of *The Greek Commonwealth*, on the modern Western World,

Alfred was committing himself to performing a much bigger stint of preliminary hard labour than *The Greek Commonwealth* had demanded of him—and that first book of his had been the mature fruit of at least eight years' persistent work on it, not to speak of the background given to him by his previous nine or ten years of classical education at Winchester and Oxford.

Alfred had taken the measure of his new enterprise, and he now set out to prepare the ground for it with the thoroughness that becomes a second nature in a well-drilled classical scholar. For his point of entry into a study of the modern Western World, he chose Erasmus's correspondence and started to read it. No choice could have been better. Alfred had the first-rate scholar's sure eye. But at this point he began to lose his way. I fancy that he did not even finish reading Erasmus's works, and he certainly did not follow up this first piece of preparatory work with any further systematic reading of sources for the study of the modern West. He was now being much sought after in many quarters for multifarious purposes. The publication of *The Greek Commonwealth* had revealed his gifts to a wider public than the academic one, and this had rightly made his intellectual stock rise high. All kinds of people now recognized his ability and his versatility, and they assumed that his resignation from his fellowship had released his working time for doing the various jobs that they had in mind for him. Thus Alfred's resolution to devote himself to a second and still more exacting piece of long-term intellectual work was challenged by numerous solicitations to him to give away his intellectual capital in small change. For someone of Alfred's temperament, these overtures were serious temptations. He succumbed to them, one after another, and his preparatory reading for *The Modern Commonwealth* ran into the sands and petered out. Years passed, and there was still no more news of any progress on what should have been Alfred's masterpiece.

This misfire of Alfred's major enterprise distressed me. My affection for Alfred was great, and so was my estimate of the intellectual potentialities of which he had given so splendid a demonstration in *The Greek Commonwealth*. How was his creative mind's second child—the projected *Western Commonwealth*—to be brought to its now long overdue birth? This problem was always exercising me at the back of my mind, and in the nineteen-thirties —when nearly a quarter of a century had passed since Alfred's resignation of his New College fellowship—I thought that I had found a solution for it.

At this date the Rockefeller Foundation generously gave Chatham House a grant for use in promoting works of scholarship in Chatham House's field. It fell to me, as Director of Studies at Chatham House, to make recommendations to the Publications Committee and the Council for projects on which our Rockefeller grant should be expended. I thought at once of Alfred's still unwritten great work, and I asked him whether I might include it in my list of proposals. To my delight he agreed, and, to my further delight, the Publications Committee and the Council of Chatham House agreed, for their part, that, if we could harvest what promised to be Alfred's major work, we should, at least as far as that went, have made the best possible use of the money that the Rockefeller Foundation had entrusted to us for spending on research. The Council authorized me to invite Alfred, on its behalf, to write his still unwritten book under Chatham House auspices. An agreement, to this effect, was concluded. But now we suffered a sad disappointment. Once again, the work failed to get under weigh. It was held up by a further succession of ephemeral short-term undertakings. By this time Alfred had allowed himself, for too long, to be diverted by one of these after another. Yielding to this temptation had become, for him, an almost compulsive habit. In the end, death overtook him, after the Second World War, with his work on *The Western Commonwealth* no farther advanced than it had been in 1913. This potential achievement of Alfred's has been lost to the world, and the excellence of his inaugural book, *The Greek Commonwealth*, gives the measure of the greatness of the loss of its projected sequel.

How are we to account for this tragedy? (Tragedy is really not too strong a word.) I think the major cause is to be found in Alfred's own nature and temperament, and a minor cause in what may have been an error of judgement on Alfred's father's part at a critical moment in Alfred's life.

I have mentioned already what seems to me to have been an unusual and distinctive element in Alfred's psychic and intellectual make-up. I am speaking of what I have called his 'psychic antennae'. The sensitiveness and perceptiveness of this special psychic organ of his was the faculty that made his Oxford lectures so stimulating and that gave his one substantial book, *The Greek Commonwealth*, its high quality both as an interpretative study and as a work of art. This special gift of Alfred's was his strength so long as he kept it under control for a long-term purpose; but it became his weakness when he allowed it to run away with him. The butterfly's temptation is to flit to the next flower before it has drained the last flower's cup of nectar. This was Alfred's temptation too, and he succumbed to it.

What was Alfred's father's mistake? At the time when Alfred was proposing to resign his fellowship at New College, he mentioned to me that his father, whom he had, of course, been consulting, had told him to do what he thought would be the best for his intellectual career without being deflected by financial considerations. His father (so his father told him in advance) was prepared to finance him if and when he ceased to draw his salary as an Oxford fellow and tutor. This was a fatherly gesture, and a natural one in itself. Alfred's father appreciated his son's gifts; he was proud of them; he was anxious that financial considerations should not stand in the way of these gifts being used to the best effect; and he commanded the necessary means for seeing to this. Alfred's father's benignity was human; yet it was also inconsequent in a father who was in a position to finance his son because he himself had made his own way financially by his own efforts; and it was also perhaps strange in a father who was presumably acquainted with his son's temperament. What Alfred's gifts needed, if they were to be made to bear fruit, was discipline. His 'antennae', which were constantly inciting him to flit from flower to flower instead of settling on any one of them, made inward self-discipline difficult for him. The alternative external discipline of financial necessity would, no doubt, have been discipline of an inferior kind; but the event showed that, for Alfred, it would have been a blessing. This was a point to which he and his father seem to have been blind. (It is notoriously easy to be clear-sighted retrospectively.)

Yes, it was surely a misfortune for Alfred that, when he was thinking of throwing up his fellowship, he was relieved of the necessity of immediately finding another paid job. If he had had to go on spending his working hours on earning his bread and butter, it seems not unlikely that he would have succeeded, in his spare time, in producing *The Western Commonwealth*. The yoke would have been a help and not a hindrance, because it would have provided the discipline that Alfred's temperament needed for working effectively either in or out of school.

I can make this point of mine *ad hominem*. Supposing that, at the time when I had to resign from the Koraïs Chair, someone had stepped in to provide me with the financial means for just following my own bent, would I have accepted Chatham House's invitation to undertake the formidable task of launching the *Survey*? And, if I had shied away from putting myself in this harness, would I ever have launched *A Study of History*?

Alfred is not the only friend of mine who has carried a precious intellectual cargo to the grave with him, after his friends had tried for years, in vain, to persuade him to give this riches to the world. Norman Baynes is, I suppose, the only English Byzantinist so far who could dispute with J. B. Bury the title to have been the greatest scholar in this field that the British Isles have produced yet. But, like Alfred Zimmern, Norman Baynes gave away, what he did give, in small change. His coin had, perhaps, a higher specific gravity than Alfred's had. The fraction of Baynes's store of knowledge that did find its way into print mostly took the form of meticulous and densely documented reviews of other people's books. Baynes did not publish any fugitive essays or ephemeral newspaper articles. His published work is all magnificently scholarly in quality. Yet, substantially, his intellectual career was like Alfred's. He died without having given to the public the masterpiece that he was qualified to write.

Baynes's weakness was the opposite of volatility; it was a hypertrophy of the scholar's conscience. Baynes had laid down a rule for himself to which he adhered rigorously. He would not publish anything of his own on any Byzantine topic till he had read everything that had been published up to date by other scholars in all sections of the field of Byzantine life: every book and every article. In Byzantine studies the output is relatively small by comparison, say, with the output in modern European history or in inorganic chemistry. Yet in our days the human ant has dwarfed himself so radically by the colossality of his product in all domains that Baynes always just fell short of being able to fulfil his enabling condition, and therefore always found himself debarred from publishing anything of his own just yet. (The publication of reviews was the only licence that he allowed himself.)

In the vain hope of being able to tease him one day into lowering his superhuman standard, I used to produce an argument that exposed the fallacy of his reasoning. 'If so industrious a worker as you are', I used to argue, 'is never able to keep quite up to date, you may be sure that your fellow-Byzantinists whose output of books and articles keeps you on the run have published without having mastered everything in the field of Byzantine studies that has already been in print at the time. They have published in ignorance and, according to your standards, this ignorance makes their published work as worthless as your own would be, in your judgement, if you were to follow their bad example. Since their works are not based on exhaustive knowledge, you can ignore them, and indeed you should; for such ignorant products will not be informative; they will be misleading. Therefore, forget about all this shoddy work that your contemporaries are doing; confine yourself to the original sources, which you have at your fingertips already; and publish something of your own, based solely on these. You can do that with a clear conscience.' Baynes always admitted, with a smile, that my critique of his rule was cogent, but of course he never dreamed of modifying his own frustrating practice.

Happily, there is another point, besides their common phobia of producing substantial works, in which Alfred's and Baynes's intellectual careers resemble each other. While both, alike, left a legacy of published work that was tragically smaller than what it might and should have been, they both also left another legacy which cannot be measured with precision, because it is one that is of an invisible kind. This other legacy is as precious, in its own way, as any published work could be. Baynes, like Zimmern, was a splendid lecturer, and he, too, had an inexhaustible kindness of heart that made of him a generous friend, and not merely an inspiring instructor, for every pupil who had the luck to come under his tutelage. The field of personal human relations was the one in which they both found fulfilment—and here their fulfilment was complete, without being marred by any paralysing inhibitions.

This was the role that I had found Alfred playing in my first encounter with him as a member of his audience in New College hall; and, though, when he passed on from speaking to writing, he remained a man of one book, his Oxford course of introductory lectures on Greek history was not his only outstanding achievement in this line. For a number of years in the inter-war period he held an annual summer school at Geneva at the season when the Assembly of the League of Nations was in session. One feature of the syllabus was a running commentary, by Alfred himself, on the Assembly's proceedings, and it goes without saying that this course of his was masterly; it gave fruitful scope for those 'psychic antennae' that sometimes led their owner a dance. The students who attended the Zimmern summer school came from the United States as well as from all over Europe. The intellectual fare that they were offered was sufficiently attractive in itself; but, when once they had attended the school, they had a double motive for coming again. They had been captivated by Sir Alfred and Lady Zimmern's human kindness—a common quality which, in both husband and wife, was irresistibly spontaneous and warm-hearted. I saw the effect of this at first hand when, one year, I was one of Alfred's lecturers.

Alfred's Oxford lectures were a worthy prelude to *The Greek Commonwealth* into which they eventually turned. His Geneva summer school was his *chef d'oeuvre* in this special line of his, in which intellectual stimulus was humanized by a kindly personal touch. His achievement in this field, which was peculiarly his own, surely mitigates the tragedy of the book that was never put on paper.

6
Sir Lewis Namier

ONE autumn morning in the year 1909, a week or two after the beginning of my third year as an undergraduate at Balliol, I observed that my 'scout', who, as usual, was bringing my breakfast up to my room, was being followed, this morning, by a procession. A second scout, carrying a second breakfast, was at my own scout's heels, and, from behind the second scout, there came a voice, saying, in a strong Slavonic accent, 'I am Bernstein; I am coming to have breakfast with you.' This vocal member of the procession was not the end of it; for the owner of the voice had come trailing clouds of Eastern Europe. These clouds floated into my room behind him, and they quickly filled it, as Bernstein's stream of talk flowed on.

This early morning *levée* that I was now involuntarily holding did not take me by surprise; for I had already heard of other men of my year receiving similar visitations from an importunate and exotic freshman. Bernstein's tactics were hazardous; for they were a breach of the rather formal rules of undergraduate etiquette. The custom was for senior men to call on the freshmen and invite them to breakfast for a date some time ahead. It was for them, not for the freshmen, to take the initiative; and here was this foreign freshman inviting himself to breakfast, unannounced, in the senior men's rooms. Some of the men who had had this experience of Bernstein had been resentful. This had been unimaginative and unmagnanimous on their part. How could the East Galician stranger be expected to be *au fait* with Oxford undergraduates' provincial conventions? And was it not natural that, now that he had become an Oxford undergraduate himself, he should take the shortest cut that he could think of towards getting acquainted with other members of this interesting fraternity? For what other purpose had he made his way across Europe to Ultima Thule? Having chosen his objective, Bernstein was making straight for it. He always knew what he wanted, and he was seldom hampered by inhibitions. In his *début* at Balliol, he was innocently unaware of the negative effect that he was making on some of those new-found fellow-undergraduates of his whose friendship he was eagerly seeking.

If some of these did rebuff Bernstein's well-meant overtures unkindly, they had some excuse. In Bernstein there was something of Coleridge's Ancient Mariner. If once you let him fix you with his eye, you might find yourself his prisoner without writ of Habeas Corpus. For example, one afternoon in pre-First-World-War North Oxford, he called, at a moment when my wife was on the point of going out, and began to recite to her the original Slav names of the cities of Germany east of the Elbe. (Bernstein was then still a Slavophil.) My wife found herself caught standing in a draught between an open door and an open window. Her mind worked quickly. 'That is quite a large piece of country, and the cities must be numerous. If I ask him to sit, and then shut that window and that door, this recital may take who knows how long.' So she stood where she was and got through in twenty minutes, at the price of contracting a chill. If Bernstein's psychic antennae had been like Lloyd George's or like President Johnson's, he would have been more sensitive to the reactions of the person whom he was addressing. Unfortunately for him, his psychic radar was as inadequate as President Wilson's. His attention was preoccupied by what he himself had to say. He had no psychic energy to spare for picking up what the other person was feeling.

My own reaction to Bernstein's uninvited visit to me was positive, I am glad to say. As he followed his voice into my room, I was instantly taken with that broad bespectacled face backed by that massive head. I divined that Bernstein was lovable, and I did not find his clouds of Eastern Europe suffocating; I found them entrancing. His monologue did not bore me; it held me spellbound. As he talked on, piece after piece of the East European nebula came into focus and then coagulated into a world that was as solid as my Winchester and Oxford world, yet, at the same time, was fascinatingly unfamiliar and complex. This was a feast for my curiosity. When my visitor left, I was eager to see and hear him again; and, during the next two years, this first session of ours was frequently repeated—on my initiative as often as not.

We got on with each other well; for our wishes were concordant. Bernstein wanted to talk; I wanted to listen. Bernstein had more to tell me than I had to tell him. Bernstein was opportunely filling a blank in my picture of the world; for, in my picture, Eastern Europe was still a *terra incognita*, though regions that were far more remote from England—for instance, India, China, and Malaya—already meant something to me, thanks to my education by Uncle Harry and by Cousin Fred. In this, I was typical of my generation and my kind in England; and most of Bernstein's and my contemporaries at Balliol persisted in their state of invincible ignorance about Eastern Europe till they were overtaken by the outbreak of war in August 1914. They failed to profit by the opportunity of learning about Bernstein's world at first hand from Bernstein himself because they were allergic to him and therefore to his homeland. They did not take him seriously, and they therefore could not recognize that his world, too, was real.

In the last academic year but one before the outbreak of the First World War in August 1914, Bernstein was still at Balliol, while I was back there again as a don. This was the year of the two Balkan wars. In one of that year's vacations—I forget whether it was at Christmas 1912 or at Easter 1913—Bernstein had gone home to visit his family, and he came back to Oxford looking worried. 'The international situation is very serious,' he reported to us. 'The Austrian Army is mobilized on my father's estate, and the Russian Army is mobilized just across the frontier, only twenty minutes' walk away. A European war is just round the corner now.' Bernstein was given no chance of enlarging on his grave theme. At the words 'European war', most of the young Englishmen whom Bernstein was addressing in Balliol front quad burst out laughing, as the Athenians had laughed when St. Paul, in his address to them on the Areopagus, came to the words 'resurrection from the dead'. Too good to be true! Ruritania was running true to form! As entertaining as a novel of Anthony Hope's!

Ruritania? But what about Utopia? Certainly, Bernstein's world and the laughers' world could not both be real; for they were mutually incompatible. Which of the two would prove to have been the reality and which would prove to have been the mirage? It was Bernstein's world, not the laughers' world, whose reality was vindicated in the event. Within three years of this fantastic conversation in the quad, half of those unfortunate laughers were dead.

The British ignorance displayed in that pre-war conversation in the quad was not the last or the most shattering example of it that Galician Bernstein was to encounter. On Armistice Day, 1918, Lord Robert Cecil, who had been the United Kingdom's war-time Minister of Blockade, kept his vow that he would resign from the Government, as soon as the war was over, as a protest against the disestablishment of the Episcopalian Church in Wales. He had then promptly been appointed head of the section of the British delegation to the forthcoming peace conference in Paris that was to deal with the setting up of the League of Nations. Lord Robert wanted to equip himself for his new task, so he sent to the Political Intelligence Department of the Foreign Office for a map of Austria-Hungary. This was Bernstein's job, and he went to Lord Robert's room, map in hand. 'That map must be wrong,' Lord Robert said to Bernstein, after glancing at it. 'Well, no, it is correct, sir,' Bernstein answered. 'But surely this long straggling piece ought to be yellow, not red.' Lord Robert had his finger on Bernstein's native Austrian Crownland, Galicia. (On Bernstein's map, Hungary was coloured yellow, Austria red, and Bosnia-Herzegóvina green. I saw the map a few minutes later, when Bernstein came staggering into my room, still holding the map, with a dazed look on his face.) 'Well, no, you see, sir, Galicia is part of Austria, not of Hungary.' There was a moment's pause, and then: 'What a funny shape Austria must be,' Lord Robert said ruminatively, half to himself. This from a Minister of the Crown who had been engaged in blockading the Habsburg

Monarchy for the last four years! Bernstein never got over the shock of that interview. 'The English: are they human?' Someone once published a book with this title. The query would seem to be iustified by Bernstein's Oxford and Whitehall experience.

Bernstein's father's estate lay in Eastern Galicia, just on the Austrian side of the Austro-Russian frontier. The neighbouring landowners had nicknamed Bernstein's father 'the Count of Jerusalem'. He was of Jewish origin, and in this he was unique among the East Galician rural gentry. The family were no longer Jews in religion; they had become converts to Roman Catholicism — Catholicism of the Latin rite; for the East Galician landowners were Poles, or at any rate had become Polonized, whereas their peasants were Ukrainians and Uniates, i.e. ex-Eastern Orthodox who had accepted Papal supremacy and had been allowed by the Vatican, in return, to retain their Eastern Orthodox rite.

The Bernsteins had embraced the distinctive nationality as well as the distinctive religion of their fellow-landowners in Eastern Galicia; but their assimilation, though it had gone far, had not been complete. Their neighbours evidently did not feel that the Bernsteins had become one hundred per cent. Polish and Latin-rite Christian. The nickname is evidence of that. Conversely, Bernstein, when I first knew him, was conscious of his family's Jewish background and was proud of it. One of the first bits of information that he gave me about his world was that he was descended from Elijah ben Solomon the Gaon of Wilno, the redoubtable enemy of the Chassidim. (The Gaon? The Chassidim? The Frankists? These figures in the history of the Jewish Pale have been part of my mental furniture ever since Bernstein put them on the map for me.)

From this point onwards, I shall call Bernstein by the name that he adopted after he had decided to throw in his lot with England permanently. Namier? The name is a hybrid. Take 'Nemirov', which was the name of the Bernsteins' family estate; drop the adjectival last syllable and replace the original vowels by the vowels of the English surname 'Napier', which in English are pronounced, curiously enough, as if they were 'e' and 'i'; and then you have a name that its inventor and subsequent bearer has, since, made famous by his achievements as an historian.

Though Lewis Namier, at the time when I first came to know him, certainly felt an attachment to his Jewish past, my recollection is that, at that stage, he saw international politics with Polish, rather than with Jewish, eyes. He was then hoping to see Poland liberated and reunited, and he was therefore hoping for the overthrow of both the German and the Russian Empire. Clearly this was the only condition on which the political resurrection of Poland could become practical politics, but, at that time, this Polish hope seemed chimerical. Even if there were to be a European war, Russia and Germany would be engaged in it on opposite sides; so presumably only one of the two oppressor powers could be defeated, and the victor, whichever one it might be, would continue to oppress its own slice of Poland as before. In the event, of course, the incredible conjuncture came to pass. By the end of the First World War, Russia and Germany were both prostrate and Poland was able to rise again, reunited at the expense of the two thunderstruck giants.

Lewis Namier's and my Balliol contemporary and common friend, Hamish Paton (Professor H. J. Paton), holds, he has told me, that Lewis's Polish feeling was never so dominant, and his Jewish feeling never so subordinate—not even in the pre-First-World-War period—as they appear to me to have been in my recollection of Lewis's political outlook at that time. Perhaps there is really no discrepancy between Hamish's impression and mine. It is possible that we may be recollecting different stages of the development of Lewis's political outlook. The time when I saw the most of Lewis was the pre-war time, when we were still undergraduates. The time when Hamish saw the most of him was during the First World War, when they were working together, for the British Government, on a minute study of the ethnic composition of the population round the fringes of the area in which the Poles were indisputably in a decisive majority. (The outcome of their joint work was the Paton Line—known to the world as 'the Curzon Line'; research-assistants, however eminent intellectually, are seldom given the credit for their work.) There is no doubt that, when Poland regained her independence, Lewis became a

Polonophobe and a Zionist. He may well have been moving in that direction already. He may have become progressively alienated from Polish nationalism as the Polish nationalists progressively showed their hand.

Lewis's transition from Polonism to Zionism, however and wherever it may have taken place, allowed of his being consistently anti-German throughout. Before the end of the inter-war period, Germany had naturally become still more hateful to Lewis as a Jew than she had been hateful to him as a Pole in the pre-war age, when the Poles, like the Magyars, had found the Jews useful as political allies. In contrast to Lewis's hostility to the Germans, his hostility to the Russians was not implacable. This is demonstrated conclusively by two positive acts that were the two most important events in his private life. Lewis twice married a wife who came from Russia, and his widow, Lady Namier, made the last chapter of his life by far the happiest. I have never seen one human being so greatly transformed by another as he was by her. 'Transfiguration' would be hardly too strong a word to describe the effect on Lewis of his second marriage. The lovableness that I had divined in him at our first meeting now shone out of his countenance unclouded. This last chapter of Lewis's life was all too short. In terms of the present-day average expectation of life, Lewis died early, when he had much still to do and still to live for. This was sad; yet that last chapter must have more than made up, for him, for his preceding disappointments and frustrations.

Lewis was invincibly lovable, from first to last; and, during the years before he was transformed by his second marriage, he needed to be invincibly lovable if a friendship with him was to last, for his character had another vein in it which, unsubdued, put his lovableness to a searching test. If you crossed Lewis on some issue which, for him, was of importance, he was capable of declaring total war on you, however old and close a friend of his you might be; and, in making war, he was always vehement, sometimes vindictive, and occasionally even venomous—*impiger, iracundus et acer*, in fact. If anyone else had been making war on one in this intemperate style, one's affection for him would have waned and perhaps have expired sooner or later. Yet there was something in Lewis that was disarming, even when he was giving considerable provocation. I can speak of my own reaction only. When he quarrelled with me, I found that I had no inclination to hit back. In the tug-o'-war between one's old affection for him and one's present annoyance with him, one's affection was an easy winner. One's affection told one that the belligerent Lewis was not the ultimate Lewis. One remembered the blue sky, even when it was hidden by rain-clouds, and one felt no doubt that, one day, the clouds would pass and the sky blow clear again.

Lewis's quarrel with me was over what I was writing, in the Chatham House *Survey*, about the history of Palestine under the British mandate; and he objected to my handling of this controversial and tricky subject because, by this time, he had become an ardent Zionist, while I, as the course of events in Palestine unfolded itself, was becoming more and more doubtful whether the mandatory power was going to succeed in reconciling its commitments to the Palestinian Arabs with its commitments in Palestine to the Jews. I feared that the Arabs were going to get an unfair deal, and I therefore felt a concern to make sure of recording in my narrative the facts that looked to me as if they were giving the Arabs reasonable cause for apprehension and therefore for resentment.

Part of the technique that I had developed, by this time, for the production of the *Survey* was to circulate chapters on controversial topics, in draft, to authorities in both the contending camps, in order to be able to consider and compare their comments and to revise my draft in the light of these, if I felt that this was required before sending the draft to the printer. When asking an authority to read one of my drafts, I used to assure him that I would give the most careful consideration to any comments and any suggestions for amendments that he might be moved to make, but I used to add that I could not guarantee that I should accept his suggestions, even partially.

When I came to have to write my narrative of Palestinian events in the explosive year 1929, I thought at once of Lewis, and sent him my draft under cover of a letter on my usual lines. Lewis's comment was furious and mountainous; and, by the time when I had revised my draft to take account of it, my additional footnotes, qualifying many of my original statements in view of the points that Lewis had made, had become as thick as those that one finds in a commentary on a play by Aeschylus or on an epistle of St. Paul's. But Lewis remained unsatisfied. What he required was an incorporation of his amendments in my text, *in toto* and *verbatim*. (Among my many commentators in the course of thirty-three years, the only other one who took offence at something less than total acceptance of his comments was Sir Samuel Hoare.) After this experience had repeated itself in one or two subsequent years, Lewis broke off relations with me. If we passed each other in the street, he would march past in grim silence; and, if Chatham House colleagues of mine happened to be with me, he would cut them, too, dead. I had brought the whole Institute and all its works under Lewis's anathema.

Lewis's motive for turning Zionist had been the chivalrous one that had also moved other people of Jewish origin who, like him, had previously sat rather lightly to their Jewishness. It was a demonstration of solidarity with Jewry now that Jewry was suffering adversity.

For the first fifteen years after the end of the First World War, the Jews' tribulations were, of course, mild compared to what they were to suffer when Hitler captured Germany and subsequently conquered most of the rest of Continental Europe. Down to the Bolsheviks' capture of Russia in 1917, Russia had been Jewry's Enemy No. 1; in 1915 the Russian armies, on their great retreat eastwards from Galicia across the Jewish Pale, had, *en passage*, robbed and evicted and, in some cases, massacred the Jewish element in the population of the territory that they were evacuating. But many of these Jewish war-victims from the Pale had found new homes in Austria and Germany; and, though Britain, by issuing the Balfour Declaration, had snatched away from Germany the advantageous role of being Jewry's principal friend, Germany under the Weimar régime still remained a comparatively agreeable country for Jews to live in. (Neither Britain nor Germany was to retain the Jews' goodwill for long.)

The countries in which the tide had already turned against the

Jews as a result of the peace-settlement of 1920-1 were Poland and Hungary. So long as the leadership of the Polish and Magyar peoples had remained in the hands of the territorial magnates and the minor rural gentry, the local Jewish community's position had been favourable. The local Gentile aristocrats had employed and appreciated the Jews' services. A Polish landowner, for instance, would have a *Hausjude* who managed his business affairs for him. But, after the reconstitution of the Polish state, the situation had changed to the Jews' disadvantage. How were the posts in the new Polish civil service to be apportioned? Here the Jews had run up against the competition of the Polish urban middle class. This middle class had been jealous and ungenerous. They had not given their Jewish compatriots a fair deal. The liberation of Poland had not turned out to mean integration or equity for this minority. That was the explanation of Lewis Namier's revulsion from Polonism to Zionism. Having been awakened to a sense of solidarity with Jewry by Polish injustice, Lewis had wanted to take his share in doing something practical for the relief of Jewish distress. Zionism had appealed to him in this aspect.

Lewis was not, I think, a Jew in the religious sense at any stage of his life, and I guess that he had never been a practising Roman Catholic either. I cannot remember our ever discussing with each other our respective attitudes towards religion, but my impression is that, from the time when he was first able to think for himself until his marriage to Julia de Beausobre, he was an agnostic. Of course, ancient religious attitudes and outlooks have a way of outliving the concomitant religious beliefs, as any ex-Jewish or ex-Christian agnostic will discover if he examines himself. So it is possible that, for Lewis, the practical value of Palestine for Jewry as a country in which Jews could now live free from penalization was enhanced by Palestine's sentimental value as Eretz Israel— the god-given homeland to which it was the Jewish diaspora's destiny to return.

A sidelight is thrown on Lewis's attitude towards Judaism as a religion by a piece of family history that he once recounted to me. In Lewis's childhood, the family had adopted a little orphan Jewish child, of about Lewis's own age; and, when this boy had grown up, they had found the money for paying his passage to the United States. Hammerling (this was the Bernsteins' protégé's name) had been grateful to the family for what they had done for him; and, after he had emigrated, his gratitude expressed itself in the practical form of a stream of presents to the household at Nemirov. The presents became progressively more sumptuous—they were running, now, to gold watches and fur coats. Where did Hammerling's American money come from? So far as the Bernsteins knew, he had become a miner. When Lewis's time at Oxford was approaching its end, it looked as if the Hammerling mystery were going to be solved; for Lewis now received a letter from Hammerling telling him that he (Hammerling) would make Lewis's fortune if Lewis would come to America and go into partnership with him in his business. He would pay Lewis's passage.

Partly out of curiosity, Lewis accepted and went, and he then found that Hammerling had ceased to be a miner long ago. He was now using his brain instead of his brawn, and the brain was proving to be much more lucrative. Hammerling had gained control over a considerable section of the foreign-language press of the United States, and he was selling its syndicated political influence to the highest bidder. Its influence was strong among voters who were immigrants of the first or the second generation, and the profits of Hammerling's business were proportionately great. The editors of a majority of his papers were the priests of foreign-language Catholic communities; so, to oil the works, Hammerling had become a professing Catholic himself.

Lewis had found all this highly distasteful. (He himself was always meticulously honest.) However, having come, he decided to stay provisionally; and his stay was overtaken by the Day of Atonement coming round. On the Day of Atonement, lapsed Jews can, by custom, attend the Synagogue without any questions being asked. 'We had better go,' Hammerling said to Lewis; and they went; but, next day, Hammerling was back in business as before, and, when the First World War started, Hammerling became a German agent. Lewis broke with Hammerling, not over religion, but over that. Hammerling was grateful to the Bernstein family; Lewis was grateful to England; so he jettisoned his chance of making his fortune in America and came back to England to enlist in the Public Schools Battalion.

Whatever Lewis's attitude to religion may have been, his Zionism was essentially practical and political. However, secular nationalists, as well as religious zealots, can be fanatics. Indeed, since the rise and spread of agnosticism as the nemesis for the Western Catholic-Protestant wars of religion, the fanaticism that has been ebbing out of religion has been flowing into nationalism as an alternative container for it. The ultra-Zionists were, and are, politically fanatical to a degree; and this spirit found a response in the belligerent vein in Lewis's temperament.

Lewis's breach with me was maintained by him for several years, and was ended only by a fluke. One afternoon we collided with each other in Lower Regent Street, and, forgetting his vow of non-intercourse, Lewis picked up a thread that he had dropped in my room in Chatham House twenty or thirty months back. 'Toynbee, that footnote of yours. . . .' But this tenacity of Lewis's was so comical that I cut him short by laughing. 'Look here, Lewis,' I said, 'this is ridiculous. We were at Balliol together, and we have been friends for years. It is absurd that footnotes should come between us, or politics either.' To my surprise, he checked himself, and the smile of the lovable Lewis broke out on the militant Lewis's face. Lewis never broke off relations with me again, though our views on the Palestine question remained as far apart as ever.

Lewis's Zionism made him quarrel for a time with me, but it never made him quarrel with England. How he managed to reconcile these two conflicting loves I do not know, but he was obliged to; for he had fallen in love with England at first sight at least ten years before he was captivated by Zionism too. England did not reciprocate his devotion in equal measure. Her formal recognition of his merit was, in my judgement, inadequate. England did, it is true, eventually give him a knighthood, but she never gave him a professorial chair at Oxford. On the other hand, the informal homage that he came to receive in England was immense. If imitation is the sincerest flattery, his heart should have been warmed by the spectacle of the legion of Namierizers that sprang up, ready armed, from the British soil on which he had scattered the dragon-tooth seed of his own particular approach to the study of history. Long before his untimely death, Lewis had lived to see the clouds that he was always trailing turn to clouds of glory. The composition of these clouds had changed since they had followed him into my room one morning in 1909. At that time they had been clouds of Eastern Europe, and few of Lewis's English fellow-undergraduates had shared my interest in these. By the nineteen-twenties they had become clouds of eighteenth-century British constitutional history, and my interest in them had declined; but the interest of a host of other British historians had been awakened.

I myself have continued to keep my eye on East European affairs, among other non-Western fields of historical study; and I had had a substantial grounding in East European studies before Lewis trained on England the searchlight with which he had previously been illuminating Eastern Europe for me. My East European education, which Lewis himself had started, had been carried farther, before the outbreak of the First World War, by Lewis's cousin Ehrlich, who had found his way to Oxford in Lewis's wake. Ehrlich's head was still more massive than Lewis's, and it was even more tightly packed with the minutiae of East European lore. In short, Ehrlich out-Bernsteined Bernstein; and Bernstein (as Lewis still was then) did not take this kindly. One of Lewis's rewards for having trekked so far afield was that, like Odysseus on the last of his wanderings, he had reached a land where he could enjoy the distinction of being unique; and now he had been robbed of this distinction through having been dogged by a relative whose resemblance to him was a caricature. In Oxford at that time, I owned a samoyed dog who, like Lewis, was locally unique and, like Lewis, appreciated this distinction of his. One day, my samoyed suddenly met his double at a street-corner. His disgust was comically like Lewis's disgust when Ehrlich trailed him and tracked him down.

After Lewis had begun to explore British history, he did not arrive either at political British history or at eighteenth-century British history straight away. His first discovery was the writings of the seventeenth-century English Puritans. Before the end of the First World War, he could, and did, recite long passages of these from memory. His analysis of the structure of British politics in the reign of George III came after that. It might seem to be a *tour de force* for a scholar who was by origin a Slavonized Jew to become the greatest of all authorities on a characteristically British institution. However, Lewis had two no less eminent precursors. One of these was a Russian Slav, Sir Paul Vinogradoff, who served his apprenticeship at home on a study of the Russian *mir*, but made his name at Oxford as a student of Domesday Book and of the English manor. Lewis's other precursor was the French Jewish scholar Élie Halévy, who became the leading authority of his time on the social history of Britain during the earlier decades of the nineteenth century. Nor was it, I believe, merely a coincidence that such outstanding contributions to the study of English politics, social life, and culture should have been made by foreign observers whose own cultural backgrounds were so unlike the English cultural phenomena that they were studying. The exotic is not only attractive; it also yields up its secrets to the determined explorer more readily than the explorer's own habitat does. When once those three Continental European scholars had made themselves at home in this exotic English field, they were in a position to inspect it with fresh eyes; and their foreign eyes could espy things—and these noteworthy things—that their English fellow-students had failed to observe because the Englishmen had taken their familiar native scene for granted.

Lewis, for instance, came to me one day, in a state of some excitement, to share with me an observation that he had just made. He had observed that the English language possessed two vocabularies to the Polish language's one. Like Polish, English had, of course, the vocabulary of everyday speech; but, in addition, English had the vocabulary of the Authorized Version of the Bible; and this second vocabulary could be drawn upon to enrich the first. This could be done in any number of graded dosages, ranging from the *verbatim* quotation of a biblical text to the subtlest nuance of a reminiscence of biblical language. By contrast, Lewis pointed out, the Polish language was destitute of a corresponding resource, because Poland was a Catholic country of the Latin rite, and therefore the authorized version of the Bible there had continued to be in the Latin Vulgate—a source on which the Polish language could not draw, because, between Polish and Latin, there is a great gulf fixed. This discovery of Lewis's was also a discovery for me, and it was one that I think I should have been unlikely ever to make for myself. Unlike Lewis, I had been brought up on the Authorized Version, and the relation between its vocabulary and the everyday English vocabulary of my time had always been so familiar to me that I had never meditated on it. Even if I had, I might not have arrived, unaided, at Lewis's observation; for I did not possess the illuminating term of comparison that Lewis possessed in having Polish for his native language.

Lewis's major discoveries about British life were made, as everyone knows, in the field of eighteenth-century British parliamentary history. This field that Lewis made his own, and in which he achieved such great things, happens, for me, to be almost as unattractive as trigonometry is. This is, of course, a blind spot in my field of mental vision, and my blindness is my loss. Yet, though I am not much interested in Lewis's *corpus vile* for its own sake, I am intensely interested in the method that he devised for dissecting it.

Lewis once pointed out to me—I forget at what stage of his work this was—that, though, since we had first come to know each other, we had gone such different ways, we had retained one thing in common: we had, both of us, been unwilling to follow the broad highway that was being trodden by most contemporary Western historians. The simile that Lewis used on this occasion was a different one. 'You', he said, 'try to see the tree as a whole. I try to examine it leaf by leaf. The general run of historians try to take the tree branch by branch; and you and I agree', he wound up, 'that this last approach, at any rate, is an unpromising one.'

I myself believe that what Lewis's way of working and my way have in common is something more than our common rejection of the usual way. I believe that we have rejected this other way because it has seemed, to both of us, to be a mythological way. We have both been trying to demythologize history. We have been trying, each along his own line, to find some way of expressing historical events in terms, not of myths, but of the realities: *wie es eigentlich gewesen ist*, in von Ranke's famous words. The reality to which I myself have been trying to relate history is, I should say—speaking the language of Lewis's simile—the whole of the tree: that is to say, the whole of the Universe, together with the ultimate spiritual presence behind the phenomena, if there is such a presence there. The single leaves, which are the realities with which Lewis sought to operate, are the individual human beings whose innumerable and intricately interwoven relations with each other produce the tangible fabric of history and offer this to us for us to grasp if only we can find a way of apprehending the web's elusive texture. I am not concerned with my own way here. I have expatiated on it in a whole series of other volumes. Lewis's way is my subject in the present chapter; and Lewis's way interests me no less than my own does. It interests me because it seems to me to go straight to the heart of what is one of the historian's crucial problems, as I see it.

As I see it, and as Lewis, too, saw it, the realities in the realm of human affairs are human beings and the relations with each other into which human beings enter. In human affairs the source of every action is some individual person. Every human action is a product of a previous act of choice, and the power to make choices is the monopoly of human personalities. So, when we say 'Harold Wilson did this or that', we are using language that is one hundred per cent. realistic. If we say 'the Prime Minister did it', our feet are no longer planted quite so firmly on the ground; for the term 'Prime Minister' is an abstraction; the title is worn, like a second-hand suit of clothes, by one human being after another; and the wearers, not their official vestments, are the realities. If we say 'Her Majesty's Government did it', we have floated off the ground into the atmosphere of mythology. What we are alluding to is the resolution of a number of real forces, namely the network of relations between Mr. Wilson, Mr. Stewart, Mr. Gunter, Mr. Brown, and several other realities in the shape of human personalities. 'Her Majesty's Government' is a mythical character; and so are its congeners the United Kingdom, the Electorate, the

Crown, the Church, the Bench, the Bar, the Trade, the Turf. These collective abstractions, to which we attribute human-like acts, are of the same order of unreality as the nereids, dryads, oreads, and other anthropomorphic divine presences in human form in whose imaginary actions the Ancient Greeks had mythologized the seas, woods, mountains, and other features of inanimate Nature before Thales reduced all these mythical beings to water.

Everyone will agree that history ought to be written, on Thales's lines, in terms of the realities, not in terms of myth. Mythical history is as inadequate a vehicle for conveying the realities of human affairs as Erasmus Darwin's vocabulary in *The Loves of the Plants* is for conveying the realities of the science of botany. Try, then, to write a passage of historical narrative in terms of nothing but human individuals and their relations with each other. You will find the experiment frustrating. You will discover that you will not be able to write a line without ascribing to mythical abstractions the authorship of actions that, in reality, were performed, as you know very well, not by these non-existent wraiths evoked from fairyland, but by human beings.

Why do we find ourselves writing about human affairs in terms which we know to be imaginary? The historians are not the only students of human affairs who are driven to defeat their own purpose in this way. The sociologists, anthropologists, and economists fare no better. All of them alike are defeated by Psyche's task—the task of coping with quantities with which a human being's unaided powers are incommensurate. This task has been aggravated in our time by a characteristic feature of the modern world. Since the outbreak of the Industrial Revolution, the quantity of everything in Man's environment—particularly the quantity of production and of population—has been increasing inordinately, while a human being's powers have remained what they always have been. The limitation of these powers is the most rigid in the realm of intellectual work, which can be performed only by a single human mind, and cannot be expedited, as industrial production can be, by team-work and by the division of labour. In the field of intellectual work, the limit of the quantity that a single mind can handle is the maximum capacity of a vigorous and industrious mind that survives to live out its full working lifetime. This maximum has been slightly increased by the recent increase in the average length of effective life, thanks to the progress of medicine; but this gain on the human side of the balance-sheet between the individual human being and his environment is derisorily small compared with the multiplication, in the field of intellectual work, of the quantity of things that there are to know. The widening gulf between these two sides of the intellectual worker's balance-sheet is the gulf that students of human affairs have, so far, found themselves unable to span.

The difficulty of describing human affairs in terms of realities is illustrated by our inability to get to grips with what really happens in an election. The only way that we have yet found of recording this is to treat an election as an impersonal event. Out of such and such a number of potential votes, such and such a number were actually cast, and, of these, such and such a number were cast in favour of this and that candidate or party. The winning majority of votes was of such and such a magnitude. This is, of course, so inadequate a way of describing the realities that it is positively misleading. The realities were not one simple impersonal event; they were an immense number of personal acts of individual human beings acting in an intricate network of relations with each other. Some of the voters' actions were negative. They ignored the election and failed to vote. Of those who did vote, some cast their votes without previous consultation; others had previously discussed the issues with their neighbours, with some of the canvassers, and perhaps with one or more of the candidates themselves. A full record of all these acts, negative and positive, would be an account of the election in terms of the realities. Why, then, does not the historian who sets out to write a narrative of the election, or the sociologist who sets out to analyse it, present his findings in these realistic personal human terms? Why does he have recourse, instead, to impersonal abstractions which he knows to be unreal? One reason for his behaviour is evident, and it is a compelling one: the quantities involved in an account in terms of the realities are so vast that, unaided, the observer cannot even begin to cope with them. He is being asked to trace the stream of feeling and thought in the psyche of every elector, and also to trace every thread in the web of intercourse between each elector and his neighbours, throughout the period of the election campaign, and perhaps also during an antecedent period that may be of indefinite length. This is truly a task that a human mind cannot hope to perform, unaided.

Lewis Namier had two virtues that are great in themselves and are cardinal for the study of human affairs. He had insight and he had courage. Lewis saw that, in this field of study, the problem is to demythologize our language by describing things in terms of the human realities; he saw that, if we are to solve this semantic problem, we have also to solve the operational problem of coping with inordinate quantities, and he worked out a plan of campaign. He decided to start operations from the side of the realities. He would make a survey of the acts, thoughts, and feelings of the individual human beings involved in the transactions that he was studying. This survey was to be so exact, minute, and extensive that it would embrace the sum total of the realities and would thus make the mythological travesty of these realities superfluous. When he had made his plan, he had the courage to put it into action. This was an act of faith; for he was relying on his own human intellectual powers alone, without aid, either supernatural or technological.

Lewis was not, of course, the first student of human affairs to employ the 'prosopographical' method of investigation. The identity of the pioneers is revealed in the technical term 'prosopography' itself. This word, which means 'the documentation of personalities', has been coined out of two Greek components, and the method had already been applied in the field of Greek and Roman history before Lewis Namier adopted it. A 'Who's Who' had been compiled of Alexander the Great's officers and another of the members of the Roman governing class, before Lewis started to compile his own 'Who's Who' of members of the Parliament of England and, thereafter, of the United Kingdom. In China, history has been partly presented in the form of prosopography ever since the pattern of Chinese history-writing was set by its father, Ssu-ma Ch'ien, in the second century B.C. Lewis, however, made a new departure which was, I should say, not only distinctive but epoch-making. His precursors in the fields of Chinese history and of Greek and Roman history had made a notable addition to mankind's stock of raw knowledge. In the corpus of Chinese historical works, the total quantity of the prosopographical material is vast. But neither the Chinese nor the Western classicist prosopographers had looked far—if they had looked at all—beyond the process of accumulating biographical information. Lewis Namier was, perhaps, the first prosopographer for whom this process was, not an end in itself, but a means to an end that lay beyond it. Lewis's objective, in plunging into prosopography, was to arrive ultimately at a presentation of history itself in terms of individuals and their relations with each other—terms which, as he had divined, would present history *wie es eigentlich gewesen ist*.

It will be noticed that Lewis's prosopographical prescription for arriving at the realities is the opposite of the sociologists' prescription for the same purpose. Lewis begins by laying hold of the realities—i.e. human personalities—and his objective is to end by leaving these alone in the field, after having crowded out and eliminated the last remnant of the mythological abstractions. By contrast, the sociologists start by analysing the abstractions; and their hope is that, by progressive refinements of their analytical technique, they will succeed in reducing the abstractions to shreds of the size of an individual human being. The sociologists' act of faith is a belief that, in this 'last analysis', their *corpus vile* of abstractions will undergo a sudden metamorphosis. It will turn, they trust, into the inter-relations and the individual acts of real live human beings. The sociologists' act of faith seems less warrantable than Lewis's, and their method therefore seems less promising than his.

How promising is Lewis's inverse method? All the prosopographers whom I have cited—Lewis, the Western classicists, and the Chinese—have been rationalists without being also technicians; and this has condemned them all to have to grapple, unaided, with an undertaking that is superhuman in its dimensions.

They have not looked for the divine intervention which, in the fairy-story, came to Psyche's rescue; and they have not commanded the services of a machine to supplement the workings of their own brain-cells. A *deus ex machinâ* may be neither procurable nor indispensable for an intellectual worker who is up against infinity. But *aut deus aut machina*; if he does not enlist either the one or the other of these two extraneous powers, what chance does the investigator stand of extricating infinity from mythology and reducing it to reality?

Evidently the unaided prosopographer's most promising fields of operation are those in which the number of effective personalities is small and in which the average amount of extant biographical information about each of them is great. These conditions come the nearest to being fulfilled in studies of oligarchical societies; and it is no accident that the Chinese, Macedonian, Roman, and British governing classes have been the objects on which the prosopographical method of research has been tried first, and in which the experiment has also met with the greatest measure of success. This success, however, has been only relative and incomplete; and it could not have been more than that in the case of these unaided prosopographical endeavours. It could not, because, even within the compass of the narrowest and most exclusive oligarchy, the quantity of the prosopographical investigator's material is still too vast to be mastered, without extraneous aid, by one mind in one working lifetime.

Lewis, before the end of his life, had cut down his own stint of work on the history of Parliament by confining its chronological limits to a span of only twenty years of eighteenth-century British parliamentary history; but, on the last occasion on which I had an opportunity of asking him how he was getting on, he was pessimistic and low-spirited. It was evident that, by now, he was not expecting to live to finish even this drastically reduced stint of work himself; and, in the end, he died leaving it uncompleted. (Happily for Lewis, it has been finished, since his death, by a colleague whom he himself had inducted into his method and who had become a Namierizer after Namier's own heart.)

Had Lewis failed? At first sight, it might seem so; for his unfinished stint of work—and this was only one among a large number of stints that he had parcelled out—was one of the steps in the merely preparatory stage of his plan of operations. Before his death, an immense amount of this preparatory work had been done by him personally or, under his supervision, by tested and approved colleagues. In the compilation of biographies, Lewis's achievement was on as heroic a scale as the god Thor's achievement was when he accepted the Giants' challenge to drain the drinking-horn that they had proffered to him. When, at last, Thor set the horn down still undrained, the Giants pointed out to him that they had surreptitiously connected up the tip of the horn with the sea, and that he had now drunk up one-third of all the water in the world's oceans. Still, two-thirds remained unconsumed; so, though Thor's performance had been heroic, Thor had lost his wager. Lewis had rivalled Thor's performance in his own task of assembling the prosopographical materials for producing a history of Parliament in the realistic terms of the lives and acts and inter-relations of human personalities, but Lewis's heroic efforts, too, had been defeated by the overwhelming quantity of the stuff that he had to master. The history of Parliament that Lewis launched has not yet entered on its second and final stage—the stage that is the objective of the preliminary operations. Lewis died before he had completed David's work on the temple, and before he had started on Solomon's.

Does this spell failure? No; for there are two senses in which Lewis did achieve his ambitious purpose. In the first place, he did succeed in writing history in terms of the human realities in one field at any rate. In this field—it is the history of the German Revolution of 1848—he succeeded by a feat of intuition in lieu of extraneous aid from a tutelary divinity or from a computer. In the second place, Lewis blazed a trail which his epigoni, equipped with computers, will perhaps now be able to follow out to its goal, but which they might never have been able to discover for themselves if Lewis had not shown them the way.

Lewis's discovery about the Revolution of 1848 is a characteristic feat of his streak of genius. The approach of the hundredth anniversary of the event had prompted Lewis to make a study of it, and naturally he approached the subject along prosopographical lines. He compiled biographies of the leading participants in the Revolution, and in this investigation he broke through to a conclusion that was as brilliant as it was illuminating.

He found that the majority of the leaders whose careers he had been tracing out were people whose native district had been transferred, in the peace-settlement of 1814-15, from one sovereignty to another. The inhabitants of these transferred territories had been arbitrarily cut off from their ancestral political attachments, and they felt no affection for, or loyalty to, the other German states whose subjects they had now involuntarily become. Like deportees or exiles, they found themselves politically uprooted. Man, however, is (in Aristotle's phrase) 'a political animal'. When he has been expatriated, he feels uncomfortable till he has found a new country to supply the missing focus for his patriotic feelings. The former subjects of the extinguished German ecclesiastical principalities who had now become subjects of Prussia (in the Rhineland) or of Bavaria (in the valley of the Main) gave the allegiance that Prussia and Bavaria failed to inspire in them to a fatherland that transcended all the German parochial states. They gave their allegiance to Germany herself. Germany, however, like Italy, was still 'only a geographical expression'—Metternich's wet-blanket phrase. If Germany was to become a political fact, the peace-settlement of 1814-15 would have to be overthrown. The German Revolution of 1848 was the first attempt at this, and it was only natural that, in this movement, the expatriates should have taken the initiative. This historical connexion between the settlement of 1814–15 and the Revolution of 1848 was perceived by Lewis, and he perceived it with no other aid than his own intellectual acumen.

In the field of British parliamentary history, in which Lewis did not succeed in reaching his goal, who is going to play Solomon to Lewis's David? Probably someone who will not have Lewis's acumen, but will have a computer. (If Lewis had lived ten years longer, he might have taken to operating a computer himself and have ridden this electronic steed to victory in his parliamentary enterprise.)

The vista that is opened up by this guess of mine is both exciting and depressing. It is exciting that Man should have acquired an instrument that promises to enable him to achieve results which, in the pre-computer age, were as far beyond his reach as the Moon, too, was at that time. It is depressing that an inanimate moron should be able to accomplish things that are beyond the unaided power of the ablest human mind.

A computer is a moron. Its 'thinking' is limited to the 'yes or no' procedure of binary arithmetic. Leibniz invented binary arithmetic as a mathematical *jeu d'esprit*, not dreaming that, within three hundred years, his toy would become a serious instrument for practical purposes. For Leibniz, this was unimaginable, since the computer's intellectual ceiling is ludicrously far below a human mathematician's altitude. The computer's *forte*, which a human mind cannot emulate, is that the computer can work so fast that, by its clumsy binary method, it can perform, in a few seconds, calculations that would occupy the full working lifetimes of a number of human higher mathematicians, employing all their most sophisticated devices.

A computer cannot, of course, frame its own questions. It needs a human mind to 'programme' it. But feed Lewis's unanswered questions into a computer, and it will churn out for you, *instanter*, the answers that Lewis did not live to find. Indeed, the mannikin with the computer will be able, with ease, to handle problems of a magnitude that Lewis himself never tackled. The computer-man will not need to confine his investigations to oligarchies. He will be able to describe an election in India in terms of the human realities, though in India the number of the voters runs into nine figures.

Lewis assaulted infinity with his bare fists, and this was Quixotic. It was magnificent, but it was not war. The computer-man is going to subdue, with his machine, quantities of the highest order of magnitude that is to be found in the field of human affairs. His victory in this vaster intellectual war will be scientific, but it will be less glorious than Lewis's brilliant successes and heroic reverses.

7
The Tawneys

THERE is a well-known parlour-game that should be a warning to incautious prosopographers. If Charles Beard, for instance, had had this game in mind when he was engaged on a prosopographical game of his own, he might not have played his own game with such rigour. Beard's game was to write the history of the framing of the constitution of the United States in terms of the private business interests of each of the Founding Fathers of the United States. This interpretation was certainly human, but it was unrealistic in being single-track. There is a mixture of motives and a tangle of contradictions in the conduct and character of even the most single-minded and self-consistent human being. Any single-track interpretation of human nature is therefore unlikely to hit the whole truth. Beard recognized this as he grew in humane wisdom and in scholarly stature. He reconsidered and modified the thesis that he had originally expounded in *An Economic Interpretation of the Constitution of the United States*, and he showed his good faith and his large-mindedness by making his second thoughts public.

In the parlour-game that I am referring to, the player thinks of someone with whom everyone in the room is acquainted, and then, without revealing this common acquaintance's name, he describes him by mentioning traits and acts and experiences of his subject's that are authentic but are misleadingly uncharacteristic. He then challenges the company to guess which of their common friends he has been describing. If the subject's personality lends itself to this treatment, and if the player knows his subject fairly well, the player may be able to baffle even people who know the subject intimately.

I am going to play this game with an old friend of mine. He was a Rugbeian, he was a Balliol man, he was a sergeant in Kitchener's Army, he was an attaché at the British Embassy at Washington during the Second World War—and now I will give him away. When I called on him at the Embassy in the summer of 1942, he was sitting among the lions and unicorns in his shirt-sleeves. I have now told you that he was not a career-man in the United Kingdom Foreign Service. One cannot imagine any permanent member of it letting himself be seen *en déshabille*, even in the sticky heat of a Washington summer. Like me at the time, my friend was just a temporary Foreign Office clerk; at the Washington Embassy he was Labour Attaché; he was Harry Tawney.

By 1942 I had known Harry for thirty-five years. He was my senior by more than eight years. He had come up to Oxford in 1899, and, at the time when I came up, he was one of the Workers' Educational Association's lecturers. This job used to bring him back to Oxford every summer term, and at Oxford we used to see a good deal of each other, thanks to Harry's friendliness. We used to paddle up the Cherwell together in a Canadian canoe; and this soon makes people feel at home with each other, even when there is some difference of age. Once, far up the river, we came on a cow floundering, shoulder deep, in the water. To try, from on board a canoe, to rescue a drowning cow is to ask for trouble. The cow did not drown, but we capsized, and getting wet through together on this forlorn hope was one of those trivial experiences that clinch a friendship.

At the time of our fiasco with the cow, Harry Tawney was already engaged to Jeannette Beveridge. Jeannette's brother William had made his mark by this time as a civil servant—one of a new kind. The Liberal Government of the day had been laying the foundations of 'the welfare state'; and this required, in the civil servants who had to translate the new legislation into practice, a rapid mastery of a mass of detailed information and also a demonic driving-force to set the heavy wheels of administration turning. Setting up the Ministry of National Insurance, for in-

stance, was a night-and-day job, as contemporaries of mine found
who were posted to this ministry in its infancy. The sense of
emergency was foreign to the traditional civil service atmosphere;
it anticipated the spirit of war-time work; and Jeannette Beveridge's brother was one of the active young men who gave this
new *tempo* to a civil servant's work. Lord Beveridge and his sister
had been brought up in India, and their mother was a distinguished
orientalist. Her translation of the Timurid Emperor Babur's
memoirs from the original Turki into English is a fine piece of
scholarship.

When I find myself miserably depressed by the spectacle of
the unwisdom with which the world is governed, I raise my
spirits again by contemplating something in the Universe that
seems wholly good. One of our human world's redeeming features is happy marriages; and, when my mind turns to these, I
think, above all, of four couples whom I have known: the Hammonds, the Webbs, the Adivars, and the Tawneys.

Jeannette and Harry Tawney were made for each other. They
had both taken naturally to an identical way of life, and this was
not the conventional way of the British middle class of their
generation. If they could have been carried back into fourth-
century or fifth-century Egypt, they could have shaken down
easily among the Desert Fathers, and in that setting they might
have become world-famous for their austerity.

Harry Tawney had not been a Rugbeian for nothing. One of
his contemporaries there had been William Temple, and they had
become lifelong friends. Both were generous-minded and were
consequently radicals; both occasionally trailed their coats and
inevitably got into hot water; and both combined their radicalism
on the social and political plane with a lasting attachment to the
Anglican Christianity in which they had been brought up. Temple
became an archbishop, and Tawney continued, I believe, to be a
more or less orthodox Anglican layman. (What? A socialist an
Old Believer? To the Mensheviks a stumbling-block, to the
Bolsheviks folly!)

Archbishop Temple's occasional hot water became hotter at
each stage of his advancement; for his success in his ecclesiastical

career did not incline him to kowtow to the established secular order. He remained radical and did not conceal this; and that exposed him, in his eminent position, to attack. In the summer of 1942, when I was travelling round the United States, making speeches to local branches of the Council on Foreign Relations, a questioner once asked me, in the same breath, whether it was not time for the British to liquidate that antediluvian institution the House of Lords and whether it was not also time for them to depose the Bolshevik who, by divine oversight, had now become Archbishop of Canterbury. My American questioner was leaving my countrymen a narrow path to walk on. Between his Georgian Scylla and his Stalinian Charybdis he was reducing the path to a knife-edge. He was going to be a difficult American for Britain to appease.

Archbishop Temple and Harry Tawney were kindred spirits; but it has never been feasible for archbishops to lead the Desert Fathers' way of life. Conversely, of course, the anchorites and stylites have never been willing to be made archbishops. However, austerity is a relative term. Archbishop Temple's predecessors in the see of York would have been unable to imagine the Desert Fathers' life, as the Tawneys lived it; and, if they could have come back to life to re-visit Bishopthorpe when the Temples were living there, they would have eyed the Temples' modest establishment with astonishment and disapproval. This plain living, they would have felt, was out of keeping with the dignity of the office. The contrast, in the Temples' time, between the grandeur of the palace and the simplicity of the occupants' way of life was, indeed, bound to strike any eye. The effect of the contrast on me was to make me feel that the dignity of the office was now being upheld more genuinely than perhaps ever before. The Temples were wholly proof against the external pomp that surrounded them at Bishopthorpe *ex officio*. Had any previous Archbishop of York and his wife succeeded in keeping themselves so clean and unspotted from the world?

Archbishop Temple once told me of his experience in staying with Harry for the week-end. The place was Mecklenburgh Square, London, but it might as well have been the desert valley of Nitria. (Jeannette must have been away at the time, for Harry alone seems, on this occasion, to have had the responsibility for entertaining his guest.) After the two friends had been talking, for some hours, about things of common interest, Harry asked William whether he would like to have supper now. William said that he would, but he wondered how it was going to be provided; he had seen no signs that it was in preparation. But Harry now went up to a stack of bookshelves and began to rummage behind one shelf of books after another. William watched to see what was coming, and what eventually came out of its lair was a brace of cold mutton cutlets.

After dining on these the two friends went on talking till it was time to go to bed. Harry then pulled out two travelling rugs and strewed them on a wooden bench that ran round the inside of a bow-window. This was to be William's pallet, and, on it, he managed to fall into a sound sleep, though the bow-window had no curtains and there was a street-lamp shining through the window from outside. (The Tawneys' flat was on the ground floor.) In the small hours, however, William awoke with a start. What had roused him was that the light from the street had doubled in intensity. Looking up, he saw a policeman's lantern trained on his face, and, behind the lantern, the policeman's face looking down at the sleeper dubiously. The Archbishop told this tale with a mixture of amusement and affection. The difference in the two friends' handling of the temporal things that are seen did not divide them in their quest of the unseen things that are eternal.

When I was seeing Harry in Washington in 1942, he and Jeannette were there together, and Jeannette was enjoying herself. She had had to meet a practical emergency, and she had been successful. In their own passage of the Atlantic the Tawneys, happily, had reached America safe and sound; but their baggage, which had been following them in a cargo-boat, had been torpedoed. The loss would have been serious for any Britons at that stage of the war, but it was doubly serious for the Tawneys. Their wardrobe had been scantier than the average, to begin with; and, in America, they were not intending to spend one cent more than they could help on replacing it. They were spending on something else every cent that they could spare; and they spared more cents than most British residents in the United States at that time would have been willing to renounce. The Tawneys were spending their American cents on sending food-parcels home to their friends in Britain. They could not, of course, get out of having to reclothe themselves, at least up to the Desert Fathers' standard. But how, in extravagant America, would it be possible to fit oneself out on the cheap? Jeannette was resourceful. She found a way.

In Washington, D.C., the local Catholic community had worked out an ingenious way of raising a community fund for charitable purposes. Well-to-do Catholic ladies would give the fund clothes of theirs—and sometimes clothes of their husbands' too—when the clothes were still as good as new. (Constant scrapping and replacing is, of course, part of the American way of life —such a key part of it that it persisted, to some extent, even in war-time.) The fund was able to sell these all-but-new high-quality clothes at bargain prices, and yet to make a reasonable profit for the benefit of Catholic good works. Appropriately, the fund's trading name was 'The Christ Child Opportunity Store'. Jeannette Tawney jumped at the opportunity, and she did mutually profitable business with the store over the telephone. When she rang up, a voice would answer: 'Christ Child speaking.' Christ Child reclothed the Tawneys at prices that did not check the flow of the stream of food-parcels that they were sending home to a host of friends.

Jeannette had got the better of the American cost of living, but she could not always keep Harry under control, and this once cost her a Waterloo.

Before Jeannette's discovery of 'Christ Child', when Harry still had only the old suit of clothes in which he had reached New York, an American friend, with characteristic American generosity, gave Harry a suit of his. The act was generous, but the suit was not a good fit. The donor was short and thin; Harry was big in all dimensions; when Harry put this gift-suit on, he could only just make buttons and button-holes meet, and the two sides of the coat pulled away tightly in protest. Harry did not notice this; Jeannette did; after all, she had a woman's eye.

Harry's job at the Embassy in Washington was the one which
Lord Bryce, when he had been British Ambassador before the
First World War, had found to be the most useful thing on which
a British diplomat in the United States could spend his time. Instead of staying in Washington and revolving there within the
narrow and exotic circle of the diplomatic corps, Bryce had
toured the country, giving lectures. Fortunately for European
lecturers, the American public's appetite for lectures is insatiable;
and, in sections of the vast country that are distant from the
capital, a visit from a foreign diplomat is particularly appreciated.
It is a gratifying sign that he has recognized that Washington is
not the United States. Harry's job as an attaché during the Second
World War was to follow in Lord Bryce's tracks; and Harry's
lectures, too, were popular; he was a first-rate speaker. Being
Labour Attaché, he used to speak mainly to trades union audiences,
and one day he was addressing a nation-wide convention of the
National Union of Garment Workers.

Harry's speech that day delighted his audience so much that
they decided at once to give him some substantial token of their
appreciation of it. 'Mr. Tawney,' they said, 'we have been tickled
to death by your message. We are going to make a suit of clothes
for you of the very best cloth in the United States. All that you
have to do is to give us your measurements.' By a double mis-
chance, Jeannette was not there (the city in which the convention
was being held was far away from Washington) and Harry happened to be wearing the misfit gift-suit. 'Measurements?' he
answered vaguely, with his mind still preoccupied with higher
things—'Measurements? Oh, I don't know what mine are. Well,
just take the measurements of this suit that I am wearing; those
will do.' For the garment workers, Harry's word was law; so,
when Jeannette opened the parcel in Washington some weeks
later, she found that the cloth was indeed superb, but that the new
suit had been given, with pedantic exactness, the inadequate
measurements of the old one. This was a tragedy for Jeannette,
but not for Harry. Fits and misfits were all the same to him, when
it was a question of mere clothes, and not of social justice.

Harry Tawney was an idealist in act as well as in theory. Upon the outbreak of the First World War, he had volunteered for Kitchener's Army, and, on principle, he had refused the offer of a commission. No middle-class privileges for him. He would serve in the ranks; and he promised himself that there, at last, he would find himself in his element. He would be quit for a time of the unedifying middle-class way of life against which he had been up in arms since as far back as he could remember. In the ranks he would have the pleasure of associating with unspoiled human nature. When Harry went into the ranks, his doctrine of human nature was more Confucian than Christian. In spite of his continuing attachment to his ancestral religion, he had come to believe that human nature, uncorrupted by the bourgeois ideology, was intrinsically good. In the ranks, however, he was surprised and disappointed to discover that, beneath the crust of diverse manners and customs, human nature was the same in a proletarian as it was in a bourgeois.

This disillusioning experience of Harry's demonstrates the strength of British class-consciousness. Harry had tried with all his might to shake himself free from the middle class's sense of social superiority, but all that he had been able to accomplish was to invert it. His idealism had endowed the 'working class' with the virtues that, in his own ancestral class, he had indignantly refused to see. What his service in the Army taught him was one of the classical tenets of his ancestral religion. He had learnt that all human beings, without distinction, are prone to Original Sin.

Harry's active service began and ended with the Battle of the Somme. On his first day under fire, he was severely wounded; and, though he recovered, his wound plagued him at times throughout the rest of his life. This physical handicap did not prevent him, though, from giving to the world the gifts that he had to give, and these gifts were twofold. Harry himself, no doubt, gave priority to his un-self-seeking labours in good causes, but he left a more tangible, and perhaps more lasting, memorial of himself in his published works. He was a productive, as well as an eminent, economic historian; and he was eminent, not only as a scholar, but as a writer. He was a master of the English language; there was a magic in his marshalling of his words; and this will surely give longevity to his books. All scholarship is destined, by its nature, to be superseded by later scholarship. Scholarship's achievements are cumulative, and successive generations of scholars perch ever higher and more precariously on their predecessors' shoulders. Works of art, on the other hand, are timeless. No later work of art can make an earlier one obsolete; and Harry Tawney was a great artist as well as a great scholar.

8

The Hammonds

IN setting out to write my recollections of Lawrence and Barbara Hammond, I have to overcome a slight inhibition. This is not because there is any need for reticence. There is nothing that I know about the Hammonds that I should shrink from making public; and the Hammonds themselves need not have had any reservations if they had ever thought of writing their autobiography (singular, not plural; for, in those two bodies, there was one spirit). The Hammonds' published confession, unlike St. Augustine's, could have reproduced their unwritten confession *verbatim*. What holds me back is not reticence; it is intimacy. Barbara and Lawrence are, for me, virtual members of my inner family circle. My feeling towards them is like that. But, in spite of this, I am going to write about them, because I believe that they are a precious part of mankind's human treasure, and that this treasure ought not to be withheld from readers who did not have the good fortune to know the Hammonds at first hand. My contribution to a knowledge of them is small, and there are other people, still living, who could tell as much about them as I can, and more. I am only one of the survivors of the band of their devoted friends. But I believe that any morsel of knowledge about them is worth preserving.

I am an admirer of the Hammonds' works, as well as of the Hammonds themselves. With a very few exceptions, such as Lawrence's study of Gladstone and the Irish question, their works were products of a partnership that entered into everything that they did. Their works are, in my judgement, of the same quality as Harry Tawney's; and if, in my view of the Hammonds too, their works nevertheless loom less large than their personalities, this is because they are numbered among the saints in my canon.

Works—in the sense of publications—seem to be subject to one of the laws of fashion that governs the fortunes of most other kinds of work as well. Anything that has won esteem in its maker's lifetime is thereby destined to go out of fashion in the next generation, and is also destined to come back into fashion in the next generation but one. In my own lifetime, I have seen these almost automatic vicissitudes of fortune overtake the Victorian horsehair-covered chair. The Hammonds' work today is in the trough from which the horsehair chair has re-emerged, and there are now signs that the Hammonds' work is beginning to re-emerge too.

The Hammonds were social historians. Their field of study was Britain after the accession of George III; and it was approximately continuous with Élie Halévy's and Lewis Namier's and my Uncle Arnold's fields, except that the Hammonds' field was not limited in its subject, as Lewis Namier's field was, to politics, and that, in Lawrence's part of it, its lower chronological limit came down to Gladstone's generation.

The series of judgements on the Industrial Revolution in Britain that have been passed by successive students of it displays a rhythm like that of an alternating electric current. The social effects of technological change in Britain in that age have been judged alternately to have been prejudicial and beneficial, tolerable and intolerable, for the British industrial workers and for the British people as a whole. The Hammonds' judgement was adverse; it has been challenged by Miss Dorothy George as being prejudiced by a sentimentality that is not warranted by the facts; and now Miss George's dissenting interpretation of the facts has been challenged in its turn by Mr. E. P. Thompson in *The Making of the English Working Class.*

If Mr. Thompson had simply reverted to the Hammonds' standpoint, one might have feared that the study of the Industrial Revolution had become caught in a cyclic rhythm in which it might go on circling without progressing, like a convict in a treadmill or a squirrel in a revolving cage. However, Mr. Thompson's rehabilitation of the Hammonds is discriminating, though his own judgement seems to come closer to theirs than to Miss George's. For the sake of the advancement of knowledge and understanding, we have to hope that Mr. Thompson has succeeded in converting a circle into a spiral, and that, out of the Hammonds' thesis and Miss George's antithesis, he will have produced a synthesis that will provide these scholars' common study with a new point of departure. The Hammonds, humble-minded as they were, would never have expected, or have wanted, to have the last word. Any scholar is sufficiently rewarded if his bucketful of water has not been lost in a whirlpool, but has gone to quicken a flowing stream.

There is another stream of history which seems, in our time, to be more gravely threatened with the fate of cyclic frustration. For some reason which I have not grasped, the feelings of British observers have been enlisted, during the last century and a half, alternately for and against each of two non-Indo-European-speaking nations in South-Eastern Europe, the Magyars and the Turks. In both cases this British partisanship has been passionate. The Turks and the Magyars have been, in British eyes, alternately devils and angels, never just run-of-the-mill human beings. Ever since Alfred Zimmern and Lewis Namier inducted me into the observation of East European affairs, there have always been two British students of Hungarian affairs at a time, half a generation apart from each other in age, one Magyarophobe and the other Magyaromane. When I first became cognizant of Hungarian studies in Britain, R. W. Seton-Watson was the Magyarophobe British Magyarist. I then saw Seton-Watson overtaken by a Magyaromane runner-up, C. A. Macartney, and I have now lived to see Macartney overtaken, in his turn, by a Magyarophobe successor of Seton-Watson's, A. J. P. Taylor. Though I may not live to see Taylor's Magyarophil runner-up rise above his horizon, I can predict his coming as confidently as an astronomer predicts the coming of an eclipse. I cannot feel so confident that British studies of Hungarian affairs are eventually going to escape from the inconclusive cyclic motion in which they have been circling in my lifetime.

When I first met the Hammonds, they had just moved from
Hampstead into a house at Piccott's End, near Hemel Hempstead,
and this continued to be their home for the rest of their lives.
They had lived in London previously, and Barbara had been
brought up there. Her father had been an Anglican clergyman
with a parish among the London Docks. Lawrence's father, too,
had been an Anglican clergyman. His parish had been in the industrial North of England, though he himself had been a Jersey-
man by origin. Thus Lawrence and Barbara were neither of them
country-born. But, after settling at Piccott's End, they developed
a phobia for urban life. For Lawrence the modern city was
physically as well as psychologically intolerable. Years after the
London Underground had rid itself of its primeval suffocating
smoke by going over from steam to electricity, Lawrence was still
unable to travel in it without feeling that he was being asphyxiated.
The Hammonds' expeditions from Hertfordshire to the reading-

*Barbara winning her first-class honours degree, as seen and drawn by a less
successful co-examinee*

room of the British Museum were necessarily frequent during the many years over which they were engaged on the research that went to the writing of their books. But these expeditions were like a diver's descents. They were trials of endurance which Lawrence and Barbara would have found insupportable if they had not made them so brief. The Hammonds' practice was to submerge in London for no longer at a time than the inside of a day between nights spent in the country.

The one person who was regularly successful in enticing Lawrence into staying in a city for a longer time on end than that was the owner and editor of the *Manchester Guardian*, C. P. Scott. Besides being a student of eighteenth-century and early nineteenth-century British history, Lawrence was a keen observer of contemporary politics, with an almost passionate commitment to the Liberal cause. He and Scott saw eye to eye; and, apart from this identity of their views about public affairs, Scott had the highest opinion of Lawrence's professional ability as a journalist. Scott was unable to induce Lawrence to accept a full-time post on the *Guardian*; but he did persuade him, and this year after year, to come to Manchester to act as Scott's *locum tenens* there during Scott's annual holiday. Scott's estimate of Lawrence's powers in Scott's own line was amply justified by Lawrence's performance in his special stints of work for the *Guardian*; and his regard for the editor extended to the paper itself. By the time of the outbreak of the Second World War, Scott was no longer alive; but Lawrence and Barbara spent the war years working for the *Guardian* in Manchester, to do duty for members of the regular staff who were absent temporarily on war-service. For the Hammonds, at the age that they had reached by then, this prolonged spell of town-life under wartime conditions was an ordeal from which they might have flinched if they had not been enduring it on the *Guardian*'s account.

Oatfield (this was the name of the Hammonds' house at Piccott's End) made the same impression of Desert-Father austerity as the Tawneys' flat in Bloomsbury as far as the human householders were concerned. At Oatfield, for many years, at all seasons and in all weathers, the Hammonds passed their nights in an open-

sided revolving summer-house, with their camp-beds exposed to
the climate of the chilly interior of England. (One reason for their
move into the country had been that Barbara had had symptoms
of tuberculosis at the time. Thanks, possibly, to her drastic open-
air cure, she lived, after all, to an advanced old age—too long a
life for her own happiness, since she outlived Lawrence.)

The Hammonds' regimen, like the Tawneys', was austere. At
Oatfield, however, the ascetic human residents were in a minority. They were heavily outnumbered by a clientèle of birds and
beasts. The kitchen window-sills were usually lined with a row of
cats; the warmest spot in front of the sitting-room fire was always
occupied by a dog; and, outside the French window opening on
to the garden (the window was apt to be open at all seasons), there
was a permanent congregation of birds, standing as expectantly
as the birds in Giotto's picture of St. Francis preaching to them.
The Hammonds' birds, like St. Francis's, were technically wild,
while the Hammonds' animals were technically domesticated;
but the birds and beasts alike were tame. They were almost as tame
as kites and vultures and monkeys are in India, and this for the
reason that made birds and beasts unafraid of St. Francis too. Like
St. Francis, the Hammonds could charm wild creatures without
the aid of Orpheus's lyre. Their instrument was inaudible but
compelling. They loved their non-human fellow-creatures, and
their love for them was strong enough to break through the
barrier between human and animal kind, and to evoke in animals
an almost human responsive feeling.

The Hammonds were arrant 'respecters of persons'. The discrimination that they made was invidious; yet it was not of the
sort that would have brought upon them a reproof from St.
James. The persons to whose detriment they discriminated were
themselves alone. As far as they were concerned, the birds and
beasts had priority. But what about the Hammonds' human
guests? Did they fare as Archbishop Temple once fared in Harry
Tawney's home? They did not; for there was a decisive difference
in the domestic situation. The Tawneys had no pets to raise the
level of their standard of human comfort. The Hammonds did
have pets; and they gave their human guests most-favoured-bird-

and-beast treatment. In consequence, their human guests fared sumptuously.

The Hammonds' non-human beneficiaries would have been indeed unperceptive and ungrateful if they had not been responsive; for the devotedness of the Hammonds' ministrations to them knew no limits.

An instance was Barbara's solution for a problem that a lark once set for her by making her nest in the Hammonds' field. How reconcile the lark's interest with the cats'? The hedonistic calculus indicated that, for once, the cats' interest must be subordinated. The cats' pleasure in hunting could not weigh against the lark-chicks' right to life. Then must the cats be immured until the lark-mother had finished raising the brood? Such harshness was unthinkable; so Barbara committed herself to a full-time game-warden's job. In daylight hours she now kept a perpetual watch on the lark's nest, to note when the mother bird flew off to forage for her young; and, whenever the chicks were thus temporarily left unprotected, Barbara would run out with one of those domes of wire-mesh that housewives use to keep flies off a joint. She would slip this covering over the nest, and then she would keep watch again till she saw the returning mother hovering above the field—whereupon she would run out again to remove the cover and so give the mother access to her brood again. This exacting task occupied Barbara for weeks, but she was rewarded for her assiduity by having accomplished both her humane purposes. The cats' freedom had never been restricted, yet the lark-chicks had not become the cats' prey.

As I watched, and assisted in, this rhythmical exercise of covering the lark's nest and uncovering it again, the operation revived, for me, the memory of another operation of this unusual kind in which I had participated once, a number of years earlier. Walking back westwards from the east end of Crete in the spring of 1912, I had stayed, on my way, for a night with an American archaeologist, Richard B. Seager. (I had blown in, uninvited, as unceremoniously as Lewis Namier had once blown in on me for breakfast in my rooms at Balliol.)

Seager had built himself a house on the northern side of the

Pakhyammos-Hieropetra Isthmus and had settled down there to
explore, from this base, the numerous sites, of many different ages,
in the neighbourhood. Seager loved flowers as much as the Hammonds loved birds and beasts, and, to keep him company in his
otherwise rather lonely life (his only human companion was his
Cretan servant 'Alî), he had surrounded his house with a garden.
To clear away the scrub, dig flower-beds, and stock these with
seeds and bulbs had been easy. But how were the flowers' lives to
be saved when they had poked their heads out of the soil? The
Pakhyammos-Hieropetra Isthmus is low-lying; it is flanked by
mountains on both sides; and the winds sweep across it, between
the mountains, with a force that would lay the hardiest flowers
flat if they were to be exposed to it. These winds had set for
Seager the problem that was being set for Barbara by her cats,
and Seager had anticipated Barbara's solution. He had imported a
ship-load of wooden boxes from Trieste—this was the nearest
point to Crete at which wood-work was obtainable in quantity
—and, whenever the wind rose, Seager would run out (this took
many journeys back and forth) to put a box over every clump of
flowers. He would run out again and remove all the boxes whenever the wind dropped low enough for it to be safe to give the
flowers a chance to breathe without risk of exposing them to
disaster.

The only return that I could make for Seager's hospitality was
to assist him, while I was with him, in a task that competed with
archaeology for his time. I worked with a will; but I found that,
between us, we could not carry out the operation of imposing or
removing those boxes in less than twenty minutes. If a prize had
been offered for human devotedness in fostering non-human life,
Barbara Hammond might have had to divide the honours with
Richard Seager.

There was a time when, if you strolled round the countryside
within a radius of a mile or two of Oatfield, you would find,
lying about, a number of queer bits of ironmongery, all of an
identical make. They were curious enough to have aroused the
curiosity of an archaeologist who specialized in the Iron Age,
supposing that he had been ignorant of these artifacts' true origin.

The existence of these objects was accounted for by an accident that had been suffered by a little dog. One of his paws had been crushed; no human being except the Hammonds could do with a lame dog; so the Hammonds adopted him. To keep this pensioner and feed him, however, was not enough; Lawrence and Barbara could not rest till they had also made the dog happy again by enabling him once more to run. They went into consultation with the blacksmith, and, between them, they and he devised an iron shoe which did the trick. This shoe gave the dog back the use of his lame leg, but the blacksmith's skill did not run to devising a shoe that would stay on. The charitable shoe soon dropped off, and the poor dog then found himself disabled again. The result was that the blacksmith always had a full order-book, and that the discarded dog-shoes in the country round Oatfield accumulated thicker and thicker on the ground.

One winter evening in the year 1919, Barbara Hammond was on her way home to Piccott's End from Paris. (Lawrence was at the peace conference as the *Manchester Guardian*'s special correspondent, and Barbara had been in Paris with him.) Before leaving Paris, Barbara had written in advance to the livery-stable in Hemel Hempstead, ordering a cab to meet her at Hemel Hempstead railway station. (The days of taxis were not yet.) By the time, however, when Barbara reached Euston from the Gare du Nord, the evening had turned so cold and raw that she realized that it was not a fit night for a poor horse to be out. Accordingly, she telephoned from Euston to the Hemel Hempstead livery-stable, countermanding her order, and from the station she walked home, carrying her bag. The distance from the station to Piccott's End must be something between two and three miles. I have walked it myself, but not on a winter evening, carrying a bag, and not as the last lap on a journey from Paris.

I have not yet mentioned the Hammonds' own horses. They were a post-war addition to the Hammonds' animal clientèle as I had first seen it. They were a sequel to Lawrence's service in the Army.

Lawrence's reaction to the outbreak of war in August 1914 had been the same as Harry Tawney's. Like Harry, Lawrence had quickly joined up, and he had found himself an officer in a battery of field artillery. This was an heroic act on Lawrence's part. Military discipline, which includes being correctly dressed, was a sufficient ordeal for him, and, in the field artillery, the officers had also to be riders. Lawrence did not get out of uniform again unscathed. One day, when he was on leave and was walking along Pall Mall, he collided with a general coming down the steps of one of the clubs. 'Where is your frog, sir?' the general roared at him. Lawrence did not even know what a frog was, and inexcusable ignorance dangerously aggravated his offence. It appeared that the general had spent the last few weeks meticulously drafting an order to make frog-wearing by officers *de rigueur*; and here was the first officer whom he had met since his peremptorily-worded order had been promulgated. What, no frog! The general's order, on which he had lavished such loving labour, was being flouted. I do not know how Lawrence escaped arrest.

As for riding, Lawrence had never managed to learn to ride even a bicycle; yet he not only learnt to ride a horse; a day came when he won kudos in the battery by a dashing equestrian performance. That day, the battery was to practise field-manoeuvres; Lawrence had turned up late at the stables; there was only one horse still left there; and this was the major's horse, which was notoriously vicious. For Lawrence, this was a crisis. If he did not mount and master that horse, his military career would be at an end. He did mount the horse and it bolted, but fate was doubly kind. The road down which the major's horse had bolted was the very road along which the battery was travelling; and, as the bolting horse drew level with the other horses, it slowed down to their pace, instead of carrying Lawrence past the trotting battery, as John Gilpin's horse had carried its rider past his waiting family. Lawrence was greeted by his brother-officers with applause. 'Well, old boy, I congratulate you. If I had managed the major's horse as you have, I should be jolly well pleased with myself.'

Though Lawrence was not quite so good a rider as the major's horse had made him appear to be, it was not any failure to pass riding-tests that took him out of the Army. Lawrence was as frail as Harry Tawney, before his wound, was sturdy; and a medical board had the discernment to foresee that, on active service, Lawrence would be invalided out before he had time to go into action. Lawrence spent the rest of the First World War doing civilian war-work; but he had been bitten by the charm of riding. It had introduced him to a new species of pet animal. So, when the war was over, Lawrence and Barbara bought a couple of horses; Barbara now learnt to ride too; and, during the inter-war years, they used to ride together, as they did everything else together till they were cruelly parted by death.

A few days after Lawrence's return to civilian life, I fell into an error which anyone but Lawrence might have taken amiss. He had invited me to lunch, and my attention was caught by the clothes that he was now wearing. 'Lawrence,' I said, 'I see that you are making the most of your relief at being out of uniform again. You are celebrating this by wearing your oldest suit.' It was not his oldest; it was his newest suit—the least shabby one that he possessed; he had put on his best for going to the club. The obvious genuineness of my misapprehension made him laugh. The joke was against me, not against him.

Every good thing in life has to be paid for; the better the thing is, the higher the price; and, since the best thing in life is love, the worst agony in life is bereavement. Lawrence's and Barbara's love for each other was unsurpassed in my experience; so, sooner or later, agony of unsurpassed intensity was in store for one or other of them.

This tragic last chapter in one of these two blended lives could have been averted if they had had the good fortune to die simultaneously. For Greeks, Romans, Chinese, and Japanese, simultaneous death presents no problem. If it does not come by accident, the survivor can correct chance's blundering instantly by an act of human choice. The survivor can commit suicide. For Christians, however, and for ex-Christians too, suicide is tabu; so they are at the mercy of chance, and their most promising chance, nowadays, is the possibility of perishing simultaneously in an aeroplane accident. This happy ending is possible in real life, though not, so I have been told, for United Kingdom Inland Revenue purposes. My heirs have not yet had occasion to discover whether this information is true or false, but I understand that the simultaneous death of husband and wife is, in Britain at any rate, a fiscal impossibility. If they both die in the same aeroplane crash, the Inland Revenue authorities deem that one of the two (it does not matter which) predeceased the other by at least two seconds. It does not matter which because, either way round, the supposition enables the Inland Revenue to levy death-duty twice over. However, Lawrence and Barbara could not have obtained this happy reprieve from sorrow. Air-travel had never come within their horizon. I believe they did not ever even board a plane, not to speak of having a chance of meeting their deaths in one together, so one of the two had to suffer the pain of surviving the other. The lot fell on Barbara. While Barbara had been emerging from under the shadow of tuberculosis, Lawrence had been falling under the shadow of heart-disease. One night, he died, without warning, in his sleep. Fate could not be merciful to them both. The easier the passage for the one, the greater the shock for the other.

Barbara's bereavement was, I believe, the lesser evil. I cannot imagine how Lawrence could have lived without Barbara. The nearest that I can come to imagining that is by analogy with the suffering that Barbara had to endure. Barbara grieved for Lawrence till, at last, Nature stilled her grief by clouding her memory. This was the remedy that Nature had eventually found for Uncle Harry's grief over Aunt Ellen. In both cases, Nature's mercy was grudging and parsimonious. Nature left her victim to suffer for the longest possible term before she brought herself to apply her anaesthetic; and, even then, her act of mercy was half-hearted. When she was extinguishing the psychic faculties that make humanity human, why did she forbear to kill the body at the same stroke?

My last visit to Barbara while she was still herself was in 1956, just before I was setting out on travels that were to last for seventeen months. When, after my return to England, I saw Barbara next, she was already out of communication with the dead and the living alike; but in 1956 her grief was still touching the quick. In the familiar sitting-room she was now sitting alone. Outside the French window, however, the congregation of expectant birds was still standing as it had always stood at the time when there had been two human benefactors on whose benevolence the birds could count. Gazing at the birds while Barbara and I were talking, I found myself imagining that the legendary sympathy of St. Francis's birds for their human friend had communicated itself to these birds of Lawrence's and Barbara's. I ventured to speak to Barbara of this fancy of mine; and she told me that this had been much in her mind too. In her bereavement, birds and beasts could give her the comfort that her most devoted human friends were powerless to provide. The birds' presence was consoling because the bond of feeling between them and her was also a bond between her and Lawrence. When she was ministering to their nonhuman clientèle, Lawrence, for her, was present too, once again, for the moment. The birds, whether they knew it or not, were now repaying their debt to the pair of human beings who had dealt so lovingly with them.

9
The Webbs

I CANNOT now remember the occasion of my first meeting with the Webbs. It must have been before the end of the First World War. That is proved by the incident, recounted later on in this chapter, of Sidney Webb's quaint double column of figures. This first meeting must have been on the Webbs' initiative. It certainly was not on mine, for I was never commissioned to do a war-time job of work for the Webbs, as I was commissioned to do one for Lord Bryce; and I should not have ventured to intrude myself either on Lord Bryce or on the Webbs; the gulf between them and me was far too great; and it was a double gulf: I was very much their junior and I was also of no particular account. If the Webbs sought my acquaintance, this was because it was their nature, as it was Harry Tawney's, to be friendly, and because, like Lord Bryce, they got over the gulf between generations by ignoring it. This was not a deliberate policy; if it had been that, no doubt it would have defeated its own purpose; I am sure that it was something spontaneous and unstudied. For the younger person for whom the Webbs thus broke the ice, this was strong evidence that the Webbs were human.

Why, then, did the Webbs acquire a reputation for not being human? A picture of them as a pair of inhuman dissectors of sensitive human tissue was widely current. The spectacle might be thought amusing or be thought horrid, but, on either view of it, its authenticity was taken for granted. This judgement on Sidney and Beatrice Webb was superficial. Before applying the word 'inhuman', one ought to analyse what one means by it. In different contexts, this epithet may have different connotations, and not all of these may be pejorative.

To begin with, one must distinguish between the realms of private life and of public service. In their private life the Webbs were not in the least inhuman. Not only did they love each other deeply; they were rather more demonstrative than most English people are in displaying their feelings for each other in the presence of their friends. They were not shy; I have seen them even playful; and their friends received their share of this engaging warmth of feeling. As for the Webbs' public life, in which they were, of course, indefatigable, the common objective of all their manifold activities was to improve their fellow human beings' lot, and one of the motives of their devoted service in this generous cause was a moral revolt against inhumanity. Beatrice Webb's father had been a contractor, and I have heard her say that an early experience of hers that had played its part in impelling her into her eventual career had been her revulsion against the inhuman way in which her father and his business associates used to talk to each other about 'labour' as if it were some inanimate commodity like timber or cement, instead of being—as she herself already recognized that it was—a dehumanizing short-title for a number of human beings whose lives were too much at their callous employers' mercy. Though Beatrice Webb was a Fabian by conviction, she had Dean Swift's capacity for *saeva indignatio*. Her feelings were strong; and this was manifest in the sphere of private life, in which she did not seek to conceal them. If people who met her in her public capacity got the impression that she was cold-blooded, they were mistaking a mask for the human countenance beneath it.

Then did the Webbs deliberately repress their feelings when they were dealing with the public sector of human affairs? I think they did. I also think that, if they did do this, they did it for good reasons. However, this practice of theirs, which, in my view, was right in principle, was, I believe, the thing that exposed them to the allegation that they were inhuman. What is more, I find this allegation not wholly unjustified, though the terms in which it has usually been put are, in my judgement, much too sweeping.

The best and clearest principles are applicable only within limits; and this truth is especially pertinent to a human being's study and conduct of human affairs. In this field the pursuit of objectivity may, at any moment, run up against issues of good and evil, right and wrong, in face of which a moral neutrality is impossible and would, if it were possible, not be right. The Webbs seem to me sometimes to have tried to push their praiseworthy pursuit of objectivity beyond the limits at which it becomes morally wrong —and also, so I would contend, intellectually misleading—to re-frain from taking sides with the right against the wrong, as one sees them.

The problem that the Webbs' practice raises has exercised me because, in a minor way, it has been my problem too in the writing of the Chatham House *Survey of International Affairs*. The Council's standing instruction was that the *Survey* was to be 'scientific', and by this the Council meant 'objective in presenta-tion' as well as 'accurate in statement'. I always did my best to follow this instruction. This was not only my professional duty; my personal convictions, as well, coincided with the Council's. I too, was convinced that objectivity was indispensable for the effective performance of the *Survey*-writer's job; and there were many current international episodes that were not difficult to handle 'objectively', at any rate approximately.

An example is the dispute between Belgium and the Nether-lands over the extent of their respective rights in the waters of the Scheldt, in that section of the river's estuary, below Antwerp, in which both banks are Dutch territory. The essence of the job here was to set out the two opposing cases, and, in this analysis of con-flicting juridical claims, there was nothing to make one's blood boil or one's hair stand on end. This was the first piece of *Survey*-work on which I tried my hand. I began with this on Sir James Headlam-Morley's advice; and I have no doubt that his experi-enced eye had picked this topic out as being a fairly straightfor-ward one for giving a beginner his first practice. Fortunately, even in the contentious field of international affairs, there are al-ways a number of topics which, like the dispute over navigation-rights on the lower Scheldt, can be handled 'scientifically', in the

Chatham House Council's sense and the Webbs' sense, without much difficulty. But what about the Italian authorities' treatment of the German-speaking population of the South Tirol after the transfer of the South Tirol to Italian sovereignty from Austrian? What about the human—not merely juridical—rights of the Arab population of Palestine? What about Italy's assault on Ethiopia? And, to take an extreme case, what about the genocide of the Jewish diaspora in Continental Europe by the Nazi? How far is it possible and, if possible, right, to aim at being 'scientific', in the sense of 'objective', in cases like these?

The last, at any rate, of the four cases that I have just cited pulls the would-be 'objective' historian up short. Does the demand for 'objectivity' require him to recite the story of the gas-chambers in the flat tone of voice that is appropriate for reciting the opposing arguments of the Dutch and Belgian jurists in their controversy over the rights of navigation on the Scheldt? Let us suppose—though this is surely an extravagant supposition—that, by some lexicographical *tour de force*, one has succeeded in recording the Nazi's atrocities in words that are morally colourless. Will one not have clung to 'objectivity' at the cost of parting company with reality? And, when reality has been lost, what substance is left for the historian's 'objectivity' to adhere to? A flat-faced account of the Nazi atrocities would be out of touch with reality because the essence of the reality here is that these acts were crimes. They were criminal acts, not unfortunate occurrences. The victims were not victims of the automatic workings of non-human nature, like the crew and passengers of the *Titanic* who were killed by an iceberg or like the victims of the eruptions of Mont Pellée and Krakatoa or like someone who is eaten by a shark. These people were murdered by other human beings; and one makes nonsense of murder if one dissociates it verbally from the wickedness of the murderers and from the condemnation of this wickedness by non-criminal consciences. Here, surely, is a case in which the proper limit of objectivity has been reached and ought not to be passed. Evidently the instruction to be 'scientific' in the sense of 'objective' has an unwritten qualification which runs 'as far as is humanly possible'.

This qualification will assert itself sooner or later because the human being whose study is human affairs is subject to an occupational risk to which the student of non-human nature is not exposed. This risk is that, at any moment, the humanist's professional duty of recording people's acts may confront him with acts which he cannot record without at the same time passing judgement on them. A human being cannot be an historian professionally without being his human self first and last; and, in virtue of this inalienable human nature of his, he has a conscience that cannot suspend judgement in a case in which the moral issue at stake is grave and the guilt is manifest.

This is the point at which the proper limit of 'objectivity' is reached. But the crux of the problem that the inherent limitations of 'objectivity' raise is the question how to discern whether the limit has been reached in a particular concrete case. There is no *a priori* rule for deciding the point. The student of human affairs who comes up against it has to decide it, *ad hoc*, for himself and at his peril. His decision, whatever it may be, is likely to be challenged and criticized. My account, in the Chatham House *Survey*, of Italy's assault on Ethiopia was criticized on the ground that I had passed moral judgements where these were out of place. Conversely, the Webbs were sometimes criticized for having refrained from pronouncing moral judgements where these ought to have been passed.

In both these situations, the debate between the student of human affairs and his critics is inevitably inconclusive. The debatable presentation of controversial human acts lies, by definition, beyond the limits within which it is common ground that 'objectivity' is attainable and desirable; so it is open to either party to dismiss the other party's contention as being 'subjective'. I shall not take up the question of my own handling of Italy's invasion and temporary occupation of Ethiopia. I am a party to the case, and anyway this question does not fall within the field of the present chapter or of any other part of the present book. My concern here is with the criticism that was incurred, not by me, but by the Webbs. In their case, too, the question whether the criticism was justified or was unjustified is a matter of opinion.

The best light that I can throw on it is to illustrate it by citing some pieces of first-hand evidence of my own. I will cite, first, several in which the Webbs might appear to have deserved the reproach that they were 'inhuman'; and then, to keep the scales in fair balance, I will cite other incidents, which I either witnessed or learnt about from the Webbs themselves direct, that tell a different tale.

One day, towards the end of the First World War, I had to see Sidney Webb on some public business—I forget what—and, on entering the room, I found him absorbed in compiling two parallel columns of figures. This arithmetical exercise on which he was at work intrigued me, because of its evident importance in his opinion, so I ventured to ask him what the figures represented. Sidney informed me that they represented cubic feet. The left-hand column was a list of the amount of cubic feet of post-war housing-construction that were going to be saved by fatal war-casualties. (The war-dead had, of course, been housed, quickly and cheaply, in six feet of earth.) The right-hand column repre-sented the amount of cubic feet of post-war housing-construction that would be needed for inhabitants of the United Kingdom who, in peace-time, would have relieved the pressure on the demand for housing by emigrating, but who, since the outbreak of war, had been retained in Britain by the Government in order that it might have them at its disposal for getting them killed if required. When Sidney's collection of figures for both columns was com-plete, he was going to find the difference between the equivalent, in cubic feet, of the total number of the men who had actually been killed and the equivalent, in the same measure of volume, of the total number of impounded potential emigrants of male sex and military age who had been saved up at home during the war-years for killing as far as might prove necessary. It looked as if this second total were going to be the larger of the two, and the simple arithmetical operation of subtracting the cubic feet of ac-tual deaths from the cubic feet of potential deaths would give the number of cubic feet of post-war housing construction that would have to be catered for.

While Sidney was expounding his figures, I was seeing the

faces of my friends who had been killed. (These were about half of my closest friends of my own age.) It seemed that they had ludicrously misapprehended the nature of the cause in which they had given their lives. Some of them had supposed that they were dying 'for king and country'; others had supposed that they were dying in 'the war to end war'; and now, when they were dead beyond recall, it turned out that they had died to make a saving for H.M.G. of x number, each, of square feet of post-war housing-construction. The discrepancy between ideal and reality was too agonizing to be coped with by taking it tragically; the agony toppled over out of tragedy into farce—and I was overcome by laughter; I found myself laughing aloud. This effect of Sidney's figures on me surprised Sidney, and it also puzzled him. 'I cannot quite see why what I am doing here strikes you as being funny. Now that I have explained the calculation that I am making, you can see for yourself that my end-figure is going to be one of the key figures for post-war reconstruction.'

About fourteen or fifteen years later, I was a witness of another such failure of two minds to meet. Once again, one of the two minds was Sidney's, while the other, this time, was Baron Meyendorff's. The Webbs had just returned from their pilgrimage to the Soviet Union; they had come back with a mass of information, largely in the form of official documents; and they were preparing to put what they had learnt into a book—the book called *Soviet Communism*, which was to become so famous and also so controversial.

The Webbs' professional technique was to take into consultation, when they were engaged on a piece of research, other students of the subject in question whose knowledge and opinions might be enlightening. (This procedure is, of course, particularly valuable, as I too have found, when one is dealing with current affairs that raise burning questions.) The Webbs were also sociable and hospitable, so their first move, after coming back to England, was to invite a small group of friends to dine with them at the London School of Economics and Political Science. (The Webbs had been the School's founders.) Baron Meyendorff was one of their guests that evening, and my wife and I were also included in the party. Baron Meyendorff had more to contribute to that evening's discussion than any of the rest of us. He was a Baltic German whose ancestral home was Estland, a province of the former Russian Empire that had now become the northern half of the successor-state called Estonia. Before the second Russian Revolution of 1917, Meyendorff had been a member and also a vice-president of the Russian Imperial Duma. After the second Revolution, he and his wife had become refugees in England, and he had been appointed to a lectureship in the institution in which the Webbs' party was being held.

During dinner, Sidney was doing the talking. He was full of his and Beatrice's experiences in Russia, and he was obviously enjoying this first opportunity of sharing these experiences with other people. After Sidney had been talking for a considerable time, he happened to notice the look on Meyendorff's face. 'Oh, Meyendorff,' he said, 'you look as if you were not agreeing with what I am saying.' 'As I listen to you talking, Mr. Webb,' Meyendorff answered, 'I seem to see the faces of my friends who are dead.' These words of Meyendorff's produced a momentary silence round the table. In my case, they went home to their mark and have engraved themselves on my memory because they were the very words that had run through my own mind on that day in the autumn of 1918 when Sidney had been expounding his two columns of figures; and now Meyendorff had spoken those words aloud. Given utterance, the words came down like the blow of a sledge-hammer. What next?

For a moment, even Sidney seemed disconcerted, but his exhilaration at recounting his Russian experiences quickly swept him forward again. His monologue flowed over Meyendorff's interjection as a torrent in flood pours over a boulder. 'Oh, yes, of course,' he said, 'it is unfortunate. One cannot have revolutions without some violence. But you must remember that the number of deaths is negligible statistically by comparison with the number of lives that a revolution is going to save and to improve when it brings in its social returns.' Sidney went on; Meyendorff gave up. Yet, if any one of us but Sidney had received Meyendorff's sledge-hammer blow, he would, I feel sure, have been stopped dead by it.

Some time afterwards, I received from the Webbs a set of galley-proofs of parts of their forthcoming book, with a request for my comments, if I had any. (No doubt they had sent a set to Baron Meyendorff too.) One of the chapters included in my set dealt, at some length, with Lenin, and I started reading this chapter eagerly, in the expectation that it was going to answer for me a question about Lenin that had always puzzled me. There seemed to me to be a fundamental incompatibility between Lenin's theory and his practice. In theory, Lenin had held the Marxian belief that the march of Historical Necessity would sweep away capitalism inexorably, yet he had devoted his life to exerting his own puny human powers on giving a push to almighty Necessity's Juggernaut-car wheels. Why had Lenin not been content to sit back and just let those wheels roll over capitalism and crush it, unaided? If Historical Necessity was really the irresistible force that Lenin, like Marx, deemed it to be, human action could not affect its operation one way or the other. It was, of course, notorious that Marxians were not the only determinists who had also been activists, in apparent disregard of their own creed. Muslims and Calvinists had behaved in the same inconsequent way; so Lenin's behaviour, in this point, was not unique. Still, this tendency for determinism to go hand in hand with activism needed explaining; and there was a second feature of Lenin's life for which I could find no parallel. Lenin was, in theory, a militant disbeliever, not only in theism, but also in nineteenth-century secular 'bourgeois' idealism. Yet, here again, Lenin's practice seemed to contradict his theory. He had lived a life of personal austerity and self-sacrifice that would have well become a Christian, Muslim, or Buddhist saint. This, too, seemed to me to need explaining. I read on, looking all the time for at least a discussion of these two puzzling points in Lenin's life and character, but I reached the end of the chapter without coming across any allusion to either of these topics.

Accordingly, in writing about the galleys to the Webbs, I mentioned the points that I have just been making here, and I suggested that they might perhaps supplement the chapter about Lenin by taking these points up and giving the reader their own opinion about them. Beatrice Webb's reply to me made it evident that this suggestion of mine had displeased her. That was not, she wrote, the kind of thing that she and Sidney were interested in considering.

Not the kind of thing? Well, the galleys had told me what kind of thing it was that the Webbs did make a point of considering in their chapter on Lenin. They were including in it circumstantial and detailed accounts of Lenin's public acts: his speeches; his manifestoes; his pamphlets; his political and administrative directives. All this was certainly pertinent and, indeed, essential; but it was also the kind of thing that was the stuff of which official documents are made; and by this time I knew enough about official documents to have realized that there are limits to their usefulness as aids to knowledge and understanding.

In the Foreign Office during the First World War, I had watched official documents being made and had sometimes myself had a hand in the making of them, and I had learnt that one purpose for which no official document has ever been made is to provide information for historians. Even when documents are made in order to inform, they are intended to inform officials and politicians; the purpose of the information is to serve as a guide to action; and the information that is given is the minimum required for taking decisions about the action that is in prospect. As official documents will never be superfluously overloaded, they will not include information that is common knowledge among all concerned. Yet things that are common knowledge among the initiated may be unknown to the *profanum vulgus*, while they may, at the same time, be key points, of which one has to be cognizant if one is to comprehend the official document's meaning and purpose. Withhold these items of unwritten but indispensable information, and the document becomes, not informative, but misleading. With this in mind, I had, since then, been sceptical when I saw scholars treating documents as if these told the whole truth and nothing but it. These humanists were relying on the contents of documents as confidingly as a geologist legitimately confides in the composition, structure, and stratification of rocks. The humanists had not realized that, *ex officio*, an official document, unlike a rock-formation, does not tell the whole of its story. This story includes unrecorded information and undivulged purposes; and, unless and until the historian has brought these missing pieces in the puzzle to light, he had better refrain from using the unsupplemented document as evidence; for he will be running the risk of being hoodwinked by it.

When I read Beatrice Webb's letter in conjunction with the galleys of her and Sidney's book, it looked to me as if the Webbs' had fallen into this academic trap. They had taken, too much at its probably deceptive face-value, the documentary evidence for Lenin's public acts, and they were refusing to consider Lenin's personal character, though this was the para-documentary evidence that was the indispensable key to the interpretation of the documents themselves. Could I be right? Could such practised researchers really be so naïve? This was, and is, hard to believe. Nevertheless, I do believe that the Webbs did fall into this trap in their work on Soviet Communism, and I think that the two errors of judgement which led them into this trap were their proneness to push their pursuit of 'objectivity' beyond the point of diminishing returns and their mistaken assumption that, in the study of human affairs, one needs to discount the human factor if one is to get at the realities. I cannot agree that this way of 'processing' the evidence is likely to achieve its purpose. Behind the housing-construction statistics, 'I seem to see the faces of my friends who are dead.' Behind the mask of the revolutionary and the dictator, I seem to see the face of a self-sacrificing human being. In all the three cases that I have now mentioned, the Webbs had committed the same intellectual sin of omission. They had omitted, and deliberately omitted, the human factor; and, to this extent, the allegation that they were 'inhuman' does appear to be justified.

The Webbs: were they human? 'The English: are they human?' The Webbs were characteristically English in being insular-minded; and I remember the shock that I was once given by the first question that Beatrice Webb put to me when my wife and I had arrived at Passfield Corner to stay with the Webbs for a week-end at some date after the first Labour Government had gone out of office. 'Did I think that there was likely to be a revolution in Germany in at all the near future?' I held up my hands in horror at the thought. Nightmare visions flashed up in my mind's eye: revolution, civil war, a victory for extremists, Right or Left, conflicts with neighbours, another world war! Was this catastrophe imminent then? Why, no. (The date was in the lull between the suppression of the Spartacists and the rise of the Nazi.) 'No, I am not expecting a revolution in Germany,' I said; 'and let us hope', I added, 'that I am right.' Beatrice looked disappointed. 'You see,' she explained (her words might have been Lionel Curtis's), 'in this country, for ever so long by now, we have had politics properly under control. We have learnt how to keep them within the bounds of moderation. So there is no danger that a revolution on the Continent might set off a revolution here; but what it might perhaps do for us here is to make just enough of a political stir to bring Labour back into office.' To get one's own party back into power in Britain: how could any responsible person reckon that this would be worth the blood and tears that would be the price of a revolution on the Continent? So callous a calculation could be thought of only by Britons for whom the Continent lay outside the real world, so that the spilling of Continental blood and Continental tears could be contemplated without any British compunction.

This rather horrifying conversation of mine with Beatrice Webb at some date in the late nineteen-twenties reminded me, at the time, of Gilbert Murray's having once observed to me that 'the Webbs had been bad about the war'. (The date of this remark of G. M.'s was pre-1914, when 'the' war was still the South African War for the British.) The Webbs, Murray told me, had taken the line that an increase in the size of political units made for an improvement in administrative efficiency, and hence for the acceleration of social progress. So let the Orange Free State and the Transvaal be incorporated in the British Empire, and do not let us be diverted from Fabian social objectives to a political side-issue.

In looking at the South African War in this cold-bloodedly impersonal way, the Webbs had not been typical Britons of that time. For most of the Webbs' countrymen the issue had not been the administrative one of increased efficiency versus stagnation; it had been the moral issue between right and wrong. The Campbell-Bannerman Liberals' reaction had been 'the war is wrong'; the Asquith-Grey Liberals' reaction had been 'our country, right or wrong'; the Conservatives' reaction had been 'the war is right'. In their judgements the parties had been at variance, but they had been in agreement in holding that the issue which was dividing them was a moral one. In this instance, the Webbs' attempt to 'de-moralize' the issue had been peculiar.

These episodes indicated that the Webbs did sometimes take an 'inhuman' line when they were dealing with public affairs. They can hardly be acquitted on the plea that they were being 'inhuman' in the cause of humanity, for this line of defence would acquit Robespierre too. Their 'inhumanity', as far as it went, cannot be whitewashed. Yet these occasional lapses of theirs into 'inhumanity' towards other human beings in the mass were at least offset by the consistency with which, in dealing with public affairs, they eliminated self-regarding human feelings which, in most people, would probably have asserted themselves importunately enough to jaundice their judgement and warp their action to some extent. I can cite a case in which the Webbs' practice of 'inhuman' objectivity, applied to themselves, went to almost superhuman lengths of self-regardlessness, and eventually had its reward in a remarkable conquest of a more humanly wayward personality.

'Can you tell me', Beatrice once asked me, 'what the word "snice" means?' 'It is new to me too,' I said, 'but how did it crop up?' 'Well, at a committee meeting last week, X said to me: "I don't want to have anything more to do with your 'snice' society." It evidently means something uncomplimentary, but I should rather like to find out exactly what the meaning is.'

In recounting this 'snice' incident, Beatrice had been speaking calmly and good-naturedly, and I found myself considerably impressed by her apparently effortless detachment; for I could see that the incident had been not just personally disagreeable for her and Sidney; it had been serious for something that mattered

5   Montague John Rendall, when he was Second Master
    at Winchester, 1907

6   Alfred Zimmern, when he was a don at New College,
    1909

to them far more than the personal affront of having been treated
so rudely, and this in the presence of third parties, by somebody
who was not their equal either in age or in distinction. 'Your
"snice" society' was nothing less than the Fabian Society, of
which the Webbs were two pillars; the youngster who had used
this language was a contemporary (and friend) of mine. Yet, for
the Fabian Society, his threatened militant secession was formidable. Though, in the world of British left-wing politics at this
date, X was still a youngster, while the Webbs were old-established
Olympians, X had had a meteoric rise, and he had earned it.
His abilities were brilliant, his personality was dynamic, and, in
this first phase of his career, his personal ambition, too, was (it is
my impression) on the loose. Young though he was, he had already gathered round him a band of disciples who were under his
dynamic personality's sway. In fact, for the Fabian Society, X
was a Lucifer. He had assumed Lucifer's role in his declaration of
war at that committee meeting in the previous week. How were
the Fabian Juppiter and Juno going to react? Were they likely to
do any better than the Lord of Hosts had done when the mythical
Lucifer had defied him? Well, they did do a good deal better.
Instead of bringing their superiority in armaments into play and
hurling Lucifer headlong down to hell, to organize a permanent
anti-heaven there at Earth's expense, the Webbs succeeded in
giving the Fabian Society's crisis a happier ending. They managed
to reintegrate Lucifer and his angels into the Heavenly Host; and
they were able to win this remarkable victory because they remained unruffled by Lucifer's personal attack on them, and un-
rattled by his sniping at their 'snice' Fabian Society, into which they
and their fellow founding fathers had put so much hard work and
so much prudent statesmanship.

Only a year or two after my conversation with Beatrice Webb
about the meaning of the word 'snice', I found that X was now
once again working with the Webbs, and this not only co-oper-
atively but amicably. The Webbs' invincible unoffendableness
had eventually taken X captive as a willing prisoner. Of course,
their serenity would not have made its effect on X, any more than
their friendliness would have on me, if it had been just a diplomatic

performance to which their true feelings did not correspond. The
Webbs' 'inhuman' freedom from self-regarding feelings was irresistible because of its unmistakable genuineness. X, for instance,
personally ambitious though he may have been at the time, had in
him, too, enough of the Webbs' impersonal devotion to the left-
wing cause to appreciate the Webbs' public spirit and to respond
to it in kind.

I really do not believe that the Webbs' impersonalness, where
their own egos were concerned, had to be achieved by any hard-
won victory over temptation. For instance, I do not believe that,
at that unpleasant and critical committee meeting, they had the
least impulse to react to X's word 'snice' by retorting: 'You
young puppy, go to hell.' Personal feelings can be generated only
by a charge of psychic energy; and in the Webbs' psyche (it was
singular, not plural, in this aspect), there was never any surplus
energy to be discharged in the form of personal resentment. The
energy that was not reserved for their altogether human relations
with each other and with their friends was entirely taken up by
their public activities—and no wonder, considering the number and
the magnitude of these public calls on their energy.

The catalogue of the Webbs' public achievements is amazing.
They were founding fathers of the Labour Party as well as of the
Fabian Society, and they were not rank-and-file founding fathers
either; they were George Washingtons. They were the founders
of the London School of Economics and Political Science. They
were the authors of a long series of learned works in the field of
social and economic history, all of which required laborious research. They worked like ants or bees. They told me once that,
after their first half-dozen years of happy marriage and intellectual
hard labour, they had decided that they needed a holiday, so they
had gone for three weeks to Warrington and had spent the time
working on the records there. They told this story against themselves because they knew that it was funny. They had the saving
human gift of never taking themselves too seriously, while always
being one hundred per cent. serious about their work. Sidney and
Beatrice had a private life as well as a public forum, and in their
private life they were human enough, as the following anecdotes

demonstrate, I think. All but one of these are either things that I
witnessed myself or things that Beatrice Webb told me.

The Webbs had once travelled in Eastern Asia, and, as was to
be expected, they had taken an instant dislike for China, and a
likewise instant liking for Japan. At that time China had been
ramshackle, while Japan had already become efficient. (What
would the Webbs feel if they could return today to find China
Communist and also on the way to becoming efficient in consequence? Would they now give China priority over Japan in their
affections? And would this pair of professing Fabians give China's
militant Communism or Russia's mellowing Communism their
preference?) Liking Japan as they did, and particularly liking the
Japanese guide who was conducting them, Beatrice and Sidney
were distressed to find, one day, that they had done something
that had seriously upset their Japanese companion. There could be
no doubt about this; the guide's disapproval was too strong for him
to be able to conceal it. They begged him to tell them what they
had done amiss, in order that they might have a chance of correct-
ing it. The guide was embarrassed, but remained reticent. Clearly
they had done something too awful for him to be able to mention
it without being gravely discourteous. At last they teased it out of
him: 'Well, please, not so affectionate.' What had happened was
that, when they had been walking up a hill, Sidney had helped
Beatrice to climb it by putting a hand in the small of her back.
Such obscene behaviour in public on the part of barbarians for
whose conduct the guide was responsible had shocked the poor
guide to the core. Beatrice's way of telling this story made it clear
that she saw that it was not only funny in itself but was a particularly funny thing to have happened to a pair who, in their barbarian native land, had a reputation for being inhuman *à la
Japonaise.*

Beatrice Webb's family, the Potters, was a large one, and the
human bonds between its members were close. Beatrice was an
admirable aunt, and she deservedly enjoyed the affection of her
numerous nephews and nieces. Accordingly, the family appealed
to Beatrice to come to the rescue when a niece, who was still at the
age of indiscretion, announced her intention of entering into a

companionate marriage and remained unmoved by her parents'
representations. Beatrice made this family crisis her concern. She
invited the recalcitrant niece to tea, and the tea-tray served to
display a set of lovely eighteenth-century tea-spoons. Beatrice, as
she told the story to me, never alluded directly to the proposed
companionate marriage. But, after she had seen her niece eyeing
the spoons, as she had intended that the niece should, she remarked
casually that, now that she was getting on in years, she was
thinking of handing on those spoons to some member of the
younger generation. 'You know me well enough', she went on,
'to realize that I am as free from old-fashioned prejudices as I
expect you, too, are. But there is a practical point that I do have
to think of. Before I part with these spoons, I have to make sure
that their new home is going to be a permanent one. They are a
family heirloom, you know.' Nothing more was said, but, while
the niece was on her way back home, Beatrice was already in a
position to tell her niece's anxious parents, over the telephone,
that all would now be well. The spoons went to the niece, and the
home that they found with her was a permanent one. The spoons
had helped, no doubt; but the trick had been done by Beatrice's
insight into human nature. Beatrice showed obvious enjoyment
in recounting this *coup* of hers in a family affair. I should guess that
it had given her as much pleasure as any of her *coups* in the arena of
public business.

A field in which the Webbs' humanity revealed itself charm-
ingly was their friendship with George Bernard Shaw. Their
attitude towards Shaw was amusing. They felt about him rather
as if he had been their adopted child—a brilliant child, in whose
success they took great pride, but still a child who had never quite
grown up, so that he always needed some parental care, no
matter what his stature might be in the eyes of a world that did
not know him as intimately as the Webbs did.

The Webbs took some credit to themselves for Shaw's success.
Mrs. Shaw had been the Webbs' friend before she had become
Shaw's wife. She and Bernard had met each other first in the Webbs'
house; the Webbs held that they had done something to promote
the courtship; and, in their view, the marriage had been as aus-

picious for Shaw's professional success as it had been for his private
happiness. Mrs. Shaw had private means that made it possible for
Shaw to give up hack-work and to devote all his time to writing
that first batch of plays that took the world by storm and made
Shaw quickly world-famous. The Webbs did not fail, however,
to mention that Shaw's eventual income from his royalties far
exceeded Mrs. Shaw's income from her investments. They were
au fait with the rise in Shaw's royalty-income over the years, and
quoted exultantly the current year's amount. (Reckoned in pounds
sterling, it was high up in the five figures, if I remember right.)
On principle, the Webbs disapproved of a state of society which
allowed private enterprise to rake in such gross profits; but their
pleasure in Shaw's success drove a coach-and-four through the
walls of their social theory. Where Shaw was concerned, the
Webbs were humanly inconsistent, unobjective, and unashamed,
because, towards Shaw, they were humanly indulgent.

The need, as they saw it, for looking after Shaw was illustrated by a story of theirs. One day Shaw announced to them
that he was going to stand for election to the London County
Council. The Webbs threw cold water on this idea; the technical-
ities of public administration were not, they told him, in his line;
but Shaw would not be dissuaded. 'I shall stand all the same,' he
said, 'and of course I shall be sending you a copy of my address to
the electors.' (It was customary for candidates for election to the
London County Council to distribute, in advance, an election
address in print, as a substitute for house-to-house canvassing.)
Shaw did stand, the polling-day arrived, and Shaw was nowhere
in the running. The Webbs found Shaw fuming. 'I cannot understand', he said, 'why I failed to get elected. I had supposed that my
election address had made my election certain. It ought to have.
I took great trouble with it, and it is one of the best things I have
written—don't you agree?'—'But we haven't seen it.'—'You
must have. I sent you a copy as I promised. We must look through
your files: yes, of course, here it is.'—'This pamphlet of yours?
Yes, that came, and we enjoyed reading it, but we still haven't
seen your election address.'—'Not seen it? Why, that is it.'—
'But, in this pamphlet you haven't mentioned the election; you

haven't even mentioned the County Council itself. It certainly makes very good reading; but how could you expect the electors to gather from it that you were a candidate and that, in this pamphlet, you were canvassing them for their votes. No wonder you weren't elected.'—'Well, I am disgusted. If the electors are so stupid that they couldn't see that this was my election address without being told that in so many words, I am sorry that I stood and am glad that I didn't get in.'

I have mentioned that the Webbs spoke with approval of the part played by Mrs. Shaw's private means in easing Shaw's passage to achievement and to fame. Their attitude towards private means in a society on which socialism had hardly yet begun to make an impression was that, in these archaic social circumstances, the possession of private means was provisionally legitimate, on condition that these means were used by their possessors for purposes that were socially valuable. That was how the Webbs themselves were using Beatrice's private means, and they were not prompted, either by conscience or by sensibility, to strip themselves, as St. Francis of Assisi stripped himself of the property that had accrued to him from his father's success in business. For the Webbs, private means were an instrument that liberated their time and energy for following socially valuable but financially unremunerative occupations. They took the common-sense view that they would have been diminishing their own usefulness to society if they had thrown away this instrument that had been placed in their hands by Chance—the deplorable but all-powerful arbitress of human destinies in a free-enterprise society. They knew, perhaps as well as St. Francis knew, what they wanted to do with their lives; and they saw, no less clearly than he did, the significance of private means in their unmercenary pursuit of a socially valuable objective. For St. Francis's purpose, private means were an impediment to be discarded; for the Webbs' purposes, they were a tool to be used. Like St. Francis, the Webbs wanted to convert the world; but they never thought of converting it, as he did, by renouncing it. Nor did they camp in the world, as the Hammonds and the Tawneys did, like strangers and sojourners *in formâ pauperis*. They did not deprive themselves of the normal apparatus of the British upper middle class of their time. As far as what the Greeks used to call 'choregia' went—the furnishings of their house and the table that they kept—you could not have told that they, too, were peculiar. Fundamentally, they were peculiar in the Hammonds' and the Tawneys' way. They spent their lives on working strenuously for disinterested ends.

Beatrice Webb was handsome. She had beautiful features which did not grow less beautiful with age. Her person called for clothes to match it, and she was always well-dressed. She understood the art. In her family there was a joke at her expense about this. At some coronation (perhaps George V's), her sister, Lady Courtney of Penwith, had had to wear a peeress's robes. These are costly, and they are unsuitable for wearing except on this one state occasion. After the ceremony was over, Lady Courtney had been proposing to sell her robes and to give the proceeds for good works. The proceeds might have been appreciable; for the material was, of course, superb. However, Mrs. Webb had intervened with a request. If her sister did not want those robes for herself any longer, would she not give them to Beatrice? Beatrice would cut them up and use the stuff for making an evening dress for herself. She could see just how the robes could be adapted for this more practical use.

One of my last recollections of Beatrice Webb is of her appearance at a lunch-party at the School of Economics that some of her friends were giving in her honour on her eightieth birthday. When she stood up to reply to the toast that one of us had proposed, she was as handsome and as well-dressed as ever, and her speech was on original lines. It took the form of a series of conjectures about what each of the men and women present would be doing ten years later. (It was evident that she had chosen a date at which she did not expect that she herself would be there to see whether her forecasts had come true.) Besides being a graceful gesture towards her hosts, this series of character-sketches—for that is what they were—surprised us by revealing to each of us how much Beatrice knew about his or her personality. It became clear to us that she had taken a greater personal interest in each of us than we had previously suspected. We were aware of the affectionate interest that she had always taken in her nieces and nephews. We had not been aware, till now, that she had made honorary nieces and nephews of us. After this, how could anyone ever again think of Beatrice as being 'inhuman'?

Beatrice was characteristically human in her impatience, which increased as she grew older, to see socialism achieved in her lifetime. At this stage of her and Sidney's lives, the difference in their temperaments, which had always been apparent, came out more sharply—though this without ever disturbing their harmony. It could not disturb that; for the different veins in their temperaments were complementary to each other, and this must have been one of the things that had drawn and had held them together. They were Fabians, both, but Sidney was manifestly an *anima naturaliter Fabiana*, whereas Beatrice, I should guess, had been a Fabian by an effort of will that had been upheld by an intellectual conviction against the natural current of her feelings. Before Beatrice died, her more impetuous temperament had asserted itself, and, under its pressure, her Fabianism had begun to wear thin.

10
Lionel Curtis

I DID not make, at the time, a note of the date of my first
meeting with Lionel Curtis. I did not then foresee that he
was going to have a decisive effect on my life. But I can
identify that date for certain. You will see why.

I owed my first meeting with Lionel to Alfred Zimmern.
After *The Greek Commonwealth* had been published and before the
First World War had broken out, Alfred had come into contact
with Lionel's 'Round Table' group. The word 'commonwealth'
itself had, perhaps, been a pass-word between the Round Table and
Alfred. Lionel and his companions were always on the look-out
for promising recruits; and Alfred, like the Athenian philosophers
with whom St. Paul fell in, was always open to the attraction of
some new thing. Already, at lunch in Alfred's flat before the war,
I had met Philip Kerr (afterwards Lord Lothian). On 3 June 1915
I was to meet Lionel Curtis, the 'Round Table' group's founder
and leader, under Alfred's auspices.

When I joined Alfred and Lionel that morning, I found Lionel
talking about federal union for the British Commonwealth.
While we were on our way to the restaurant where we were to
eat, Lionel was still talking about federal union for the British
Commonwealth—so commandingly that neither Alfred nor I
ventured to interrupt him when we passed, in the street, an alarming newspaper-poster. 'Russian garrison of key fortress Przemyśl
encircled', the poster blared out at us. Lionel was still talking about
federal union for the British Commonwealth during lunch and
when, after lunch, we were returning by the route by which we
had come. The newspaper-vendor was still standing at the same

point, but the poster that he was now displaying was a new one. 'Przemyśl falls', the new poster said. 'One hundred and twenty thousand Russian troops surrender, 310 pieces of heavy artillery captured'. (I do not, of course, remember the exact figures, but those that I have fabricated were of the true figures' order of magnitude.) This second poster was too much for Alfred and me. The German break-through, here in Western Galicia, a few days back, had been bad enough; but the re-capture of the great Austrian fortress Przemyśl, with this huge haul of Russian prisoners and war-material, surely spelled sheer disaster on the Eastern Front. Our jaws dropped and our tongues were loosened. 'Oh, look here,' we began to say; but 'the Prophet' cut us short. ('The Prophet' was Lionel's nickname in the inner circle of his disciples.) 'A merely ephemeral event,' he said; and he went on talking about federal union for the British Commonwealth till we parted to go back to our respective war-time offices.

'A merely ephemeral event.' Why, that was what St. Paul said to the crew when the ship was going to pieces on those reefs off the coast of Malta. And St. Paul's serene appreciation of an apparently desperate situation had proved correct. Everybody on board, crew and passengers and all, had reached dry land alive. 'The Prophet'! What was one to think of this man, who had been talking at us, rather than to us, continuously for two hours without a pause, even for the fall of Przemyśl? Was he a great man of Pauline stature? Or was he just a monomaniac? If it is the mark of a prophet to make improbable predictions and to prove to have been right, Lionel Curtis, like St. Paul, was proved a prophet by the event. On longer and closer acquaintance with Lionel, I came to the conclusion that, like St. Paul, he was a great man and a monomaniac too.

There are monomaniacs whose primal monomania stays with them for life. Mr. Dick, whom David Copperfield met in his aunt Betsey Trotwood's house at Dover, was a monomaniac of that steadfast sort. Lionel Curtis's and St. Paul's monomania, like Professor Margoliouth's, was of a transferable kind. St. Paul transferred his monomania from the persecution of Christianity to the propagation of it at the dramatic caesura in his life. Lionel's monomania, like Professor Margoliouth's, was punctuated by more transfers than one. Lionel was preoccupied, successively, with the federation of the British colonies in South Africa after the South African War; the federation of all the 'white' peoples in the British Empire (an objective that led him to impose a new meaning on the historic word 'commonwealth' and to institute the 'Round Table' group, with its journal of the same name); self-government for India as a member of the Commonwealth; the Royal Institute of International Affairs; self-government for Ireland as a member of the Commonwealth; the Institute of Pacific Relations; and a crusade against 'sky-writing', least as well as last. Lionel did not, of course, become indifferent to all his old loves when he was on with a new one; but his attention was always monopolized by the love of the moment.

This combination of monomania with seriality was characteristic of Lionel's relations with human beings, as well as of his service of causes; and this made relations with him hazardous for anyone except the members of his small inner circle. Lionel's friendship with them was sacrosanct for him. This circle had formed round Lionel while its first components had still been undergraduates at New College, and it had been further compacted by membership in Milner's 'kindergarten': the group of younger men whom Milner had gathered round him as his aides for the reconstruction of South Africa after the end of the South African War. An apt name for the nuclear group of Lionel's disciples would have been 'the Apostles', if this title had not been appropriated by a contemporary group whose sphere of interest was different. Some of 'Prophet' Lionel's apostles were Robert Brand (Lord Brand), Philip Kerr (Lord Lothian), Geoffrey Robinson (afterwards Dawson); John Dove; (Sir) Edward Grigg; Hugh Wyndham (Lord Leconfield); Geoffrey Gathorne-Hardy. These were all men of mark; and, naturally, each of them went his way on an individual career of his own that gave him an individual experience and outlook. Lord Brand, for instance, became an eminent banker in the City of London; Geoffrey Dawson became editor of *The Times*; Philip Kerr became a member of Lloyd George's war-time staff at 10 Downing Street and, in the Second

World War, war-time British Ambassador at Washington. John
Dove was perhaps the only one of those whom I have named of
whom it could be said, in the words of a Balliol rhyme, 'me the
Master quite absorbs'.

These intimate friends had always been able to laugh at
Lionel. His nickname 'the Prophet' was of their making. (Outsiders would not have ventured to coin a nickname for Lionel,
still less to use one in speaking of him.) In a great man there is
often a comic incongruity between the greatness that makes him
unique and the inalienable human nature that he necessarily
shares with the rest of his kind. To recognize, and smile at, this
incongruity is, of course, compatible with affection, admiration,
and even veneration. However, some of Lionel's apostles were
able, not merely to smile at his foibles, but to criticize his stand on
important points of public policy. In the later years of Lionel's
and Lord Brand's lives, I occasionally heard Lord Brand criticize
acts of Lionel's with seeming severity. But differences of view over
public affairs did not weaken the bond of personal friendship.
This was lifelong.

Lionel also needed, and recruited, a supply of younger assistants
for his successive public activities; and it was for these that the
seriality of his monomania made relations with him always tricky,
and sometimes dangerous. Lionel, like President Franklin Roose-
velt, had a way of picking up and dropping his lieutenants as a
mechanic picks up and drops his tools. Unlike the members of
Lionel's nuclear group, these human tools of his were valuable to
him primarily as instruments for getting on with the particular
job that he had in hand at the time. As soon as the job required the
use of some different human tool, Lionel would drop the tool
that he had been holding. This was callous; for, in employing a
human tool, utilitarianism is not enough; one contracts human
obligations which outlast the tool's usefulness and which cannot
be repudiated with impunity.

The danger that Lionel, in his obsession with his impersonal
public aims, might inflict injustice on human beings was enhanced
by other traits in his character. His judgement of people was
fallible, and, in all that he did, he went to extremes. For him,

people were either white or black, without any intermediate
shades; and one might turn from white to black (though never
vice versa) in a twinkling of Lionel's eye.

If one was going to do business with and for Lionel, one's
prospects of survival were better if one was an 'egg-head' than
if one was an 'executive'. Lionel had found, by experience, that
academics could produce, by peculiar and partly mysterious pro-
cesses, results that were valuable for his purposes and that could
not be produced by 'practical' men. Accordingly, he treated 'egg-
heads' with some forbearance and even indulgence. At a series of
meetings, convened by Sir Arthur Salter in his rooms at All Souls
in the late nineteen-thirties to discuss whether a second world war
could be averted, I have seen Dr. A. L. Rowse repeatedly risk his
neck within pouncing-distance of Lionel and yet come off alive.
My schoolfellow Sir Reginald Coupland survived, unscathed, a
collaboration with Lionel that was a good deal longer and closer
than mine was. I escaped unscathed too, though Chatham House,
for which I was working, was Lionel's child.

One of the most intriguing features of Lionel's personality was
common to him and Cato the Censor. Like Cato, Lionel was a
bundle of inconsistencies and contradictions.

For instance, he was a man of action, and a superb one; yet he
chose to live among academics; and, since he had a genius for
making people do what he wanted, he made the intellectuals want
to have him living with them. He was elected a fellow of All
Souls, and he never forfeited his fellowship, though he was prone
to the fault of monopolizing the conversation by holding forth
on his monomania; and this, at All Souls, might have been expected to be an unforgivable sin. (N.B. the coveted honour of an All
Souls fellowship was never attained by Lewis Namier.) Again,
one of the actions that were nearest to Lionel's heart was the
transformation of the British Empire into a federal union; but the
effect of his acts was to transform the Empire into a congeries of
states that were all independent, virtually if not formally. His
forte, as a man of action, was salesmanship; if he had hired himself
out to Madison Avenue, he could hardly have failed to make a
fortune. But he was indifferent to money, and to honours as well.

He was devoted, heart and soul, to the promotion of his series of good causes, and he used his talent as a salesman solely for this disinterested and unremunerative purpose. Most paradoxical of all, he could not speak a word of any language except his native English, yet he founded a British institute of international affairs.

What were Lionel's greatest acts as a man of action? In my judgement, two stand out which were not executive acts, but were acts of imagination that were potent enough to have far-reaching consequences in the executive field.

His first act of this kind was the new usage that he gave to the old word 'commonwealth'. This literal English translation of the Roman term *respublica* had been used in seventeenth-century England to designate a political community in which the citizens governed themselves as each other's equals, without being subject to the rule of a king. Lionel employed the word to mean, by analogy, an association—ideally a federal union—of political communities, in which the constituent communities were to govern themselves, as each other's equals, without being subject to the hegemony of a dominant partner. His new usage of the word was a re-definition that was also a programme.

Lionel's second act of imagination was his thesis that the 'political verities', as he called them, on which the ideal and the practice of democracy were founded, held good universally for all human societies in all times and places. He divined that these were 'verities', not just for an Ancient Greek society or for a modern Western society, but for all mankind, because these 'verities' were implicit in the spiritual constitution of human nature. This thesis demanded that the transformation of the British Empire into a commonwealth (in the Curtisian sense) of self-governing nations was not to be limited to those peoples in the Commonwealth that were European in race and Western in civilization; self-government was to be extended progressively to all the other peoples of the Commonwealth, of whatever race and culture.

Both these ideas were great, but the second was the more original of the two and the more profound. Lionel gave the British Commonwealth of Nations its name; but this political structure had been in process of taking shape for the best part of a century

before Lionel began to make it his concern. The true founders of
the British Commonwealth had been the founding fathers of the
United States; for it had been they who had taught the British
people the lesson that it is better to give a subordinate or subject
people self-government voluntarily, without waiting for this boon
to be wrested from the hitherto dominant power by force. Canada, Australia, and New Zealand were already self-governing before Lionel took up the cause of self-government in South Africa.
As for the idea that the self-governing peoples of the Commonwealth ought to be on a footing of equality with each other, this
derived ultimately from the doctrine of the equality of states,
which had established itself in the Western World at least as
early as the seventeenth century.

By contrast, Lionel was surely the first political thinker in the
Western World to hold and declare that non-Western peoples had
the same human right to self-government as Western peoples and
also the same inherent human capacity for governing themselves,
so that the grant of self-government to them was not only a moral
duty but would prove to be practical politics. This thesis of Lionel's
was profound as well as original; for its foundations went down
to the bedrock of human nature, and the thesis therefore applied,
not only to the British Commonwealth, but to the whole world.

These acts of imagination were Lionel's greatest acts; but they
might have remained hovering up aloft, like Plato's utopia, in the
intellectual world of ideas, if Lionel had not been a more effective
man of action, in the ordinary executive sense, than Plato proved
to be when he missed his successive chances of bringing his utopia
down to earth at Syracuse. Lionel's tactics for carrying his ideas to
victory were those of the Romans and the Scottish highlanders. He
would open an engagement by 'softening up' the opposing force
with a discharge of missiles, and he would then swiftly close in
to overwhelm his shaken opponents in hand-to-hand fighting.

Lionel's preliminary missiles were books. His books would, I
believe, have brought him lasting recognition if they had been
the only memorials that he had left. But Lionel was a writer
only incidentally. His books were not ends in themselves; they
were preludes to direct action in hand-to-hand encounters. This

took the form of button-holing key people *viritim*; and Lionel had an unerring eye for potential converts whose conversion might turn the tide of public opinion in favour of the particular cause that was his monomania at the time. About half-way through the First World War, I met Lionel in London when he was on the point of leaving for India after having issued his private declaration of self-government for India by stages. My visual memory of him on this occasion puts a carpet-bag in his hand; but here my memory may be playing me a trick; for he had reminded me, at that moment, of one of those Northern 'carpet-baggers' who descended on the South in the reconstruction period after the American Civil War. His expedition sounded quixotic to me. He was proposing to go round India, 'selling' his idea to senior members of the Indian Civil Service. The sequel showed that he knew what he was about.

Lionel's response to a call for action was as instantaneous as a greyhound's reponse to the sight of a hare. In a split second, he was off the mark. I have had personal experiences of his speed—experiences in which I was the fortunate beneficiary. For example, before I had finished writing the first volumes of the Chatham House *Survey* on a non-renewable *ad hoc* allocation of funds for my salary, Lionel had secured a permanent endowment for carrying on the *Survey* and for keeping me on as the writer of it. There was, however, going to be a gap of several months between the date at which the *ad hoc* funds would run out and the date at which the income from the new endowment would begin to come in. This hiatus was awkward financially for me, as there would be no hiatus in the demands on me for household and educational expenses. When this point was put, on my behalf, to the Chatham House research committee by its chairman, Sir James Headlam-Morley, Lionel instantly solved the problem. He was going to be one of the lecturers at a forthcoming session of the Williams College summer school on international affairs at Williamstown, Massachusetts. He was sure that he could obtain an invitation for me to be one of the lecturers too. (And, of course, the lecturership would carry a fee that would tide me over that summer.) Lionel cabled to Williamstown that afternoon, and the organizers of the

7 The author as an undergraduate at Balliol, about 1911

8 Lewis Namier as an undergraduate at Balliol, about
   1911

summer school took me on trust on his recommendation. (At that date, I was unknown in the field of international affairs. The first volumes of the *Survey* were not published till I was already cross-ing the Atlantic under Lionel's wing.) This transaction not only kept me afloat financially; it also gave me my first opportunity of visiting the United States—an experience that was, of course, invaluable for all my subsequent work, both on the *Survey* and in other fields.

Lionel's ardour for action, like his appetite for causes, had in it a touch of fanaticism that sometimes betrayed him into commit-ting absurdities. I have mentioned his crusade against sky-writing. The sight of an aerial advertisement as he landed in Britain after an absence in America sent him straight into righteous action against this violation of the purity of the skies. That cause was not a bad one, but it was surely too trivial to deserve to occupy Lionel's time and energy. At that moment, Lionel must have been action-mad; for, when I saw him after his arrival in London from that Transatlantic voyage, he thrust a large bunch of cotton-wool into each of my hands. 'An American on board gave me these,' he said. 'It is cotton that he has grown on his farm. Do something about them.' I did the only sensible thing that could be done. I went back to my room and put the stuff in my waste-paper basket. I felt sure that, on reflection, Lionel would not have wanted me to divert my time and energy from work for Chatham House to marketing his American chance acquaintance's random cotton-samples.

It is also true that Lionel's action sometimes back-fired. For instance, his crusade for turning the British Commonwealth of Nations into a federal union resulted, instead, in its becoming a more and more tenuous association of mutually independent states. Two sensational back-fires were produced by Lionel's suc-cessful action for bringing the four British colonies in South Africa into a federal union with each other. In this first essay in federation, his aims were enlightened and laudable. He wanted to assuage the bitter feelings that were the legacy of the South African War by reconciling the Dutch-speaking South Africans politically with their English-speaking fellow-countrymen and with the people of the United Kingdom; and he also wanted to avert a threat that the military war which was just over might be followed by a tariff war between the four separate British colonies that were now on the political map of South Africa as a result of Britain's recent annexation of the Orange Free State and the Transvaal Republic. In the creation of the Union of South Africa, these two constructive aims were duly achieved; and, within a decade, this achievement had saved the situation in South Africa for Britain after the outbreak of the First World War. Lionel probably deserves more credit than any other single person for all this; but the weakness of his 'single-track' mind was its inability to pay attention to more than one thing at a time. While he was preoccupied with his successful endeavours to reconcile the two estranged 'white' communities in South Africa, he had no eyes for the African majority or for the Indian minority of the 'non-white' population. In consequence, this enthusiast for democratic institutions paved the way for the eventual conversion of the Union of South Africa into a police-state by thinking of democracy, at this stage, in terms of a franchise for the 'white' minority only; and he also unwittingly set a political avalanche rolling in India.

In a little book called *Satyagraha*, the Mahatma Gandhi has affixed to Lionel Curtis the responsibility for having launched Gandhi on his political career. The outbreak of the South African War had found Gandhi practising law in the Indian community in South Africa. In Britain's local crisis, Gandhi had seen an opportunity for the South African Indian community to help the cause of self-government for India by doing something for Britain that might win her gratitude and might therefore incline her to do something for India in return. Gandhi had therefore organized a South African Indian ambulance corps for the British Army in South Africa, and, after serving in this corps himself throughout the war, he was on his way to Durban with a steamer-ticket for Bombay in his pocket, when he happened to notice in a newspaper the announcement that a young Englishman called Curtis, who was then Town Clerk of Johannesburg, had just issued an order that all Indians within his jurisdiction were to register their fingerprints. The young Englishman was 'selling' to the Afrikaners his 'grand design' for the reconciliation of the two 'white' communities in South Africa by playing up, at the Indian community's expense, to Afrikaner racial prejudice; but naturally the young Indian did not see this action with the Englishman's eyes. What Gandhi saw was an exhibition of British ingratitude to the Indian community that aroused his indignation. Gandhi sacrificed his steamer-ticket; stayed in South Africa to fight the Town Clerk of Johannesburg's order; lost his battle on this South African field; and eventually returned to India to continue his championship of Indian rights in a vaster arena.

This Indian back-fire from an African act of Lionel's grew into a mighty blast under Gandhi's inspiration, and, when once Lionel had become aware of the problem of Indian self-government, he found himself on Gandhi's side. Lionel did not become a convert to non-violent non-co-operation. (This arch-activist could hardly have been expected to realize that the Mahatma Gandhi's Quaker-like political strategy might be as effective as his was.) But Lionel did make enough important British converts to a scheme of his own to move the United Kingdom Government to adopt this Curtisian scheme for inducting India into self-government.

The scheme that Lionel succeeded in selling was 'dyarchy', and the success was deserved, for the strategy was ingenious. Once again, Lionel had ferreted out an old name from the historians' store-cupboard and had made this name do new work by giving it a new application. 'Dyarchy for India' was as brilliant a coinage as 'a Commonwealth of Nations' had been. Both names were feats of analogical imagination; and the historical analogy drawn in each of them suggested a programme for current political action. As a slogan for working on the minds of British civil servants and politicians, the word 'dyarchy' was a masterly choice. For these classically-educated British minds, the meaning of 'dyarchy' was familiar and its historical associations were reassuring.

The historic 'dyarchy' is the scheme that 'the crafty nephew of Julius' had devised as a political safety-valve for averting a repetition of the explosion that had cost Augustus's uncompromising uncle his life. Augustus had been concerned to save the face, and give some scope for the energies, of the Roman nobility who had been deprived by his high-handed predecessor of their old-established prerogative of being the rulers of the Roman Commonwealth. Augustus had accomplished his purpose by handing back to the Senate certain fields and functions of government that were not fraught with political or military power, while prudently retaining in his own hands those powers that carried with them the mastery over the Roman state. Besides being familiar to the British minds to which Lionel was laying siege, this episode of Roman history was also reassuring for them; for the sequel showed that Augustus's seemingly generous renunciation of some of his almost plenary powers had not jeopardized the princeps's *de facto* supremacy. The fields and functions that Augustus had handed back to the Senate did not provide the Roman nobility with an adequate launching-pad for attempting a counter-revolution; and, as time went on, it was the imperial authority that increased and the senatorial authority that decreased. The British could be induced, as Lionel had calculated that they would be, to swallow this well-tried Roman half-measure. Had Lionel also calculated that, just because dyarchy was a half-measure, it would not satisfy the Indians, and that, if once the process of transferring British powers in India to Indian hands had been set going, it would be impossible to bring the movement to a halt till the transfer had become total? Thus a back-fire from an act of Lionel's in South Africa had led, eventually, to his taking action, and this most effectively, in India too.

The means by which the effects of Lionel's action were produced was his extraordinary power of enlisting or conscripting other people to do what he wanted. It was amazing to see him captivating people whose temperaments and outlooks were so different from his that they seemed to offer him no hold for getting a purchase on them. It was fascinating to watch him stalking his intended prey. Lionel was a master of the salesman's fine art of making the maximum display with the minimum outfit. Once, in the early days of Chatham House, Lionel had lured a potential benefactor to visit the Institute in order that he might be shown the works, such as they were, and, when the day arrived, Lionel made an urgent appeal to me for stage properties. All that I had to give him was a few clutches of the galley-proofs of the first volume of the *Survey*; and I was depressed at the thought of his having to go into action so poorly equipped. Peeping round the door of Lionel's room, however, I saw him waving my galley-proofs, like a hypnotist, in front of the visitor's face, while the visitor stood open-mouthed, listening, spellbound, to Lionel's earnest allocution. I realized that, in Lionel's hands, those galleys were ample material; it was Lionel's personality that was producing the desired effect. Not long after that, I myself was being waved by Lionel for the edification of Sir Daniel Stevenson. The outcome of Lionel's production, this time, of a live exhibit was the Stevenson research professorship in international history: a University of London chair located in Chatham House.

What was it in Lionel that gave him this hypnotic power? His manifest sincerity and disinterestedness were, of course, compelling. Here was a remarkable man obviously devoting himself, heart and soul, to some cause that was bringing him no personal profit or advantage; and this fact suggested that the cause must be one that deserved support. However, I doubt whether sheer sincerity and disinterestedness alone could have moved the mountains that Lionel did move into the exact positions in which he wanted to have them. Lionel's magic effects were produced by collusion between his virtues and his magnetism.

Lionel's magnetism was brought home to me when, in 1929, I kept a rendezvous with him in the International Settlement at Shanghai. (Lionel had come from England across Canada and then by Canadian Pacific, while I had come overland across Europe and Asia to Basra, and by ship from there.) I found the Curtises installed in the house of a Shanghai merchant, Mr. Brown. The house, the household, and Mr. Brown himself were all at the Curtises' disposal. Lionel and Mr. Brown had been unknown to each other before they had boarded the same Canadian Pacific boat at Vancouver; but it was impossible to remain unaware of Lionel's presence for long if you were his fellow-passenger on a Transpacific voyage. On the first day out, Lionel had organized, for the passengers, a daily seminar on federal union. Before the boat had reached Shanghai, Mr. Brown had begged the Curtises to be his guests for as long as his hospitality might be of service to them for the promotion of the cause. When, on arriving at Shanghai in my turn, I came upon the Curtises in Mr. Brown's house, and heard how this had come about, I felt as if I had stepped into the narrative of Part II of the Acts of the Apostles. Once again, as at my first encounter with Lionel, I had been transported from our world to St. Paul's. Mr. Brown had now qualified for finding a place on the roll of names that had, unknowingly, been made famous by their pious owners when these had taken Paul into their homes and had helped him forward on his busy way; and I felt as if I were some latterday Titus or Timothy who had been privileged to catch up with the servant of the Lord at a halting-place on one of his seminal missionary journeys.

Lionel was not only the founder of the Royal Institute of International Affairs; he gave a considerable part of his working life to the hard labour of nursing the Institute through its teething stage, and this makes his phobia of foreign languages the more extraordinary. He once told me that, in his early childhood, his family had lived for a year or two somewhere in the French-speaking part of Switzerland. Lionel must have successfully resisted this golden opportunity for becoming bilingual, and perhaps it was this early battle that had made him allergic to all languages except the one with which he had started.

Lionel's allergy to French was certainly extreme. I once happened to be in Paris on one of those very rare occasions on which he visited that city. (It was characteristic of Lionel that he was coming over to France to see, not any Frenchmen, but an officer of the Rockefeller Foundation whose itinerary happened to have routed him via Paris, not, as it ought to have, via London.) From London, Lionel, before starting out, had made a signal to me in Paris to meet him at the Gare du Nord. I did meet him there, I dealt with the porter and the taxi-driver, and I delivered Lionel at his hotel. As we set foot in the lobby, Lionel told me to ask the head-porter: 'What is the earliest morning train back the day after tomorrow?' Of course I had no need to translate. The head-porter could not have held down his job if he had not been able to speak English far better than I could speak French. 'Five forty-seven a.m., sir,' the porter answered immediately. Lionel would not acknowledge that a Continental foreigner could really speak the Chosen People's language. 'Tell him', he said to me again, 'to reserve me a seat on that.' When the head-porter had promised to do so, but only then, Lionel went to the desk to register. He had not been going to commit himself to spending a night beyond the pale till he had secured his line of retreat.

Lionel was critical of British civil servants in India and British consular officers in Eastern Asia who had acquainted themselves with the classical languages and literatures of the countries in which they were stationed. Their scholarship, he had found, had made them too much enamoured of these Asian countries' deplorable undemocratic pasts, and, in consequence, these orientalists in office were unresponsive to the 'political verities' that it was Lionel's mission to propagate *in partibus infidelium*. Preposterous, one is tempted to protest. Why, since the days of Sir William Jones, the service of the British East India Company and the British Crown had bred generations of scholars who had shed glory on Britain in the Republic of Letters by a series of distinguished contributions to learning. Yet Lionel's philistine critique of these cultivated countrymen of his may not have been altogether unjustified. Classical scholarship may be conducive to political conservative-mindedness. Lionel felt that he was being obstructed by political stick-in-the-muds, and, when one has allowed for his prejudice against the gift of tongues, one still cannot be sure that there may not have been some sense in his, at first sight, extravagant thesis.

Lionel's phobia of foreign languages and foreign countries was most acute vis-à-vis Continental Europe. He accepted the overseas world as being redeemable. Indeed he embraced it as a vast mission-field for the propagation of 'the political verities' of democracy in the medium of the English language. By contrast, the Continent, as Lionel saw it, was invincibly ignorant of both these means of salvation. Realizing that he could never convert the Continent, he ignored it.

I once ran into André Siegfried in Oxford just after he had

been spending a week-end as a guest at All Souls, and I found him laughing over his conversations in college with Lionel. Siegfried was the leading French specialist of his day on the English-speaking peoples. He had had a good start for becoming an Anglo-Saxonist. His father was an Alsatian Protestant who had emigrated to Le Havre after 1871; and Le Havre lived by doing business with England. Siegfried had not only visited all the English-speaking countries; he had also published at least one book on each of them. Siegfried's reaction to 'Anglo-Saxon attitudes' was not unlike Margoliouth's reaction to Islam. His subject was, on the whole, displeasing to him. In Siegfried's eyes, Anglo-Saxon culture was inferior to French, yet the baser metal was threatening to drive the purer out of circulation. At the same time, Siegfried found the inferior culture so fascinating that he devoted his working life to the study of it. 'I really believe', Siegfried declared to me on this occasion, 'that, if Curtis were ever to land at Calais, he would say to himself "Here the niggers begin." ' At the moment, I took Siegfried's quip as being an expression of pique rather than a matter-of-fact observation. But I found that I had done this sober-minded French Anglo-Saxonist an injustice when, on picking up a new book of Lionel's next day, I read in it the words 'some Brahmins are as white as Frenchmen'. So, after all, Siegfried had not been exaggerating. Lionel really did believe that, just across the Straits of Dover, visible to the British white man's naked eye, lay the first of the lands in which the colour of human skins was perceptibly sub-fusc. Lionel cannot ever have crossed a rather wider sea to make a landfall at the Norman port in which blonde André Siegfried had grown up. In Normandy, Nordic Man is so thick on the ground that Lionel himself could not have overlooked his presence there.

I ought not to have doubted Siegfried's word, for, by that time, I had already seen enough of him to appreciate his prowess as an observer of public affairs. He was as keen as ever on the scent when, in Paris during the peace conference of 1946, I saw him for the last time before his death. I had been wondering, with some anxiety, how he had fared during the German occupation, and I now made contact with him at the first opportunity. He was looking old, frail, and starved, but he was animated by a glow of intellectual exhilaration; and, before I could ask him how he was, he was telling me, eagerly, some of his war-time experiences. He had had the professional good fortune to be living at a point in Paris from which he had had a full view of the fighting during the last days of the Germans' presence in the city. The Siegfrieds' apartment—No. 8, Rue de Courty—overlooked the Ministry of Foreign Affairs, and, from his windows, Siegfried had been able to watch the German shells exploding on the nearest corner of the building. (The Quai d'Orsay had just been seized and manned by the Resistance.) And then Siegfried had seen the people of Paris pouring out into the streets and throwing up barricades of torn-up flagstones and cobbles. When the frail old man got to this point in his lively narrative, his face lit up. 'I had never dreamed', was the climax, 'that I could ever see 1830 and 1848 and 1871 with my own eyes, and now I have had this good luck.'

While Siegfried was speaking, I had been looking at his daughter's face. (She had come with him to have dinner with me at the British delegation's hotel.) Like Baron Meyendorff on an earlier occasion, when Sidney Webb had been holding forth, Mlle Siegfried did not see, with the same eyes, the experience that the speaker was recounting with such gusto. Mlle Siegfried's job had been a tougher one than her father's. She had had to keep the octogenarian observer alive; and I suspected that her anxieties had been increased by his indifference to the danger to which he had been exposing himself by craning out of the window for fear that he might miss some detail of the history that was being made before his eyes.

In terms of British party politics, Lionel called himself a Liberal; and it is true that the ultra-Conservative *Morning Post* denounced him every other day for years on end as the villain who was liquidating the British Empire. However, the *Morning Post*'s denunciation of Lionel could not make him a Liberal *de facto*. Temperamentally, Lionel was conservative-minded, like his bugbears the British administrators and consuls in Asia. As a party man, Lionel was in truth neither a Liberal nor a Conservative (Labour hardly came into his picture). He had a party of his own

—the federal union party—and in this party he was a host in himself. He would continue to follow this party's programme, even if the official parties were to fall behind and were to leave Lionel marching on as the world-federalist movement's solitary vanguard.

Lionel was a parson's son, and he used to wear a cross on his watch-chain. He would have classified himself, I suppose, as being an unorthodox Christian, while I should have classified myself as being an un-de-Christianized agnostic. On the gamut of varieties of religious experience, I used to feel myself to be at least several points farther over towards unbelief than Lionel was. Yet it was I, not Lionel, who was shocked at the other's conception of religion.

When Lionel and I were crossing the Atlantic together in the summer of 1925, Lionel was putting the final touches to the script of a lecture that he was going to deliver at some place in Michigan before we assembled at Williamstown, Massachusetts, to attend the summer school there. The subject of Lionel's Michigan lecture was: 'If Christ were to come back to Earth, where, in the present-day world, would he find that his precepts were being best practised?' Lionel invited me to guess the answer that he was going to suggest. 'Well, not, I take it, in the churches.'—'No, not there, of course.'—'Well, perhaps, then, in the lives of humble people who have never been heard of.' But I could see that, in my groping, I was getting colder, not hotter, so I gave it up and asked Lionel what the right answer was. 'Why,' said Lionel, 'the answer is: "In the British Commonwealth". The relation between the peoples of the Commonwealth is the best attempt to carry out Christ's teaching that the present-day world has to show.' Obviously Lionel was surprised at my stupidity at not having seen this obvious answer for myself; but he could not have been more surprised at my blindness than I was at the considered view of a professing Christian.

Four years later, at Shanghai, I was a guest at a meeting of the local Rotarians at which Lionel was the speaker. Lionel was telling the Rotarians about the mission to which they had dedicated themselves (so 'the Prophet' informed them). Their mission, he declared, was to convert China to democracy through the shining example of the municipal constitution of the International Settlement at Shanghai, in which the 'verities' of democracy were being put into practice, for all China to admire and to embrace. As Lionel's audience listened to their speaker giving them this surprising news about themselves, their faces were a sight to see. These Western businessmen had become hardened, long ago, to being denounced, by left-wingers at home, as mercenary-minded exploiters; they had never before heard themselves being lauded to the skies as idealists. It was manifest that they were receiving Lionel's benediction with mixed feelings. They were flattered—how could they not be?—at being so well thought of, and this in such unmistakable good faith, by so distinguished a visitor; but their self-satisfaction was tempered by alarm. Might not Lionel, in all innocence, be committing them (disturbing thought) to a quantum of idealism that would threaten to cramp their style in their future commercial transactions?

For my part, I found myself, as I listened, being shocked, as I had been in 1925, and, this time, to the core. I was shocked now because my own impression of the International Settlement and the French Concession at Shanghai bore no resemblance at all to Lionel's impression of them. This great city that had been conjured up on Chinese soil by Western commercial enterprise had made a horrifying impression on me. As I saw it, the founding fathers of Shanghai had transplanted the body of a Western city to Eastern Asia, but had left the city's soul behind. Shanghai seemed to me to be giving me a pre-view of what Western cities on Western soil were going to be like when the last lingering vestiges of the medieval soul that had originally dwelled in them and redeemed them would have evaporated, leaving nothing there but a gross, sordid, sprawling carcase. The British Commonwealth Christ's Kingdom! That had been comic. But, now, Shanghai the City of God! This was blasphemous.

These had been my pagan reactions to a Christian idealist's recipes for establishing the Kingdom of Heaven on Earth. But was it I, or was it Lionel, who had been right? Had Lionel's vision really been the comedy or blasphemy that it had looked like, to me, at first sight? Had not Christ himself used the similes of the action of salt and leaven when he was trying to convey to his disciples the way in which the Kingdom was to come? And what follows from that verse in the First Epistle General of St. John: 'He that loveth not his brother whom he hath seen, how can he love God whom he hath not seen?' The Long Bar at Shanghai! Publicans and harlots! Yet Christ had announced to these sinners, as Lionel had announced to the Shanghai Rotarians, that, whether they knew this or not, they were the Lord's servants, and that they had been brought into the world to do the Lord's work. When the descending Heavenly Jerusalem makes its impact on the sordid Earth, the juxtaposition of these two incongruous societies cannot fail to be startling. But something that is startling is not comic or blasphemous *ipso facto*. What is startling may also be sublime. Is it possible that the unconventional Christian had seen farther than the conventional agnostic?

I I

Lord Bryce

I WAS in some trepidation while I was on my way to Lord Bryce's flat at 3 Buckingham Gate. Lord Bryce had been receiving first-hand reports, from American missionaries in Turkey, of the recent deportations of the Ottoman Armenians, and he had agreed to a request from His Majesty's Government that he would make a collection of these documents for publication in a Blue Book. Lord Bryce had agreed on condition that H. M. G. would provide him with an amanuensis. I had been given the job.

At the time, I was unaware of the politics that lay behind this move of H.M.G.'s, and I believe Lord Bryce was as innocent as I was. Perhaps this was fortunate. For, if our eyes had been opened, I hardly think that either Lord Bryce or I would have been able to do the job that H.M.G. had assigned to us in the complete good faith in which we did, in fact, carry it out. Lord Bryce's concern, and mine, was to establish the facts and to make them public, in the hope that eventually some action might be taken in the light of them. The dead—and the deportees had been dying in their thousands—could not be brought back to life, but we hoped (vain hope) that at least something might be done to ensure, for the survivors, that there should never be a repetition of the barbarities that had been the death of so many of their kinsmen.

After the Blue Book had been compiled and published, I gradually became aware of the politics that had lain behind H.M.G.'s request to Lord Bryce. The date was 1915. In the spring of that year, the Germans had made that colossal break-through on the eastern front that had drawn from Lionel Curtis his pro-

phetic dismissal of the surrender of the Russian garrison of Przemyśl as 'a merely ephemeral event'. As the Russian armies had
retreated across the Jewish Pale, they had committed barbarities
against the Jewish diaspora, and, when the pursuing German
armies had occupied the evacuated Russian territories, they had
cashed in on the Russians' indiscretion. (The Russian barbarities
were also that. From the point of view of public relations, 'they
were worse than a crime; they were a blunder'.) At that time, the
Pale (i.e. the ex-Polono-Lithuanian dominions of the Russian
Empire) was still the centre of gravity of World-Jewry. For the
Jews, the Pale was then what the North-Eastern United States is
now. Yet, by 1915, the naturalized ex-East-European Jewish community in the United States was already numerous and prosperous
enough to be a power in American life—and a political power at
that, owing to the strategic importance of American Jewry's
geographical distribution on the map of the electoral districts of
the United States.

The German General Staff had lost no time. It had invited a
party of about thirty American journalists—including a Jewish-
American contingent, no doubt—to visit the German-occupied
Russian territories; it had shown the journalists round; the Russian
barbarities had lost nothing in the Germans' exhibition of them;
the American journalists' dispatches to their papers had been lurid;
and, when the clippings of these had been received in London,
H.M.G. had been seriously perturbed. Though, at this time,
World-Jewry had no quarrel with Britain herself, the West European members of the anti-German alliance would suffer inevitably
for the misdemeanours of their ally; and the possible consequences
might be serious indeed. American Jewry might retaliate against
the Allies by throwing its weight into the anti-British scales in the
debate in the United States about the lengths to which American
policy should go in disputing the latitudinarian British doctrine
about a naval power's rights of blockade. Besides, the revelations
about Russian anti-Semitic acts would, no doubt, give the important Jewish communities in Germany and Austria-Hungary an
additional motive, besides patriotism, for supporting the cause of
the two belligerent Central Powers whose citizens they were.

In Whitehall it was recognized that some counter-action must be taken quickly by H.M.G., and, opportunely, H.M.G. was now presented by the enemy with counter-propaganda ammunition. At the very time when the Russians had been committing barbarities against their Jews, the Turks had been committing considerably worse barbarities against their Armenians. If Russian barbarities were telling against Britain and France, would not Turkish barbarities tell against Germany and Austria-Hungary? This line of reasoning in Whitehall lay behind H.M.G.'s application to Lord Bryce to produce a Blue Book on what the Turks had been doing to the Armenians.

H.M.G.'s counter-move to the German General Staff's move indicates that, by 1915, Whitehall was just beginning to become Madison-Avenue-minded. Yet, even by the date of the end of the First World War, Whitehall had not made much progress along this broad way. Throughout the First World War, Whitehall was still naïve in its approach to the problems of public relations. (The new science of analytical psychology was then still in its infancy.) When H.M.G. took action for procuring a Blue Book on the treatment of the Armenians in the Ottoman Empire, they overlooked two material points. One was that human beings are likely to be considerably less indignant about barbarities committed against other people than they will be about barbarities committed against the members of their own community. The second material point that H.M.G. overlooked was the disparity in numbers and influence between the Jewish and the Armenian diaspora.

No doubt, Lord Bryce's Blue Book would produce the same desired effect on the Armenian diaspora as the American newspaper-correspondents' dispatches, which the German General Staff had procured, were already producing on World-Jewry. But, if H.M.G. were reckoning that the Jews' indignation against the Allies on account of the ill-treatment of Jews by Russians would be cancelled out by Jewish indignation against the Central Powers on account of the ill-treatment of Armenians by Turks, their reasoning had stumbled into a *non sequitur*. A human being who felt himself to be a citizen of the world first and foremost would, no doubt, have abominated any atrocities—whoever might be the

perpetrators and be the victims—and, if this imaginary global
humanitarian had employed a Sidney Webb to do two addition
sums and to work out the difference between their respective
totals, he might have concluded that, while each of the belligerent
camps was collectively guilty, the Central Powers' collective
guilt showed an excess over the guilt of their opponents.

In 1915, however, there were few people alive (there are few
in 1966) who had either the moral sensibility or the imagination
that are required for attaining this global humanitarian view. The
number was (and is) too small to be an appreciable quantity in the
calculus of public relations. The great majority was (and is) rather
narrowly nationalist-minded. In schematic numerical terms, one
can perhaps put it that ninety per cent. of a human being's human
sympathies are still bestowed on members of his own particular
community, leaving only a paltry ten per cent. at his disposition
for extending to the huge alien majority of the human race. The
Jews were not more global-minded than any other tribal fraction
of mankind. It would have been unreasonable to expect them to
be. So, as far as World-Jewry was concerned, H.M.G.'s Armenian
Blue Book was predestined to fall flat. World-Jewry's indignation
would continue to be concentrated on the barbarities that had
been committed by the Russians against Jews in the Pale. The
sufferings of the still more barbarously treated Armenians would
be, for World-Jewry, *le cadet de ses soucis*. It was naïve not to have
foreseen this, and it would be most unfair to blame the Jews especially for a narrowness of heart which was just as characteristic of
all the other representatives of the human species.

Disillusioned by the failure of their first essay in propaganda,
H.M.G. thought again; and at last they took the obvious point
that, in order to solve their Jewish problem, they must find a solution in Jewish, not in Armenian, terms. The negative effect on
Jewish feelings of the bad thing that the Russians had done to the
Jews could be counteracted, if at all, only by some positive act, on
the Western Allies' part, to the Jews' advantage; and this good
thing that the Western Allies would have to do for the Jews must
be of a magnitude that would outweigh the Russian barbarities
decisively. Zionism was the key. The Western powers must make

themselves agents for the fulfilment of the Zionists' aspirations. Here was something that might swing Jewish sympathies over to the Allies' side—at any rate in the United States, and perhaps also in Central Europe, though, ironically, Zionism had little appeal for the Jews of Britain and France.

When H.M.G. noticed this trump card in their hand, they were, of course, eager to play it; but first they would have to surmount two obstacles. Palestine was not yet in their possession for them to deliver to Zionism, and there was a Russian veto on any project for making Palestine Jewish. (The Russian Imperial Government's position was that a Jewish Palestine would no longer be a Holy Land fit for being trodden by Russian pilgrims.) The first obstacle fell when Allenby entered Jerusalem; the second fell with the fall of the Tsardom. The promulgation of the Balfour Declaration followed. This was indeed a trump card for the winning of the First World War. It was to prove to be a joker in the pack in the inter-war game of international power politics. That, however, is another story, and I am going to steer clear of it in this book.

If this political spider's web had been visible to Lord Bryce when he had been asked by H.M.G. to undertake the production of an Armenian Blue Book, I believe he would have declined. His integrity was notorious; and this, even more than his access to the American information, and than the esteem in which he was held in the United States, had been, I should guess, his special qualification for the job in H.M.G.'s eyes. I know that, if the political background to the commissioning of the Blue Book had been visible to me when I was on my way to Lord Bryce's flat, I should have felt doubly uneasy.

My private trepidation was bad enough without its being aggravated by misgivings over the public aspect of the job that had been assigned to me. Within the next few minutes, I should be in the presence of one of the most eminent men now alive in Britain.

I had first become aware of Lord Bryce as the author of *The Holy Roman Empire*. A prize essay (and this book had been that originally) seldom proves to be a work of lasting value; but this one had been a notable exception. Since its publication in 1864, it had deservedly gone through numerous new editions; and, in most of these, the author had made revisions and additions that had kept on adding to the book's value. I had read *The Holy Roman Empire* at a fairly early age in my mother's copy of it. I had found *The American Commonwealth* in Moberly Library at Winchester, and I had learnt much about the state governments, as well as the federal government, of the United States by the time I had finished reading those three informative volumes. I knew, too, that Bryce the famous historian was only one of this many-sided personality's facets. There were also Bryce the traveller, Bryce the mountaineer who had made the ascent of Mount Ararat, Bryce the member of Mr. Gladstone's Cabinet, and, above all, Bryce the British Ambassador to the United States—a post from which he had returned home in 1913, after having filled it in an original and most effective way of his own. And now, by this time, there was also Bryce the septuagenarian. When I had first read *The Holy Roman Empire*, Lord Bryce had, for me, been already an historic figure; he had seemed to belong to a receding Victorian past; and now here I was having to present myself to him as the amanuensis that H.M.G. had allocated to him. How was I to live up to the part for which I had been cast? If the difference in age had been the only difference between Lord Bryce and me, that would still have been formidable. It was a difference of fifty-one years. In 1915, Lord Bryce was seventy-seven and I was twenty-six.

I took the lift, rang the bell, and went in, and I was quickly reassured. Lord Bryce's presence was not at all alarming. With his penetrating eyes peering out from under bushy eye-brows, he reminded me of a Scotch terrier, and his movements, too, were still as brisk as that. His manner was unassuming, and this was reassuring too, though it was an unassumingness that had nothing in common with a nonentity's. It was the simplicity of someone who was incapable of being pompous and who was effective enough, just as he was, to feel neither the need, nor the temptation, to assert himself. Lord Bryce did not need, either, the support of honorific letters after his name. Some months after my first meeting with him, when I was putting together the title-page for the forthcoming Armenian Blue Book, I lifted the list of honours bodily from *Who's Who*; and, when the proof of my manuscript page came in from the printer, the string of abbreviations and initials took up nearly half the printed page. When I submitted this heavily-loaded proof to Lord Bryce, he gave it one glance and then deleted the whole phalanx of his honours with one stroke of his pen (and in Lord Bryce's treatment of proofs, deletions were rare). I took it upon myself afterwards to put just a few of the most distinguished of his honours back without consulting him about this again.

Another characteristic of Lord Bryce's that made a deep impression on me was his perennial youthfulness. This was not the distressing youthfulness of an old man who has never quite grown up. It was the refreshing youthfulness of someone whose arteries—metaphorical as well as literal—had not hardened with the passage of time. I have never met anyone to match Lord Bryce for this except Sri Jawaharlal Nehru, and Pandit Nehru's youthfulness did not have an equal staying-power. Though Nehru's life was shorter than Bryce's by a little more than eight years, Nehru eventually had the misfortune to outlive his long-sustained vitality. No doubt, the odds were not equal either. Nehru died in a prime minister's crushingly heavy harness, whereas Bryce was able to spend the last years of his life in triumphantly completing his literary *magnum opus*.

Lord Bryce's body and spirit kept in step with each other from beginning to end. They both retained their youthfulness to the last. I have mentioned that Lord Bryce, in his late seventies, moved with the briskness of a terrier. His London flat was on two floors, and the upper floor housed many of his books and papers. When he needed to fetch some document from up aloft, he would, not walk, but run upstairs, and this two steps at a time. On his errands when he was in the country, at his house in Forest Row, he was still riding a bicycle. In the garden at Forest Row there were trees, planted by the Bryces, which they had lived to see grow tall. Lord Bryce liked to point out the height that those trees had reached. He told me once that, when the time had been approaching for him to retire from his ambassadorship at Washington, he and Lady Bryce had decided that they would like to test how much physical exertion and hardship they could still stand. (He confidently spoke for Lady Bryce as well as for himself, and it is true that she was considerably younger than he was; but for keeping up, even just physically, with her seventy-five-years-old husband, Lady Bryce will have needed all the advantage that she had over him in chronological age, since, in Bergsonian durability, Lord Bryce had the advantage over all comers.)

The test that the Bryces (or one of them) had selected was to travel back to Britain from Washington, D.C., via one of the transcontinental American railroads and the Pacific Ocean and the Trans-Siberian Railway, instead of making the humdrum Atlantic crossing. I will not tell the story of that long journey here. H. A. L. Fisher has told it in some detail in his life of Lord Bryce, and I am not a first-hand witness. In brief, the Bryces found the Trans-Siberian train too comfortably appointed to provide the test that they were seeking; so, part way across Eurasia, they switched on to a branch line heading southwards, changed into a horse-carriage at railhead, and pushed on to within sight, at least, of the Altai Mountains. (They got that far, even if Bryce the mountaineer did not add Altai's scalp to Ararat's, as a culminating trophy.)

I feel sure that Lord Bryce regretted this omission. It is one of my own regrets that I had not been assigned to him as his amanuensis before he had left Washington, so that I did not have the chance of serving as his courier on his Siberian endurance-test. In consequence, I have not even seen the Altai Mountains yet, not to speak of ascending any of their peaks. However, the recollection of Lord Bryce's exploit still gives me hope; for, even now, I am only seventy-seven. My knowledge of what feats Lord Bryce performed at what ages has set me a standard of performance for myself in my accumulating but not, so far, I hope, declining years. I find this a splendid stimulus; but my wife, being concerned to preserve me alive, complains that Lord Bryce's successful defiance of physical age has set me a thoroughly bad example.

If Lord Bryce's physical unageingness was impressive, what

epithet does his mental unageingness demand? Fresh thoughts were continually sprouting in his mind. They sprouted fast enough to create a problem for his printer and his proof-reader. When I was seeing the Armenian Blue Book through the press, Lord Bryce added as much again, on the galleys, as there had been in his manuscript, and as much, once again, on the page-proofs, as there had been on the monstrously swollen galleys. At each successive stage of production, Lord Bryce made the proofs burst at their seams. I have been told that, when the Oxford University Press was publishing a book of his, their policy was to scrap each of the heavily corrected proofs and to set up the whole of the type afresh. They had found, by experience, that this procedure cost them less than trying to insert the massive corrections and additions on the existing proofs. But this was before the onset of a progressive rise in prices that has been continuing, by now, for half a century. I fancy that, today, even Lord Bryce would be called to order by his publishers if he had not learnt, by now, to mend his ways.

This practice of Lord Bryce's gave evidence of the activity of his mind, but it was not propitious for his literary style. The difficulty that he found in refraining from piling third thoughts on second thoughts tended to make his writing top-heavy and, in places, even clumsy. Yet few passages of English historical writing can vie, in point of style, with the opening paragraph of *The Holy Roman Empire* or with the description, towards the end of the same book, of the ravens wheeling over the crags at Berchtesgaden while tormented Germany waits for Barbarossa and his knights to emerge, as her saviours for the second time, from the cave in which they are provisionally sleeping. (I presume that Hitler owed his unfortunate acquaintance with this legend to some original German source and not to a German translation of Lord Bryce's famous book. Lord Bryce would not have wished to be responsible for Hitler's having ensconced himself, like a sinister hermit crab, in Barbarossa's romantic hide-out.)

The best index of mental activity is curiosity, and Lord Bryce's curiosity never flagged. His major literary ambition had been to write a book about democracy, not limited, this time, to an account of democracy in the United States, but embracing the history, structure, and working of democracy in all societies and in all ages in which it had ever made its appearance. However, by the time he had become ready to get to work on this vast enterprise, the calls on him for important public service had become so frequent and so pressing that, again and again, his projected *magnum opus* had to go to the wall. First came his ambassadorship, then came his war-work. (The Armenian Blue Book, on which I had the good fortune to work for him, was only one of many war-time tasks that were required of him.) It was not till after the end of the First World War that he was able, at last, to give priority to his big book on modern democracies.

By this time, Lord Bryce was far on in years; and, at best, *ars longa, vita brevis.* It might have been expected that, by now, his ideas about democracy would have become hard set, and that, in any case, he would have become impatient to gather in the harvest that was already standing in his field, without waiting to look in the by-ways and hedges for stray sheaves. Lord Bryce felt, in a high degree, the sense of urgency that is the mother of productivity but that can also be the enemy of thoroughness. Other people who found themselves in the position that Lord Bryce was in at this late hour might have allowed urgency and age to work together to head them off from running after any new thing. If they had been writing on democracy, for instance, a report of some novel form of democracy or of some new knowledge or understanding of old forms of it might have thrown them on the defensive and even have aroused their hostility. They might have been inclined to close their eyes and shut their ears. Lord Bryce, however, had not grown old in any but the irrelevant chronological sense, and his curiosity was strong enough to be able at will to keep his sense of urgency waiting.

I had first-hand evidence of this at the time when his big book on democracy was on the stocks. One day, in talking with Lord Bryce, I happened to mention Douglas Cole's name. Oh, did I know Cole personally? Lord Bryce inquired. I told him that we had been contemporaries at Balliol and that we were friends. Then could I put him in touch with Cole? He had heard of a new thing called Guild Socialism, with which Cole's name was associated. No doubt, Cole could give him information about it. He wanted to be sure not to leave Guild Socialism out of his survey of theories of democracy, economic as well as political. I did put Lord Bryce in touch with Cole, and when, eventually, the big book on democracy appeared, I looked to see whether a notice of Guild Socialism was included in it. Sure enough, there it was, and I am confident that the author would have found ways and means of stowing in this stop-press piece of information, even if it had not reached him till after he had passed for press what the printer had intended to be the final set of page proofs.

To encourage his sense of urgency to hold its own against his curiosity, Lord Bryce had invented for himself, long ago, a psychological equivalent of the dog-track's electric hare. Thinking over the list of the historical topics on which his mind dwelled the most lovingly, he had picked out the life (like the Hammonds' life, it was singular, not plural) of the imperial couple, Justinian and Theodora. Of all possible subjects, this, he judged, was the one that he would find the most enjoyable; so he decided, early, to save Justinian and Theodora up to serve him as his ultimate literary target. After that, whatever book he might be writing at the time was the penultimate piece of work standing between him and Justinian and Theodora. But, as soon as each successive penultimate book had gone to press, his policy was to slip in another—leaving the ultimate Justinian and Theodora, to which he was always looking forward, still just beyond his reach. *The Life of Justinian and Theodora* was never written, and this is, no doubt, a loss. But *Modern Democracies* was written (its author just lived to see it published); numerous other books had been written by Lord Bryce before that; and the writing of each book in turn was accelerated by the alluring prospect of Justinian and Theodora in the offing. An electric hare's function is, not to be caught, but to speed up the racing hound's pace by being so stimulatingly elusive. For Lord Bryce in his activity as an author, this was the role that his beloved pair of Byzantine sovereigns was made to play.

It is no wonder that Lord Bryce's literary output was prolific, in spite of his working-time being so frequently impounded for public service or for private travel. Lord Bryce was a wide-ranging traveller in an age in which travel was much slower—though consequently much more rewarding—than it is today. His travels, unlike his public service, did not put a brake on his pen; for most of his travels generated books.

The story of the last weeks of Lord Bryce's life was told me, I remember, by Gilbert Murray. Lord Bryce had gone, for the summer, to Switzerland, and there he had still been able to do things in which he had taken a lifelong pleasure. This summer, as before, whenever he came across a mountain that took his fancy, he climbed it, whatever its altitude; whenever he came across a lake that took his fancy, he took a dip in it, whatever its temperature. (He was a Scotsman, so, for him, a low temperature was no deterrent.) By the time when he had taken his fill of his accustomed physical exercises, the summer-holiday season was over and the Swiss holiday-makers had gone back home. Lord Bryce then descended from the Swiss mountains to tour the Swiss cities. In each city that he visited, he was welcomed by the leading citizens, and he found time to have a talk with each of them about each one's avocation and interests, whatever these might be. After that, Lord Bryce came home and died peacefully in his sleep.

'Call no man happy until he is dead'? Though death was unusually slow in coming to James Bryce, I could have called this man happy confidently within his lifetime.

12

Sir James Headlam-Morley

I WAS fortunate, in the First World War, in finding my way into the Political Intelligence Department of the Foreign Office. I do not know whether the so-called 'Ministry of All the Talents' had fully deserved its name, but in the P.I.D., a century later, there was a concentration of talent that was immensely stimulating. Among my colleagues there were R. W. Seton-Watson (still in a corporal's uniform), Lewis Namier (no longer in the uniform of the Public Schools Battalion), and the Australian brothers Rex and Allen Leeper (both of whom went on to become permanent members of the Foreign Service, though Allen's career was cut short, far too early, by death). But our *doyen* was Headlam, as he then still was.

Like the rest of us in the P.I.D. at this stage, Headlam was a temporary Foreign Office clerk, but, unlike any of the rest of us, he was already a permanent civil servant, with a distinguished official career to his credit. However, it was not *quâ* civil servant, but *quâ* scholar, like us, that Headlam was now serving in a wartime department of the Foreign Office. Headlam's own department was the Board of Education—a department whose field of activity was unwarlike because it was civilized. Before the end of the First World War, the Board of Education had been elbowed out of its offices in Whitehall to make way there for a school of trench-warfare; and, though, in its temporary war-time quarters, the Board was now engaged in preparing H. A. L. Fisher's epoch-making Education Bill, it still had officers to spare. Accordingly Headlam had been seconded to the Foreign Office because his personal experience, together with his pre-war scholarly pursuits 'out of school', had equipped him for performing timely war-time services.

Besides being an experienced professional administrator in the field of education, Headlam was, in private life, an historian and an expert on Germany. His knowledge of Germany was intimate. Like Sir Eyre Crowe, he had married a German wife. And what more effective step than that could any man take for getting to know a foreign country from the inside?

In the First World War the British people vented its feelings in a vulgar hatred of the German people to which it did not succumb in the Second World War, when Britain's position was more grave and when Germany's conduct was more atrocious. In the Second World War, it would, no doubt, have been difficult, in Britain, to be indiscriminately anti-German, considering that the country was then giving asylum to large numbers of German refugees who had been victims of Nazi persecution. In the First World War, however, there were people in Britain who let their anti-German feelings run to fantastic lengths. For instance, one of the mistresses at my sister Jocelyn's school told her class one day that she hoped that German would become a dead language; and I was once startled, at a war-time tea-party, by an old lady's asking me if I did not think that it was about time to get rid of all those Germans in the War Cabinet. (All? The War Cabinet was only four men strong, all told. I found that the silly old lady was gunning for Lord Milner. He had had a German stepmother, and, though she was long since dead, she had made an honorary German of Lord Milner for life in that British old lady's eyes.)

His Majesty's Government was, however, wiser and fairer-minded in the First World War than the British public was. H.M.G. appreciated the value, for winning the war, of two civil servants whose personal link with Germany was, in each case, a living wife, not a deceased stepmother. In the course of the war, Headlam was seconded from the Board of Education to the Foreign Office, and Eyre Crowe, who was already a senior permanent Foreign Office official, was promoted to the post of Permanent Under-Secretary of State (the top post for an official, ranking only just below the Secretaryship of State for Foreign

Affairs itself). These well-judged acts of H.M.G.'s were also courageous; for, during the First World War, Ministers went in fear of
the Press—and this not without reason, for the Press was then still
a power that could, and did, sway public opinion. (By the time of
the Second World War, the British public had become just
sophisticated enough to see through the Press and to discount it,
and this made H.M.G.'s task in the Second World War that much
less difficult.)

Before the outbreak of the First World War, Headlam had
drawn on both his knowledge of Germany and his knowledge of
history for writing an excellent life of Bismarck in Putnams'
'Heroes of the Nations' series. In 1914, this was the standard bio-
graphy of Bismarck in English. There could be no doubt about
Headlam's qualifications for taking charge, in the P.I.D., of its
German section, which was, of course, the most important section
of all. Headlam's first war-time job was to write a history of the
immediate diplomatic antecedents of the outbreak of war. *The
History of Twelve Days, July 24th to August 4th, 1914* was the earliest
account, published by a British historian, of that critical passage
of history. (Within the last half-century, the literature, in many
different languages, on this perennially controversial subject has
swollen to almost unmanageable dimensions.) After the First
World War, Headlam's transfer from the Board of Education to
the Foreign Office was made permanent, and the new post of
Historical Adviser to the Foreign Office was created for him. He
continued to hold this post till he reached the age for retirement.
(Unfortunately the post was then allowed to lapse.)

It will be noticed that Headlam owed the second stage of his
official career—and this stage was the more important stage—to
the mark that he had made, during the first stage, by his non-
official activities. This fruitful interplay between the private and
the public sector of a civil servant's life, which is exemplified in
Headlam's career, would probably be less easily practicable now.
Headlam, however, was, I should say, a typical civil servant of
his generation.

Headlam had been fortunate in entering the Civil Service before the end of the golden third of a century that had begun with

the substitution of competition for patronage as the key to entry and had ended with the setting up of the National Insurance Commission. I am grateful to the Liberal Government that took office in December 1905 for what it did towards laying the foundations of 'the welfare state' in Britain. (Actually, the first foundation-stone had been laid thirty-five years earlier, when, in Britain, primary education had been made compulsory and simultaneously been provided at the public expense.) In the past, the state has been primarily an institution for making war on foreigners and for protecting the private property of a privileged minority at home. If the state can be transformed progressively into an instrument of social justice, that will be a notable advance towards civilization. All the same, I take 1905 as the terminal year of the British Civil Service's golden age, because the birth of 'the welfare state' introduced a new rhythm into a civil servant's work—a hectic rhythm which was incompatible with leisure, or, at any rate, was incompatible with a creative use of it. From 1905 onwards, the civil servant's previous leisure was engulfed in an unremitting series of emergencies, which began with the strenuous work of bringing the earliest of the public welfare services into operation and continued thereafter in successive cycles of war, reconstruction, crisis, and war.

The competitive examination that has been the method of making appointments to the United Kingdom Civil Service since 1870 was, in its original form, very like the competitive examination by which Chinese civil servants were selected for at least thirteen centuries, also ending in A.D. 1905. In Britain originally, as in China throughout, the subjects in which candidates for the Civil Service were examined were the staple subjects of higher education in that period, and the weightage given to each examination-subject in terms of marks corresponded more or less to the relative esteem in which that subject was currently held in 'polite society'. This remarkably close resemblance between the two systems of selection may not have been altogether fortuitous. The mid-nineteenth-century decades in which the British were hotly debating the question of Civil Service reform at home were also the decades in which British officials and business men were discovering China after having broken open China's doors in the Opium War. Some of the features of Chinese life that they discovered were appreciated by some of them. For instance, the Chinese system of filling the vacancies in the Civil Service by competitive examination is described, and is also commended as an example that Britain might follow, by a member of the first batch of British consuls in China, T. T. Meadows, in a book called *The Chinese and their Rebellions* which was published in 1856.

Like the Chinese civil servant again, the Late Victorian British civil servant was not only appointed on account of his proficiency in scholarship; he was also expected, and indeed encouraged, to keep up his scholarship thereafter, side by side with his official work. This made sense, for, under the pre-1905 conditions, there was time in a British civil servant's life for both activities; the administrator and the scholar could be two natures in one person if the civil servant was hard-working and methodical (and most of the civil servants who had been appointed on their merits in a competitive examination will have been virtuous in both these ways). Moreover, the two activities not only did not get in each other's way; the pursuit of each was positively beneficial to the other. The scholar in the civil servant broadened the civil servant's outlook and so saved him from shrivelling into a mere bureaucrat. Conversely, the civil servant in the scholar put method into the scholar's work, and this sometimes enabled him to produce greater results in his margin of spare time than he might have produced if he had been a don with more time to spend as he chose but with less practice in self-discipline.

Sir Arthur Hirtzel, for instance, who rose, as a civil servant, to become Permanent Under-Secretary of State at the India Office, also rose, concurrently, to become the foremost Virgilian scholar of his time in Britain. Hirtzel's contemporary J. W. Mackail, who could have obtained, for the asking, any post in the classical field that he might have chosen at Oxford, preferred to spend his working life as a scholar civil servant in Headlam's department, the Board of Education. In the office, Mackail rose to the post of Assistant Secretary; in scholarship he had few peers at any of the universities; and it was for his scholarship that he was awarded the Order of Merit; for this rare honour is not given for meritorious service in the public administration. (Other high honours are given for that.) The conferment of the Order of Merit on Mackail shows that his feat of combining eminence as a scholar and man of letters with distinction as a civil servant counted to him for righteousness in the sight of the higher powers. This was the goodly company of Confucian-like Late Victorian scholar-administrators of which Headlam, too, was a notable member.

I have called the epoch of these 'semi-leisured' civil servants the golden age of the British Civil Service because I believe that they were in a position to do their official work better than it can be done by their successors who have no leisure for doing scholarly or literary work of their own. The civil servants of the old school might do better, because they had a better chance of retaining—or developing—a sense of proportion; and, in work of all kinds, a sense of proportion is a necessity for which mere expenditure of time is no substitute.

The British civil servants of the golden third of a century were not less conscientious than those of the subsequent hectic age, but their conscientiousness took a different form. They were conscientious in taking pains to single out, and concentrate on, the issues that were of first-class importance. They took care to give themselves time to think over each of these crucial issues thoroughly before recommending action on it to a distracted minister; and, if they did sometimes let trivial matters slide, little harm was done by that. By contrast, today the civil servant is almost as paralysingly distracted as the minister himself whose hand it is the civil servant's function to hold. During the last half-century the increasing efficiency of the registries in British government offices has swollen to a flood the flow of files that used to pass in a trickle across the Late Victorian civil servant's desk; and conscientiousness is now apt to take the form of treating all files with impartial deference but, at the same time, inevitably, allocating a smaller and smaller amount of time and attention to each file as the number of the files to be dealt with increases. This egalitarian doctrine of 'the equality of files' is havoc-making, as the doctrine of 'the equality of states' is, and this for the same reason. The doctrine is at variance with reality. The Late Victorian civil servants were more workmanlike when they drew their distinctions between issues that mattered and issues that did not. When these distinctions are flattened out, the trivial file gets more attention than it needs, while the crucial file gets less attention than it requires. This failure to discriminate is inimical to genuine efficiency, but it is a weakness that is hard to combat; for the docket on a file-jacket has the same psychological effect as a newspaper headline. It standardizes the contents of all files to the same dead level, and conditions the user to taking them all at this false egalitarian valuation. When the speed of the passage of the series of files across the clerical worker's conveyor-belt becomes as rapid as the flicking of a cinematograph-film, the conditioning of the civil servant's mind becomes hypnotic.

Since Headlam was a civil servant of the classic school, in contrast to the epigoni of my generation, to work under Headlam's guidance at Chatham House was an education for me; and this came just at the right time, when we were getting the Chatham House *Survey* going and were having to feel our way, by trial and error, towards finding a workable form for the presentation of current international history. I learnt much from Headlam the historian, but, since I am an historian myself, I perhaps learnt even more from Headlam the civil servant, with his fine flair for points of procedure. Besides being my mentor, Headlam was also my shield. My work had to run the gauntlet of the Council of Chatham House; a majority of the councillors were men of action in the conventional sense; these did not altogether understand the nature of academic work; and they therefore sometimes demanded the impossible. I myself had no direct access to the Council, but Headlam, as chairman of the Council's Research Committee, was a councillor *ex officio*, and, in his hands, my case was safe.

How did I come to have the chance of profiting so much by Headlam's help? To put the same question in another way: How did Headlam come to devote so much of his time to Chatham House? The answer is that public spirit was one of the characteristic virtues of eminent intellectuals in Headlam's generation. Lord

Bryce, Lionel Curtis, and Gilbert Murray are other examples of this; and some of them carried their public spirit to the point of self-sacrifice. I have already described how Lord Bryce gave precedence to one piece of public service after another over the writing of the big book on democracy on which his heart was set—and this in his old age, when the risk of losing his opportunity once for all was mounting with the passing of each further year. Headlam, too, had a big book to write, and the voluntary service that he gave to Chatham House diverted that much of his leisure time from the pursuit of his own work.

Ever since the swift production of his war-time book on the immediate antecedents of the First World War, Headlam had been planning to write a definitive work on the same subject on a much larger scale. He proposed to take account of all the original documents that had been published in the meantime, and I daresay he would have extended his period backwards in time from the last fortnight before the outbreak of war in 1914 to the day after the end of war in 1871. His work at the Foreign office, and to some extent also his work for Chatham House, did, of course, bring grist to his mill; but, so long as he was carrying on these two activities simultaneously, he did not have enough spare time to make it possible for him to do any systematic work on his vast private project. When he reached the age for retirement from the public service, his road seemed at last to be clear; but Headlam was less fortunate than Bryce had been. Headlam, too, now addressed himself to his *magnum opus* with all the zest and expectancy of someone who finds himself actually embarking on a cherished enterprise that has been long deferred. If Headlam-Morley had lived to Lord Bryce's age, he would have had the time that he needed; but he had hardly raised his pen when a fatal illness struck him down. His untimely death was a tragedy for him and for the world. Headlam died without having had his chance of giving the world the masterpiece that he had in him.

13
Field-Marshal Jan Smuts

I DID not see more of General Smuts than I saw of Lord Milner or of Lord Halifax, and I have not felt that my acquaintance, if I can call it that, with either of them calls for a separate chapter. I have made a separate one for General Smuts because I did some jobs of work for him too; because I owe much to a book that he wrote; and because I was one of the recipients of an honorary degree from him on an historic occasion.

The principal job that General Smuts set me was at the opening of the Paris peace conference of 1919. Almost as soon as I had arrived in Paris, I received an urgent instruction from him to reduce to a far smaller compass my papers on H.M.G.'s commitments in the Near and Middle East, which had been printed (in the Foreign Office's confidential press), and been circulated, before we had left London. I had worked hard to make those papers concise, and I had supposed that I had succeeded. I surely had succeeded by any academic standard. But conciseness is a relative concept, and its interpretation varies in accordance with the degree of the pressure, per square inch, on the time and attention of the person for whom the document is intended. The mental pressure on a statesman is comparable to the physical pressure that is borne by those deep-sea creatures whose bodies would explode if they were ever to be hauled up to the surface.

My task for General Smuts was to reduce my peace-conference papers to about a quarter of their original size. I brought him my abridgements; he asked, very kindly, how I was; and I made the mistake of admitting that I was tired. (This urgent unexpected extra job had compelled me to sit up for two nights running, after

my previous six weeks of working in the Foreign Office under
forced draught.) My imprudent admission drew on me a gentle
rebuke, and I felt abashed. I was nineteen years younger than
General Smuts, so I had no excuse for not being as resilient as he
was. I realized then that a statesman could not reach the summit
that Smuts had attained if his capacity for ignoring fatigue were
not inexhaustible.

The book by General Smuts to which I owe so much is his
Holism. I read it in the early summer of 1927, when I was poised
for starting on my first long-vacation stint of work for my own
book *A Study of History*. The comprehensive view of the Universe
that *Holism* opens up was just what I was needing at that moment
to give my thoughts an impetus—but not at that moment only;
this book of General Smuts's has continued to be one of my
guides on my own mental voyage of exploration. The spirit of
the book seems to me to reflect the author's personality, and its
substance certainly illustrates his many-sidedness. This precious
and delightful quality was more common—or, at any rate, was
more frequently developed—in the giants of the Graeco-Roman
World and of Renaissance Italy than it is in modern Westerners,
who have put their treasure and trust in specialization. Themi-
stocles was criticized by his contemporaries for having made himself nothing but a consummate politician. Lloyd George's contemporaries took his Themistoclean professionalism for granted.
To find living exponents of many-sidedness, even in the modern
West, is refreshing; and General Smuts's many-sidedness out-
classed even Lord Bryce's. Each of these two exceptionally versa-
tile modern men was a lawyer, a politician, and a writer; General
Smuts was also a farmer, a soldier, and a philosopher; and his
philosophy was fortified by a more than amateur acquaintance
with the progress of modern science. If Bryce beat Smuts in any
field, it was as a traveller.

The year and the place in which I received an honorary degree
from General Smuts were 1948 and Cambridge. Smuts was then
Chancellor of the University of Cambridge; he had made a
special journey to Cambridge from South Africa in order to
preside at the degree-giving ceremony. (This was, I believe, the

last of his visits to England.) The occasion was historic, because the principal recipient of a degree was Winston Churchill.

'The English: are they human?' Well, this occasion demonstrated to my satisfaction that they are, but it also suggested to me that it takes a Churchill to make the English forget to keep up the psychological guard that usually covers their human feelings. When Mr. Churchill entered the Senate House, the professors' wives, as well as the professors, jumped up and cheered and waved their programmes. They must have been surprised at themselves, but it was too late; they had given their feelings away. After the degree-giving was over, when the academic procession was walking from the Senate House to Trinity, in whose hall we were to have lunch, the population of Cambridge poured out of their houses and their shops to line the streets and to cheer Mr. Churchill as he passed. Like the professors' wives, they had forgotten, for the moment, to act in character.

After lunch, when the guests' healths had been proposed on the University's behalf, the spokesman for the guests could, of course, only be Mr. Churchill; and this gave him an opportunity for a sally at my schoolfellow Sir Stafford Cripps, who was one of those guests who had just been honoured. 'Think of all that he does for you,' said Mr. Churchill, pointing at him. 'And on how little he does it! Just a glass of water and one or two nuts.' The glass of water, at any rate, was correct, but one thing was surprisingly out of keeping. At that moment the ascetic Wykehamist was incongruously smoking a cigar. The fact is not in doubt. My wife, who was sitting next to him, was a witness. Yet Mr. Churchill did not draw the company's attention to Cripps's lapse into this Churchillian self-indulgence. Had Stafford Cripps's cigar not caught Mr. Churchill's eye? Or had he seen it but been too chivalrous to mention it? My guess is that it was artistry, rather than chivalry, that sealed Mr. Churchill's lips. After the glass of water and the nuts, the cigar would have been an anticlimax that would have ruined the orator's trope; and Sir Winston, like Demosthenes, was, above all else, an orator.

This characteristic of Churchill's has a bearing on the more serious topic that he took up next. Eyeing Smuts now, instead of

Cripps, Churchill began to talk about his experiences in the South African War. He had taken the field as a newspaper-correspondent, not as a soldier, but he had found himself taking part in the fighting, and he had been taken prisoner. This much was as indisputable as Cripps's cigar. It was, in fact, common knowledge. Churchill went on, however, to tell us how the Afrikaner soldier who had captured him had taken him to an officer to ask whether this enemy civilian was to be shot for having been caught fighting in plain clothes, and the officer had said: 'Oh, no, don't shoot him.' At this dramatic point, Churchill looked at Smuts harder than ever, and added: 'The soldier who took me prisoner was Louis Botha, and the officer who said that I was not to be shot was Jan Smuts over there'—and he pointed at Smuts in his turn.

In identifying his Afrikaner captor with General Botha, Churchill was repeating a statement that he had published, long ago, in his account of his early life; but, in telling us that his life had then been spared by General Smuts, he had been giving us news; and this news was sensational; for, if the sequel to his capture was now being correctly reported, it had made history. If that man there had ordered this man here to be shot on 15 November 1899, what would have happened in June 1940? With no Churchill on hand to take the lead, would the British have held out after the French had given in? Might Cambridge have found itself under German domination? It was now Smuts's turn to speak, and we waited eagerly for his comment on Churchill's sensational story. He made no comment on it. His speech was a fine one. He spoke admirably on many interesting points. But he said not a word about the point that was now uppermost in all our minds. Why?

Smuts's silence was open to two interpretations. He might be taken to have tacitly confirmed Churchill's story by giving it no *démenti* when he had the chance. Alternatively, he might be taken to have tactfully impugned it by saying nothing about it. The second of these two possible explanations is favoured by two points of 'internal evidence' and, even more, perhaps, by a recognition of the power of the artistic vein in Churchill's temperament. How could General Botha have been skirmishing, like a common soldier, in the front line? And how could any combatant Afrikaner have thought of shooting a British prisoner-of-war for having been fighting in civilian clothes, considering that the Boer commandos themselves were doing just that? However, the most telling consideration is the likelihood that Churchill the artist would pass over from *Wahrheit* into *Dichtung* as and when his art called for this. His silence over Cripps's cigar may or may not have been negative *Dichtung* in the sense of being a *suppressio veri*; the dramatic parts played by Smuts and Botha in Churchill's account of his being taken prisoner may have been thrust upon them by an artist's creative mind. The drama that Churchill had been rehearsing aloud to us required the other *dramatis personae* to be figures of the protagonist's own stature.

Whether the details of Churchill's story were historical fact or were dramatic fiction, the scene in the hall of Trinity was both dramatic and historic, and, in this drama that was being played in England, not in South Africa, the protagonist was the South African, not the English, hero. The spectacle brought home to me how extraordinary Smuts's career had been. Here was a man who had first distinguished himself as one of the leaders in a lost war of independence; and this same man had lived to become one of the leaders of the country that had once conquered and annexed his fatherland. Smuts's brilliant success in this new role testified to the greatness of his many-sided abilities; his initial decision to take up his new role testified to a rare generosity of spirit.

This generosity was, of course, primarily Smuts's own; but credit must also be given to three other personalities: on the Afrikaner side to Botha and, on the British side, to Curtis and to Campbell-Bannerman. Botha, who had fought side by side with Smuts in the South African War, had also taken the same post-war decision to work for a reconciliation, and he and Smuts had continued to be colleagues and comrades till they had been parted by Botha's death. Churchill, in his speech at Cambridge, had been right in associating Botha's name with Smuts's, even though the particular episode in which he had brought the two men together may have been unhistorical. On the British side, Campbell-Bannerman had held out the hand that Smuts and Botha had grasped. After having opposed the war in South Africa wholeheartedly while in opposition, Campbell-Bannerman had given back to the two conquered Afrikaner states their forfeited powers of self-government as soon as he himself had come into power in Britain. As for Curtis, he had had the imagination to plan, and the determination to push, for the union, with dominion status, of the four South African territories that were now all under the same British flag—a feat of political engineering which gave self-government a greatly enhanced value for the 'white' minority in South Africa—Dutch-speakers and English-speakers alike. Smuts had not been left to play a lone hand; but the part played by the statesmen who co-operated with him does not make his own part any the less imposing.

Smuts himself had summed up his career, and had put his finger on its political and moral significance, in one sentence of a speech that he had made in Edinburgh on 11 April 1917, when he was being given the freedom of the city. (He was in England as a member of the War Cabinet of the United Kingdom.) 'The cause I fought for fifteen years ago', he had said, 'is the cause for which I am fighting today. I fought for freedom and for liberty then, and I am fighting for it now.'

Long before the date at which Smuts was giving Churchill a degree at Cambridge, it had become evident that Smuts and Botha had carried only a small fraction of the Afrikaner community with them along their own path of reconciliation. Indeed, there may have been a dissenting voice within Smuts's own household. I have been told (I cannot vouch for this) that Mrs. Smuts never consented to visit Britain, and that what she had not forgiven was the death of one of her children in a British concentration-camp. Unforgivingness is always an unhappy state of mind, but in this case, at any rate, it is understandable.

The camps to which Afrikaner women and children were forcibly removed from their homes by the British military authorities in the last phase of the South African War were, of course, not death-camps in the sense of those that were afterwards operated in Europe by the Nazi. It would also, I should say, be unjust to apply to them the satirical lines in Clough's *New Decalogue*:

Thou shalt not kill, but need'st not strive
Officiously to keep alive.

The British medical officers serving in the British concentration-
camps in South Africa did their best, I expect, to cope with sick-
ness and to save life. Their ill-success was due, not to callousness,
but to incompetence and to lack of the necessary equipment. The
responsibility lies at the door of the British military authorities
and their principals, the government of the day in the United
Kingdom. The women and children had been taken from their
homes for a military reason; and the order had been given without
waiting to make sure that the camps in which the deportees were
to be concentrated were fit for human habitation. The military
reason was cogent in military terms. The intention was to deprive
de Wet and his long-enduring guerrilla-fighters of the food and
shelter that they could find in the farmsteads as long as the women-
folk were in occupation of these. But, according to the accepted
code of 'civilized' warfare, military considerations do not justify
inhumanity in the treatment of non-combatants, and Campbell-
Bannerman's denunciation of the internment of the Afrikaner
women and children, with its deplorable consequences, as 'methods of barbarism' was as well-deserved as it was courageous.

General Smuts had his opponents and his critics. His strongest
opponents were the Afrikaner nationalists; and, on this issue, any
non-Nazi will be entirely on Smuts's side. Afrikaner nationalism
and racialism have now gone to lengths that make the barbarism
of the British concentration-camps in South Africa seem mild in
retrospect. This Afrikaner nationalist and racialist barbarism, like
German Nazi barbarism, is deliberately malign. Indeed, in 1966,
Mr. Vorster's régime was the nearest thing to Hitler's régime
that was then in existence. General Smuts's critics are mostly non-
South African. The main fault that they have found in him is the
slipperiness for which he had a reputation, and a nickname, among
his own people. He has been criticized, as Jawaharlal Nehru, too,
has been criticized, for failing to live up, as a prime minister, to
the principles that he professed as a citizen of the world. It has
been charged against him, for instance, that, during his years in
office in his own country, he displayed an unedifying skill in

skating round the issue of racial discrimination without ever quite involving himself in it. He has also been charged with being the main inventor of the ingenious devices by which the terms of the reparations chapter of the Treaty of Versailles were kept within the letter of the 'no indemnities' stipulation in President Wilson's Fourteen Points (to which the Governments of the Western allies had committed themselves in the armistice agreement), while the spirit of the President's stipulation was being flagrantly violated. If this second charge is justified, and if it is also true, as has been alleged, that Smuts defended himself by saying that he had been asked for a counsel's opinion and had given this without having become a party to the decision to act on it, it must be conceded that the charge is serious and that the defence is inadmissible. The morally unwarrantable inflation of the reparations bill was a breach of faith; and, for a statesman of Smuts's standing, to advise that the fraudulent act was legally allowable was tantamount to recommending it and incurring responsibility for it.

I do not know whether either of these charges against Smuts is valid, or, if the charges are valid at all, what the extent of their validity may be. In any case one may take it that Smuts's political record is not altogether free from blemishes. One may assume this without doubting that Smuts was a great man. Great men and women are human beings, and to be human is, among other things, to be imperfect.

Smuts's personality had so many sides to it that his severest moral critics and his strongest political opponents will have found some things in him to respect and admire. This point is illustrated by a story that is told of General Herzog, Smuts's Afrikaner nationalist opponent. (Herzog's nationalism looks moderate in retrospect, against the foil of his present successors' Nazi-like ideology.) After a visit to London, when General Herzog was boarding his ship for his passage home (this was in the days before the advent of air-travel), one of the representatives of the United Kingdom Government who were seeing him off asked him casually what he had taken with him to read on the voyage. 'Why, Smuts's new book, of course,' was General Herzog's unexpected but engaging answer. Herzog's disagreement with

Smuts's politics did not prevent him from appreciating Smuts's philosophy.

The visual image of General Smuts that is impressed the most clearly on my mind is the sight of him in Paris, in 1919, taking a stroll with General Botha during one of the intervals between the sessions of the peace conference. One often saw the two comrades in each other's company; and Botha, who was then already a very sick man, would be leaning on Smuts's arm, while Smuts would be helping his old friend along tenderly. Their affection for each other was moving. This long friendship drew out, in Smuts, a quality of loving-kindness that adorned his manifold gifts and went far to redeem his relatively few short-comings.

14
Colonel T. E. Lawrence

FOR a number of years past, 'debunking' T. E. Lawrence has been a fashionable literary exercise. By now there is a row of books on this theme. The impulse to write such books has not flagged, and the market for them, when they appear, is buoyant. Let us suppose that all the statements, prejudicial to Lawrence, in all these books can be substantiated. What has been demonstrated? Only something that we knew, and were bound to know, before. The 'debunkers'' discovery is that Lawrence was human—as anyone must be, if he is to be anything else besides. Lawrence did have something in him besides the human nature that is common to us all. He had in him an element of greatness; and the exposure of human weaknesses in him will leave the greatness in him still standing, undemolished, when the debunkers' batteries have fired their last shot.

Greatness is palpable when one meets it, but elusive when one tries to analyse it and to define what it is. I have no doubt that I have met it in both T. E. Lawrence and Lionel Curtis. Of course there are different degrees of greatness, and I would not maintain that either of these two men was great superlatively. I will claim no more for them than that there was a streak of greatness in each of them; but this streak of it in each of them was, to my mind, unmistakable.

What we mean by greatness, of any degree, in a human being is, I should say, the power, in some measure and in some field, to move other human beings. There are as many fields in which greatness can operate as there are faculties in human nature, and, in different fields, one person's effect on others will have different ranges of action and will make itself felt in different ways.

The greatest souls within our knowledge are the prophets and preachers of the higher religions. The most recent of these, the Prophet Muhammad, has been dead, by now, for more than 1,300 years; Zarathustra and Deutero-Isaiah have been dead for more than 2,500 years, and Siddhārtha Gautama the Buddha for perhaps a hundred years less than that; yet like Jesus—whose traditional birth-date is accepted by most of the world today as the axial date for its time-reckoning, both forwards and backwards—those long-since-dead prophets are, at this moment, influencing the lives of far many more people, and this far more deeply, than any person now alive. Religion is the field in which greatness has proved to have the widest range of action, in both time and space; and the way in which religious greatness makes its effect on human hearts is the subtlest. Saintliness draws rather than drives. Greatness in creative art and greatness of intellect resemble greatness in religion both in their way of making their effects and in their range of action. These three kinds of greatness seem akin to each other in their common contrast to greatness in the field of practical affairs—the field of economics, politics, and war. Greatness in this field has a comparatively short range of action, and it drives rather than draws.

Every human soul, great and small, is a spiritual battle-field in which good and evil are perpetually contending with each other for mastery; so greatness may aim at either good or evil ends; and an evil-minded greatness may prove potent by appealing to the evil that is present in all of us. In our own time, we have seen a great people, with a long tradition of Christian civilization, captured by an evil man who was a genius as a demagogue. There is no guarantee that good will prevail over evil, yet the good has two advantages over evil in their struggle for the possession of human souls. One thing that tells in favour of the good is that we recognize it, and pay tribute to it, even when we are doing evil.

> Video meliora proboque,
> Deteriora sequor.

This is one of Man's spiritual tragedies, but it is a tragedy that is not conclusive. It does not close the door on the possibility of repentance. The second advantage that the good has over evil is that egotism is repellent, and therefore the evil that springs, as so much of human evil does spring, from self-centredness has an inherent tendency to defeat its own ends. An egotism that was complete and completely transparent would have no power at all to move the egotist's fellow human beings; but, of course, egotism can captivate on false pretences by simulating altruism; and complete egotism is rare, perhaps non-existent. Most human souls, including most great souls, are morally complex; and a devotee of some altruistic cause who has a greatness in him that can move mountains in his cause's service may still have a vein of egotism in him. The altruistic cause itself may serve his egotism as its vehicle.

In so far as T. E. Lawrence and Lionel were great, there was, I should say, some of this alloy of egotism in the greatness of each of them; but, though present, this weakness in them was subordinate. Their common field was the political province of practical affairs. Lawrence's range of action was wider than Lionel's. Lawrence was a scholar and a soldier besides being the champion of a political cause; Lionel's field was politics only, though he could quote Scripture to his purpose when required. On the other hand, Lionel's political objective was the larger and the more important of the two. Lawrence was the champion of a single nation. He was, in fact, one representative of a particular type of British political idealist—the type that, since about the beginning of the nineteenth century, had made protégés of one or other of the subject nationalities of the Ottoman and Habsburg empires. The Arabs, whose cause Lawrence had taken up, had had a number of notable, and noble, British champions already. This peculiarly British form of political idealism is admirable, but the vision that inspires it is limited. By contrast, Lionel's vision embraced the whole of mankind, and his objective was nothing less than the union of all the peoples of the Earth in a federation that would enable mankind to liberate itself at last from the self-inflicted scourge of war. In the Atomic Age, the translation of Lionel's ideal into practice may well be our only alternative to destroying ourselves; and the pertinentness and timeliness of Lionel's lifework are indexes of Lionel's greatness in his own field.

Whatever the assessment of these two extraordinary men's power may be, it made itself felt impressively. It made a strong impression on me, at any rate. It was the kind of power that makes its effect in Napoleon's way rather than in Orpheus's; and this is not surprising, since Lawrence's and Lionel's field of action was a province of practical affairs.

At the Paris peace conference of 1919 and in subsequent years, I had a number of opportunities of seeing Lawrence in action. The following two episodes, of which I was a first-hand witness, illustrate the nature of his power.

I was crouching in the back row of seats in the meeting-room of the Council of Ten on the afternoon on which the Amir Faysal, one of the sons of King Husayn of the Hijâz, was to make an exposé to the Council of the political aspirations of the Arab populations that had hitherto been under Turkish rule or suzerainty. My seat gave me a good view of everyone in the room, since the number of participants was not large.

I found myself crouching next to Sir Maurice Hankey (Lord Hankey); and this was luck for me. It was Lord Hankey's habit, at a session of the Council, to scribble comments on the proceedings on scraps of paper and to pass these round to his fellow back-benchers; and these comments were worth having; for Lord Hankey was the master of an art of which he had also been the inventor. Hankey was the first holder of the post of secretary to the Committee of Imperial Defence (i.e. the Cabinet of the United Kingdom Government, with some supplementary members).

The story was that Hankey owed this appointment, which he turned to such good account, to his having been thought stupid when he was a boy. In the belief that he would be unable to qualify for entry into any other service, he had been sent into the Marines; and, when the Committee of Imperial Defence had been instituted, and a secretary had to be found for it, the job had to be given to a marine because the Navy and the Army could not agree to the appointment of a member of the rival service.

Hankey's achievement reminded me of Kipling's description of the tactics of Indian elephant-tamers. Hankey's wild elephants were ministers of state, and it must have been fascinating to watch him herding these majestic creatures into his stockade so discreetly that they were unconscious of what was being done to them. Hankey's elephant-taming instrument was his minutebook. When once he had induced ministers to allow him to keep minutes of their proceedings, he had them under his control. In writing up his record of what ministers had said and had decided, Hankey knew how to put as much order into their rambling deliberations as would be consistent with verisimilitude; and, though this necessary limitation set bounds to the good that he could do, it still left him scope enough to enable him to rationalize and expedite the Cabinet's proceedings appreciably. Deftly prodded by Hankey's ankus, the elephants now moved slightly less slowly and less erratically. It was fortunate for the United Kingdom that Hankey had been in action long enough before the outbreak of the First World War to have the Cabinet already well in hand by then.

Sitting opposite to the Ten on the occasion that I am describing, there were three figures in Arab dress. One was Faysal, another was Lawrence, and the third was a Moroccan who had been stationed there by the French. The Moroccan observer's duty was to memorize what the Amir Faysal was going to say in Arabic, in order that the Moroccan's French employers might be able to verify, afterwards, whether Faysal's speech corresponded to what Lawrence had given as a translation of it. The French had taken this precaution because they had received intelligence of Lawrence's and Faysal's procedure, a few days before, at Edinburgh. On that occasion, Faysal had recited the Chapter of the Cow from the Qur'ân, and Lawrence had then put the Arabs' current political case in a telling speech in English. This way of working had saved Faysal and Lawrence the trouble of having to draft an identical speech in two languages. The Moroccan's presence (of which they had had intelligence in advance) had forced them, this time, into a procedure that had been more laborious. This time, Lawrence had written an Arabic version of his speech, for Faysal to deliver, as well as the English version for subsequent delivery by Lawrence himself; so, this time, the Arabic and the English corresponded with each other to a nicety.

When the moment arrived, Faysal recited Lawrence's speech in Arabic, and Lawrence followed him with a recitation of it in English, but then there was a hitch. Clemenceau understood English and also spoke it (an accomplishment that gave him a valuable advantage over his Anglo-Saxon and Italian colleagues); but the Italians were as ignorant of English as all the Ten were of Arabic. The only foreign language that the Italians understood was French. President Wilson then made a suggestion. 'Colonel Lawrence,' he said, 'could you put the Amir Faysal's statement into French now for us?' After a moment's hesitation, Lawrence started off and did it; and, when he came to the end of this un-prepared piece of translation, the Ten clapped. What had hap-pened was amazing. Lawrence's spell had made the Ten forget, for a moment, who they were and what they were supposed to be doing. They had started the session as conscious arbiters of the destinies of mankind; they were ending it as the captive audience of a minor suppliant's interpreter.

For those few seconds, the British and French members of the Ten had even forgotten their current conflict with each other, though by this time the conflict had become lively and the Arab World was its arena. It is notorious that a victorious coalition is apt to split after the defeat of their common opponent if his defeat has been apparently decisive. This had happened at the Vienna peace conference in 1814, and in 1919 it had happened again. This time, the fissure in the victorious alliance cut across the quadrangle in Whitehall on which the Foreign Office and the India Office buildings both abutted. The India Office and France were now in alliance with each other against the Foreign Office and General Allenby. The India Office and France had been brought together by a common interest. Each of these two powers was afraid that, if the ex-Ottoman Arabs were to be granted genuine independence, this might have an unsettling effect on France's subjects in North-West Africa and on the India Office's subjects in its Sub-continent. France and the United Kingdom did not carry their post-war colonial rivalry in the Middle East to the length of engaging in hostilities, but the India Office and the Foreign Office were less self-restrained. In May 1919, they fought each other by proxy in Arabia, on the border between the Najd and the Hijâz, at a place called Turâba. In this battle, the India Office's Arab ('Abdarrahmân ibn Sa'ûd) defeated the Foreign Office's Arab (King Husayn al-Hâshimî); but the Foreign Office then appealed to its ally General Allenby; Allenby threatened to send some whippet tanks to the Foreign Office Arab's aid; and the India Office prudently advised its own Arab to retreat.

The sinews of war, on both sides, were the subsidies that the two British departments in Whitehall had been paying to their respective Arab henchmen out of the British taxpayer's money. It would have been cheaper for the British taxpayer, and more manly of the civil servants in the two belligerent departments, if these had fought each other direct. They were each other's next-door neighbours; their common quadrangle could have served as a ready-made arena, and they could have saved the British taxpayer much expense if they had done battle with each other here with halberds, swords, staves, and the other simple weapons with which the London borough councils had fought each other in G. K. Chesterton's *The Napoleon of Notting Hill.* This, however, would have been a breach of Civil Service decorum; so the taxpayer had to pay. Since then, the Administration at Washington has streamlined Whitehall's roundabout procedure. Whitehall had given its Arab satellites money for buying the arms for fighting each other; Washington has 'cut out the dollar sign' and has given Pakistan and India the arms for fighting each other straight out of America's store-cupboard.

My second first-hand experience of Lawrence's power was in 1922—this time in my flat in London. This was at the moment when Mustafâ Kemâl Atatürk and his companions had completed their preparations for the Turkish counter-offensive against the Greek invaders of Anatolia. When the counter-offensive was eventually launched, it was successful beyond the Turkish general staff's most sanguine hopes. The Greek armies were shattered, and the balance of power in the Near East was reversed overnight.

Beforehand, however, the Turkish nationalist authorities had been doubtful about the projected offensive's prospects, and they had also been eager to save the Turkish people, which, by this time, had been almost continuously at war for nearly ten years on end, from having to suffer any further military casualties. Accordingly, before launching their offensive against the Greeks, they had sent a mission to London to find out whether the United Kingdom would now be willing to consider terms for a peace-settlement in the Near East that would come close enough to the Turkish nationalists' demands to provide a basis for negotiation without need for any further fighting.

Unfortunately for all concerned, this Turkish peace-mission to London drew blank. They were refused an interview by Lloyd George, and they were rebuffed by the Foreign Office. At this critical moment, H.M.G. were inexcusably blind. Either their military intelligence was at fault, or they themselves were guilty of ignoring it. If they had appreciated the realities of the military situation in Anatolia at this date, they would have jumped at the chance, which the Turks were now offering to them, of negotiating for peace while the Greek armies, whose *moral* had already sunk low, were still physically intact. Within a few weeks of Lloyd George's refusal to meet the Turkish envoys, the Turkish military victory had brought him down. His failure to foresee it, and his subsequent failure to face its consequences realistically, gave the Conservatives their opportunity to break up the coalition government of which he had been the almost omnipotent head for the past half-dozen years, and to put him out of office, never to come back. For once, Lloyd George's sensitive political flair had failed him, with unfortunate results.

This public affair involved me personally because, at the time, I was one of a rather small number of people in Britain who were in sympathy with the Turkish nationalist movement. The year before, I had spent some months in the Graeco-Turkish war-zone as a special correspondent for the *Manchester Guardian*, and, since then, I had been doing what I could to put the Turkish case before the British public. I could do little; for, though I had some first-hand knowledge of the current situation in the Near East, I had no political influence in Britain. When the Turkish peace-mission arrived in London, headed by a friend of mine, Fethî Bey Okyar, I did my best to help them. As was to be expected, I had no success at all in my efforts to persuade people in official positions to see them. Downing Street and Whitehall had decided to be intransigent, and nothing that I could say could move them to change their minds. All that I could do was to introduce the Turkish envoys to any non-official people to whom I had access who seemed likely to be able to help them more effectively than I could if they were so disposed; so, one evening, my wife and I invited the Turkish delegation to our flat to meet Colonel Lawrence and Sir Samuel Hoare.

When my Turkish friends had explained their mission to our two British guests, Lawrence spoke, and my hair stood on end, for he spoke roughly. Without mincing his words, he told Fethî Bey and his colleagues that Turkey was a defeated country and that she must take the consequences. When Lawrence had finished, my wife and I held our breath. Lawrence had been giving the Turks, at this time of day, the very treatment that had provoked them into taking up arms again in 1919. The Turks were not in a mood for standing any more nonsense from the victors of yesterday. How could they let Lawrence's laceration of them pass? Was there going to be an explosion? There was a moment of silence, and then one of the Turkish delegates said quietly: 'Monsieur le colonel a raison.' So Lawrence had done it again! He had captivated these Turkish nationalists now, as I had once seen him captivate the Council of Ten. Of course the Turkish envoys did not leave it at that; but what followed was a constructive discussion, between them and Lawrence, about what their peace-terms should be and how they should present them. The advice that Lawrence gave them was good, and they were receptive to it. If the British Government had been as open to reason as they were, that evening's conversation between them and Lawrence might have provided the starting-point for a peaceful agreement.

A third illustration of Lawrence's power is so amusing that I cannot resist telling the story, though, in this case, I was not a witness, and the original teller of the tale must have been Lawrence himself. The only other person who could have told it was Clemenceau; and, bitingly witty though Clemenceau could be at other people's expense, I fancy that he would have kept silence when the joke was against himself.

At Paris in 1919, the French had been finding Lawrence's activities increasingly annoying. Lawrence had the ability to do any new thing that might be required of him by his mission, which was to promote the Arab cause. His impromptu translation of his English speech for the Council of Ten was a case in point. Among other things, he had proved an adept at organizing press conferences and inducing the newspapers to put things in the way he wanted. Finally, Clemenceau complained of Lawrence to the British delegation, and the British were embarrassed. Though Lawrence was technically a member of the Hâshimî delegation— as he signalled by wearing Arab, not British, military uniform— the British Government could not credibly disclaim responsibility for him. Moreover, they themselves had already gone to the limit of prudence in provoking the French on their own account. They had, for instance, already pocketed the Mosul district, which, according to the war-time agreements between the Allied Powers, had been one of those Arab territories whose 'independence' was to be under French, not British, control. In diplomacy, possession is nine-tenths of the law, and, after the conclusion of the Turco-British armistice, a British force had raced across the armistice line in 'Iraq to Mosul while the French high commissioner designate for Mosul had been kept waiting at Basra. Eventually, Clemenceau had resigned himself to renouncing Mosul, but he could not be expected to stand much more. After all, he was 'the Tiger'. Accordingly, the British delegation made a show of washing their hands of Lawrence when Clemenceau announced that he was proposing to send for that young man and give him a talking-to. Lawrence's countrymen at Paris knew Lawrence well enough by now to feel sure that, even in the Tiger's jaws, he would be able to take care of himself.

The command from Clemenceau arrived, Lawrence obeyed it, and the engagement was soon over. 'You know, Colonel

Lawrence,' said Clemenceau as his opening gambit, 'you know
that France has been interested in Syria ever since the Crusades.'
'Yes,' Lawrence answered, 'but the Syrians won the Crusades, and
they have never forgotten that.' Apparently this had not occurred
to Clemenceau before. He had no reply ready, so the conversation
ended there.

> The man recovered from the bite;
> The dog it was that died.

Replace 'dog' by 'man-eater', and you have the tale of Clemenceau's discomfiture at the hands of the young man whom he had
rashly challenged to meet him in single combat.

Lawrence's power revealed itself visually. Lawrence was, in
fact, like a chameleon. When he was not in action, he had a
deceptive appearance of being insignificant. His height was below
average, his hair was mouse-coloured, his eyes were grey; but,
the moment he went into action, all this changed. His eyes shone
blue, his hair glistened golden, and his stature towered menacingly
above his dismayed opponent. In action, Lawrence's spirit, like
Achitophel's, 'o'er informed the tenement of clay'.

It was a tormented spirit. In Paris Lawrence had, I think,
already realized that, however many tactical successes he might
achieve in his campaign on behalf of the Arabs, he was not going
to win his war. Independence for the ex-Ottoman Arabs was not
an issue over which Britain was going to break with France.
The point had been put tellingly, though not disinterestedly, by
France's ally the Permanent Under-Secretary of State at the India
Office, Sir Arthur Hirtzel. Britain, he had pointed out, was going
to continue to need her alliance with France in the post-war years,
and this major British interest would inevitably have to be given
priority over the details of British desiderata in the Middle East.
Here Hirtzel had put his finger on a consideration that was going,
willy nilly, to be decisive for the determination of H.M.G.'s
policy. Britain would scrounge as much territory and influence
in the Arab World for herself as she could without making the
French turn savage; but in the end she would concede to France,
in the Middle East, the substance of what she had undertaken to

concede to her in the war-time agreements between the Allies, and France's pound of flesh would mutilate the independent Arab Asia that was the Arabs', and Lawrence's, objective. For Lawrence, this was a bitter pill; but his pain did not extinguish his sense of fun, for he had in him a streak of impishness, besides his streak of greatness.

I saw this impish side of him come out once when, as we were walking along a corridor on our way to some meeting, we passed the door of a Treasury official's office. The door was open, and the official was visible within, busy writing at his desk. Lawrence walked into the room, whipped out a dagger from under his robes, and held up the handle in front of the Treasury man's face as the harassed man looked up from his work. 'Guess what this is,' Lawrence said. 'I have no idea,' said the Treasury man. He looked uneasy. When one was under attack from Lawrence, one never knew what was coming next. Lawrence gave the Treasury man the answer to his riddle: 'A hundred and fifty of your sovereigns.' To see that Treasury man wince, you might have thought that, instead of just dangling the gold handle of the dagger in front of his nose, Lawrence had thrust the steel blade between the poor fellow's ribs. Why did that beautifully chased gold dagger-handle give the Treasury man such a shock? The sight shocked him because it was a jarring reminder of one of the Treasury's more painful war-time reverses.

Upon the outbreak of war, the Treasury had called in all our familiar gold sovereigns and half sovereigns. (We have never seen them again.) It had fobbed us off with paper money. (Before 1914, we had seen none of that in any denomination lower than the lordly five-pound note.) The Treasury had then hoarded our gold in the vaults of the Bank of England, with intent to keep it all impounded there. Other belligerent treasuries, on both sides, had done the same, and, in their dealings with their own obedient subjects, they were all able to impose the same high-handed policy. Housman's 'mercenary army', for instance, 'that saved the sum of things for pay', had been lionlike in battle but sheeplike in consenting to take their pay in depreciable notes. There were, however, two 'backward' (I mean 'developing') peoples, the

Albanians and the Arabs, who showed their naïveté by taking an original line of their own. Unaccustomed, as they too were, to paper money, they declined to adapt themselves to it. They insisted on continuing to be paid in gold as before, and also insisted on receiving their gold payment in advance; and the belligerent treasuries ruefully complied with the Albanians' and the Arabs' stipulations, because the belligerent governments were in competition for hiring these knowing warriors as mercenaries.

The Albanians and the Arabs were willing to be hired, so long as they were duly paid in gold in advance. They did not mind which side they hired themselves to. They had no intention of earning their pay by fighting seriously for any of the European belligerents. They wanted the gold in order to hire each other to fight each other, and this made economic sense. Spent in this way, the gold would circulate inside Albania and inside Arabia without leaving either country. The British Treasury made efforts to recover the gold that it had paid out to Ibn Saʿûd through the India Office's nose and to King Husayn through the Foreign Office's nose. At the crisis of the German submarine campaign, the Treasury coaxed cargo-space out of the Ministry of Shipping for bringing Indian textiles to Arabian ports, in the hope that the Arabs might be tempted to part with some of their gold in exchange for these attractive foreign commodities. But there was nothing doing. Arabs could not be bribed with textiles to fight each other. Only gold would work; so the Arabs held on to their gold, and the rejected Indian textiles had to be shipped back to where they had come from.

This was the historical background to Lawrence's chased-gold dagger-handle that had sprung to the Treasury man's mind when he had winced. The dagger performed the function of the Bank of England's vaults. Steel safes were rarities at that time in broad Arabia; yet, everywhere, gold reserves have to be defended till the time comes for putting them to their destined use. The Arabs had found an elegant solution for this security problem. A gold ingot can defend itself if it is married to a steel blade. But, being still only a 'developing' people, the Arabs could not be content with anything that was starkly 'functional'; so they had given their gold dagger-handles an economically superfluous chasing.

Lawrence was not the only British Middle Eastern star that found its way to Paris in 1919. His senior colleague, D. G. Hogarth, arrived from the Arab Bureau at Cairo; Gertrude Bell and Arnold Wilson arrived from 'Iraq (then known, in British officialese, as 'Mesopotamia'). Hogarth was a distinguished archaeologist of the previous generation to Lawrence's. Gertrude Bell was a queen. Make a composite photograph of Zenobia, Á'isha, and Hester Stanhope, and you have her. Arnold Wilson was a king—no, an autocrat; one might almost say, a tyrant. He was then reigning over Mesopotamia as the India Office's civil administrator of it. I should guess that, in Sir Arthur Hirtzel's mind, Arnold Wilson's mission was to groom this ex-Ottoman dominion for being turned into an additional province of the British Indian Empire, but no doubt Arnold Wilson had his own ideas about his objective.

Hogarth and I were academics; we were not in competition with the masterful three; so we sat on the sidelines and watched them. At their first encounters, they bridled at each other like a pride of lions boxed up together in a coal-cellar. The broadest paddock would not have given them room to coexist. To express their personalities adequately, each of them would have needed to have a monopoly of the entire Middle East.

It was an awesome spectacle to see the peace conference gradually breaking these three lions' imperious spirit. In their respective Middle Eastern dominions, they had each, like the centurion in the Gospels, been able to get things done. When they had said to this man 'come', he had come; when they had said to that man 'go', he had gone; when they had said to that other man 'do this', he had done it. They had assumed that, in Paris, they would still be able to transact their business in the same effective way. Weaklings from Europe and America might fail, but these British Middle Easterners would carry all before them. So they had imagined. But, of course, like every participant in any peace conference, the British Middle Easterners were frustrated in Paris in 1919. They struggled violently against fate, but, inch by inch, they sank deeper in the mire till they were as deeply bogged down as the rest of us. They had started as each other's rivals; they ended as each other's companions in misfortune.

In the parlour-game of 'debunking' Lawrence, one of the well-known hits is to castigate him for transmuting himself into 'Aircraftsman Shaw'. On this score, Lawrence has been convicted of being mentally unhinged or, alternatively, of being a calculating exhibitionist. It is true that, if Lawrence had employed a Madison Avenue publicity man, and if this advertising expert had hit on the idea of the change of name, that would have been the master-stroke of the expert's professional career. From Lawrence's publishers' point of view, for instance, could anything sell better than the magic name 'T. E. Lawrence' on a title-page? Yes, one thing could: the name 'Shaw' with 'T. E. Lawrence' printed below it between quotation-marks and brackets. Was this a deliberate publicity 'stunt' on Lawrence's part? Lawrence had demonstrated his capacity for making publicity when he had made it for the Arab cause in Paris. Did he afterwards stoop to making it for himself? Not consciously, I believe. Well, a case of unconscious exhibitionism, then? This last charge would be difficult to rebut; for, by definition, one's unconscious motives are unknown to one unless and until they are dragged up into consciousness by psycho-analysis. The charge is, as far as I know, non-proven; but its very nature makes it almost impossible to disprove. I am content to leave it at that. This may be one of the explanations of Lawrence's change of name and occupation; but, if so, it is, in my judgement, only one explanation among several, and this a minor one. I can think of three other explanations, all mutually compatible, which, to my mind, are both more convincing and more illuminating.

What has to be accounted for in the last phase of a life that was prematurely cut short is Lawrence's inability to settle down, after the First World War, to civilian life in one of the lines that his education and upbringing indicated as natural careers for him. After the war, Lawrence was elected a fellow of All Souls, and he was offered a high post in the new Middle Eastern Department that had been set up in the Colonial Office to supervise the administration of the mandates for 'Iraq and for Palestine that had been allocated to the United Kingdom in the peace-settlement of 1919. Lawrence was both a man of action and a scholar. He was now being offered a particularly attractive position in each of his fields of activity; and, if he had committed himself to either of these choices for a post-war career, he could still have kept a footing in his other field. Why did he leave Oxford and refuse to enter Whitehall? At All Souls, Lawrence had found, in Lionel Curtis, a kindred spirit who understood him and appreciated him. Lionel was good to Lawrence; and, if anyone could have helped Lawrence to anchor himself in the privileged position in academic life that an All Souls fellowship provided, Lionel would have been the man. Yet even Lionel was unsuccessful in this instance. Why?

One explanation is, surely, the notoriously unsettling effect of active military service. It is easy to put civilians into the army in war-time; it is difficult to put them back into civilian life after the war in which they have been combatants is over. This after-effect of war is one of the more serious of war's innumerable evils. In Roman history, for instance, the story of the unstable last century of the republican régime is, in essence, a tale of peasant-conscripts who were never successfully reintegrated into the rural life from which they had been uprooted. The difficulty of readjustment to peace-time was experienced, in some degree, by every other soldier, besides Lawrence, among the millions who had been combatants on one side or the other. In so far as Lawrence was suffering from malaise induced by the transition from war-time life to peace-time life, he was experiencing the common lot, and there is no mystery.

Lawrence, however, had not been an ordinary soldier. He was an ex-soldier who had distinguished himself exceptionally by individual exploits, and he had reached this peak of distinction in early manhood. In the First World War the nature of the fighting, which was mainly trench-warfare, made conspicuous individual exploits rare; and their rarity heightened the fame of the few individuals who were able to achieve them. The air-'aces'

won high fame through being few, but at least they were in the
plural number, whereas, in that war, Lawrence was the sole
famous guerrilla-leader. To be sole is to be solitary, and solitary
fame is difficult to carry. In the Second World War there were
perhaps as many famous guerrilla-leaders as there had been air-
'aces' in the First World War. (The second war was mainly a war
of movement, and the movement was three-dimensional: guerrilla-leaders were dropped on their fields of glory by parachute.)
I am acquainted with two guerrilla-leaders who, in the Second
World War, distinguished themselves in Lawrence's style. One
of them has succeeded in integrating himself into civilian life by
accepting, and embracing, jobs of the kind that were offered to
Lawrence after the First World War. The other Second-World-
War guerrilla-leader whom I have in mind has had a post-war
history that is more like Lawrence's; but who knows whether
he may not eventually succeed in re-integrating himself, like the
comrade of his whom I have mentioned? He needs, above all,
to be given time, and Lawrence was not given time. Lawrence's
life was cut short by an accident.

Lawrence and his two Second-World-War counterparts whom
I have drawn into comparison with him all had to contend with
the same difficulty. They had all reached their war-time peak
at an early age; and this peak was so high, and the circumstances
in which they had reached it had been so unusual, that it might
well be doubted whether they would ever have a chance of
achieving any success of comparable magnitude in later life, however long they might live. The psychological problem of having
to live with the memory of a dazzling early success is not, of course,
peculiar to cases of early success achieved in war. In peace-time
life, the same problem arises for a man who has reached a peak
while still a schoolboy, as captain of his school or as captain of the
school's football team, or who has reached a peak at the university
as a 'blue'. If he fails afterwards to cap these juvenile achievements
by adult achievements of comparable magnitude and distinction,
he, too, like the famous young 'ace' or the famous young guerrilla-
leader, will be in danger of falling into a backward-looking stance.
He may become the prisoner, for life, of a nostalgia for the past

which, it if captures him, will inhibit him from living in the present and from turning his face towards the future. Lawrence was surely hard beset by this problem, and, if so, that will be another explanation of his post-war restlessness.

War-time deracination? Premature success? Are these two experiences enough to account for Lawrence's repudiation of his identity? What did move him to camouflage his celebrity under the pseudo-obscurity of 'Aircraftsman Shaw'? Was not this escape an escapade? And could this escapade have been the act of a mentally normal man? Well, if 'man' is understood to mean 'twentieth-century Western man', mental abnormality might be a necessary supplementary explanation for Lawrence's action. But this understanding of the word 'man' is arbitrary, and the narrowness of it may be misleading. An alternative possibility is that modern Western man's conventional *Weltanschauung* may be abnormal, and that, in seeking to turn himself into 'Aircraftsman Shaw', Lawrence was a human being who was behaving in a normal human way.

I will put my point like this: if some medieval Western man could be raised from the dead to give us his opinion on whether Lawrence's attempt to withdraw from the world was normal or abnormal, I believe he would unhesitatingly pronounce this to have been a normal act for someone who had undergone Lawrence's experience. Obviously, my imaginary medieval umpire would say, the latterday Western World was an unpropitious environment for the practice of withdrawal, but, in these unfavourable circumstances, Lawrence's assumption of the unknown name and the modest avocation of 'Aircraftsman Shaw' was the nearest approach that Lawrence, in his world, could make to becoming an anchorite. I myself believe that this explanation hits the truth, and that it also goes farther than either of my two other suggestions to account for what Lawrence did.

What is an anchorite? The Greek word signifies a human being who has withdrawn from his world in order to expiate some sin of his, real or imaginary, by voluntarily doing penance for it. An imaginary sin, of course, will drive a human soul into the wilderness as compulsively as a real sin, if the soul is convinced of the sin's reality. Did Lawrence, at the time when he withdrew from the world in his twentieth-century way, feel that he had a serious sin on his conscience? I have the impression (it is no more than this) that he did feel something like that when, after the war and the subsequent peace-settlement were both over, he looked back at his record as an intermediary between the government of his own country and the Arabs with whom he had negotiated on his government's behalf.

I fancy that Lawrence's conscience reproached him for having promised to the Arabs, in the United Kingdom Government's name, an independence that, in the event, had been withheld from them; and, if this charge had been addressed, not to Lawrence himself, but to his principals, there would have been some substance in it. It is true that the British authorities had made a territorial reservation in their correspondence with King Husayn before his insurrection against his Turkish suzerains. The British undertaking to King Husayn to recognize and uphold the independence of the Arabs within certain territorial limits had expressly excluded the territory to the west of 'the vilayets of Aleppo, Hama, Homs, and Damascus' (in whatever way this ambiguous formula is to be interpreted). This strip of territory, however, was small in extent compared to the Arab territory, east of that line, that had also been under Ottoman sovereignty or suzerainty. In respect of this far larger Arab territory, the British undertaking had been unconditional. The British authorities had not told King Husayn—and, without being told, he could not have guessed—that, in a subsequent agreement with France, they were going to interpret 'independence' for the Arabs to mean a substitution of British and French for Turkish political control over them.

If Lawrence had been cognizant of this Anglo-French deception of the Arabs (it amounted to that), then he had been an accomplice in the fraud; if he had not been cognizant of it, he had been the Arabs' fellow-victim. Either possibility remains open, in default of decisive evidence one way or the other; and I have no evidence on this point. I cannot say, for certain, whether Lawrence's sense of guilt was justified or not. My guess is that it was not justified; but I also guess that, whether warrantably or not, Lawrence did feel guilty, and that this explains his rejection of the attractive and appropriate positions in the world of public admin- istration and in the world of scholarship which were at his disposal in the post-war years.

I believe that Lawrence could not bear to profit personally from a war-time career of his which had ended in the betrayal of his Arab comrades in the field in which he had achieved his fame. This will have been unbearable to him if he believed that he himself had been an instrument, even unknowingly, in the perpetration of the Anglo-French fraud at the Arabs' expense. In assuming the role of 'Aircraftsman Shaw', Lawrence will have been obeying his conscience by divesting himself of all personal gain from his war-time record. The Arabs had come out empty- handed. Then so would he. I offer this reconstruction of Law- rence's motives without being able to prove that it is correct. But, if that is something like the truth, it would follow from this that Lawrence's conduct is no evidence of mental abnormality. On this hypothesis, he will have acted as most human beings would have acted in his situation at most times and places except, perhaps, in the twentieth-century Western World.

Anchorites in the past have not all followed the same course after going into retreat. Some have remained in the wilderness for the rest of their lives. Others have undergone in the wilderness a spiritual rebirth that has eventually brought them back into the world with a new task to perform and with their power renewed for performing it. Which of these two kinds of anchorite would Lawrence have proved to be? We cannot tell. The spiritual re- birth that leads to a return after a withdrawal requires time for the anchorite's contrite spirit to revive and to re-orient itself; and this gift of healing time was denied to Lawrence.

15
Professor W. L. Westermann

'MY great-great-grandfather had his head cut off out there,' said Professor Westermann. He was pointing through one of the windows of the Hôtel Meurice that looked out on to the Place de la Concorde. The Hôtel Meurice was housing the United States delegation to the 1919 peace conference of Paris. Will Westermann was head of the Turkish section of the delegation, and he had asked me to lunch with him in order to make my acquaintance because I was joint number two in the corresponding section of the British delegation. (My colleague was a permanent Foreign Service man of my own age, Eric Forbes-Adam, and our chief was Sir Louis Mallet, who had been British Ambassador at Istanbul at the time when Turkey had intervened in the First World War on the German side.)

The first thing that Will and I discovered about each other was that we had both arrived at present-day Turkey from the same starting-point. We had both been concerned professionally with the history of Ancient Greece and Rome before we had become temporary civil servants. Will was Professor of Papyrology at the University of Wisconsin; I had been an ancient history tutor at Oxford. Our common concern with the past history of the Levant had given us both an incidental interest in current Levantine affairs; and this had been the qualification—rather a slender one, perhaps—that had carried me into the wartime Political Intelligence Department of the Foreign Office and had carried Will into the Inquiry—the organization that had been set up by the Administration at Washington to make preparations for American participation in the peace conference.

My American colleague's surprising family connexion with the Place de la Concorde had naturally excited my curiosity, so Will had told me his family history. His unfortunate ancestor had been an Alsatian French general in the army of the Revolution who had not done very well in the field and had paid for his ill-success by being guillotined on the spot that Will had pointed out to me. The Westermann family had afterwards migrated to Baden, had gone down in the world, had re-emigrated from Baden to the United States, and had settled in Wisconsin. In Will's generation, the family fortunes had been taking an upward turn again.

The friendship between Will and me that had started in Paris in 1919 was to last for life, and we learnt much from each other not only about each other but about each other's countries. I learnt, for instance, how Will, as a child in Wisconsin, had longed to be simply an American little boy, not a German-American little boy. However, his hyphen had not barred the way to his career, and, by the time when I first met him, he had long since come to recognize the value of his German background. This had, I am sure, been an important asset for him. His family may temporarily have gone down in the world, but they must have preserved their hereditary German intellectual standards, for these had certainly been inherited by Will. In Will Westermann, as in another distinguished American friend of mine, Reinhold Niebuhr, the American and German intellectual traditions were blended with happy results. A German intellectual thoroughness was balanced by an American openness of mind that could bubble up, on occasions, into a salutary irreverence. Will's and Reinhold's powerful minds and massive learning might have been portentous in their ancestral German setting, but, transplanted to America, they were enlivened by a twinkle in the eye which told you that this learned man was a human being first and foremost.

Will Westermann had an irrepressible sense of humour, which came out on one occasion when he was getting into the same hot water that I fell into. Our war-time concern with present-day

Turkey had produced the same effect on both of us. It had made us see the Turks, not in the abstract, as a race of 'unspeakable' monsters, but as human beings, 'of like passions' with us, who had not forfeited their human nature because some of them had committed crimes of which some of us Westerners were not innocent. At the time of the Graeco-Turkish War after the First World War, when the Greek invasion of Anatolia and the Turkish resistance movement had become a burning question, we both found ourselves engaged in controversy over this. Each of us was taking the stand that the Turks were human beings with human rights, and that they therefore had the same inalienable right to justice and fair play as the Greeks or anyone else. This stand was bringing each of us up against a wall of traditional 'Christian' prejudice against unbelievers: the 'Jews, Turks, and infidels' for whom an Episcopalian Protestant Christian prays once a year in one of the collects for Good Friday in the Book of Common Prayer. This prejudice was being played upon, in both the United States and Britain, by members of the local Greek diaspora, who, being human too, were moved to champion their country of origin, 'right or wrong'.

The Greek diaspora was thicker on the ground in the United States than it was in the United Kingdom, and it was consequently more vocal there in public in debates in which the rights and wrongs of the Graeco-Turkish issue were being canvassed. At one meeting at which Will Westermann was a speaker, he was interrupted by shouts from Greek-Americans in the audience. 'You have been bribed by the Turks,' they were shouting. 'No honest man could defend the Turks as you are doing.' At the first pause in the uproar, Will answered in a flat tone of voice but with a beaming smile: 'Why of course. Please remember how poorly paid a professor is. We professors must live, mustn't we?' Will's joke brought the house down, and the Greek-American hecklers' guns were spiked by his witty *reductio ad absurdum* of their extravagant accusation.

While the 1919 peace conference was still in its early days, I was learning from Will not only about himself but also about the American way of life. One discovery in particular which surprised me was that, on the social side, American officialdom was more hierarchical than its British counterpart was. Not long after my lunch with Will in the Hôtel Meurice, Will was lunching with me in the Majestic Hotel, in which the British delegation was housed. In the middle of our conversation, Will stopped to point to the far side of the large dining-room and said to me: 'Why, that man over there looks just like Mr. Balfour.' 'He *is* Mr. Balfour,' I told him. 'What? Your principal delegates eat in the same room as you? Why, ours would never do that.'

Will then went on to tell me that he and the rest of the American delegation had come over from America to France on the *George Washington*, on board which President Wilson, too, was travelling. The members of the delegation had been saying to each other: 'What a good idea of the President's this is, to have arranged to spend a week at sea with us. He will have time, before we land, to make himself acquainted with us personally, and to tell us something about his policy, so that we may know what line he wants us to take when the time comes for us to do business with our French and British and Italian opposite numbers.' This expectation had surely been natural, but it had been disappointed. From beginning to end of the voyage, the President had kept himself interned in his suite of staterooms and had never seen, or been seen by, one of his official staff. This had non-plussed them and had made them feel uneasy; and no wonder. The President's travelling-companions on the *George Washington* were to be his executants—his eyes and ears and hands. Yet apparently it had not occurred to the President that neither they nor he could do their respective jobs effectively if he did not take the initiative in establishing human relations between them and him. He was leaving them, without guidance, to work for him in the dark.

This gulf between the senior members of the American delegation and their subordinates was never closed, and one of its unfortunate results was Will Westermann's resignation before the peace conference was over. This happened after I had left Paris, so I did not hear of it till later, when I was told about it by Will himself. On instructions from his immediate superior, Will, in the committee on which he was serving, had been taking a particular stand against the representative of one of the other delegations (I forget which, and I do not think I ever heard what the point at issue was). Will was then summoned, one day, to his superior's office. He found there the foreign representative whom he had been opposing, according to his instructions, on the committee, and the tycoon now told him, in this foreign representative's presence, that the instructions had now been reversed and that Will was to take the same line as the foreign representative henceforward. This was the first that Will had heard of his principal's change of policy, and these were the circumstances in which he was informed of it. That was too much for Will to submit to. It would have been too much even for someone who was less independent-minded and less spirited than Will was.

I got a whiff of the hierarchical atmosphere of the American delegation myself one day when I had to bring some papers to the house in Paris in which President Wilson was living. The house belonged to a wealthy Frenchman; the richness of its appointments was almost ludicrous; and the owner's property was being jealously guarded by his staff of servants, who had remained in occupation and, as it proved, in command. We had hardly set foot inside the front door when a major-domo pointed furiously at an oil-stain on a costly carpet and accused each of us in turn of having deposited it. We had to prove our innocence by showing that there was no oil on the soles of our shoes. This was a surprising and embarrassing way of being received.

Officialdom is, perhaps inevitably, hierarchical always and everywhere, but this common spirit can express itself in different ways, and I found the difference between the American and the British expressions of it interesting for the light that it threw on national manners and customs.

In the war-time American public service, the hierarchy of rank was heavily stressed, as Will Westermann's experiences show. On the other hand, the American career-men did not seem to me to draw the rigid caste-distinction between themselves and their temporary amateur colleagues that I encountered in the corresponding British trades union.

In 1918 I had been working in the Political Intelligence

Department of the Foreign Office, with the Near and Middle East for my province. Six weeks before the Armistice of 11 November 1918 I had received the following instructions: 'Tell the Registry to send up to you all the papers dealing with the commitments that His Majesty's Government have made during the war regarding the Near and Middle East; report what these commitments are; and write an opinion on whether they are compatible with each other.' Mountains of files appeared on my desk; and I have never again had to work so desperately hard against time; for, though we could not predict the date of the coming armistice, we did know that hostilities were now nearing their end.

To cope with my Psyche's task, I was now working for about ten hours a day on seven days in the week. One Sunday morning, early, I had just settled down again to attack those stacks of files on which I seemed to be making no impression, when my telephone rang. It was a call from outside, and it had been put through to me because, at the moment, I was the only even temporary first-division officer in the place. 'Is that the Foreign Office? This is Reuters,' said a voice (it was trembling with excitement). 'The German Chancellor, Prince Max of Baden, has just made a speech; he has said so and so and so and so; it means the end of the war; we have the full text.' My voice was now trembling too, as I answered. 'Do please', I said, 'bring the text round here as soon as you can. I am only a temporary worker here, but I will tell the first permanent official who comes in what you have just told me, and I will also tell him that you are on your way.' I then rang off; rang through to the porter to ask him to ring me again when the first permanent clerk came in; and got back to my work, as far as I could now keep my mind on it.

Soon the telephone rang again. Two cypher-clerks had just come in, and the porter had put me through to them. I started to tell them the tale with the same excitement as before. 'Reuters have rung up; Prince Max of Baden has made a speech; he has said so and so; it is the end of the war; I have told them to come round with the text.' My breathless flow of words was cut short by an icy voice. 'You do not mean to say that you have invited the press to the Foreign Office?' And that was how the news of the end of the First World War was received by the first two permanent Foreign Office clerks who heard it.

I suppose that even their feelings must have been stirred, if ever so faintly, by the thrilling news. If their feelings were anything like as strong as Reuters' representative's feelings and mine were, their self-control was as heroic as the Spartan boy's who, rather than give himself away, let the fox, hidden under his shirt, tear out his entrails, without showing any outward sign of his agony. Before those two cypher-clerks could let themselves feel or think about the war coming to an end, they had a paramount duty to perform. They had to castigate a temporary colleague for a raw amateur's characteristically egregious breach of Foreign Office etiquette. If I had broken the rules unknowingly, my ignorance was culpable enough; if I had known the rules and ignored them, my offence was unspeakable. When Reuters' representative arrived, I timidly put my head round their door to announce him. They would not see him. I had to see him in the corridor and to tell them—after he had left again—what he had said. 'These soldiers were once men,' a child said, when it was reporting this improbable discovery to its parents, according to an anecdote recounted by Tolstoy. Later on that Sunday morning in October 1918 Sir Eyre Crowe and Sir William Tyrrell came in. These two seniors were eminent enough to be able to afford to break their own rules. They telephoned to Reuters to ask the agency's representative to call again with his document, and they saw him themselves—and this, not in the corridor, but in Sir Eyre Crowe's own room.

If I had been an American temporary civil servant and had done the same thing in Washington, I fancy that I should have been commended for my zeal instead of being reproved for my breach of etiquette. I do not believe that American career-men would have repressed their natural human interest in such an earth-shaking piece of news for the sake of putting a temporary colleague in his place.

'Out of school', on the other hand, those two Foreign Office cypher-clerks would, I should guess, have treated even a junior temporary Foreign Office clerk as their social equal, considering that this was how their most exalted official superiors behaved. Mr. Balfour took his meals in the Majestic Hotel dining-room, surrounded by the less eminent members of the British delegation, as a matter of course; and the Permanent Under-Secretary for Foreign Affairs, Sir Eyre Crowe, once put me at my ease, the first time that I had to meet him personally in order to submit some drafts to him, by telling me, gruffly but reassuringly, to address him as 'Crowe' and not as 'Sir Eyre'.

At the Majestic Hotel in 1919 there was one invidious distinction that was neither social nor hierarchical; it was international. Members of the United Kingdom delegation had to pay for their drinks. Mr. Balfour himself would have had to pay for his if he had ever committed the vulgarity of ordering one. On the other hand, the drinks ordered by members of the Dominions delegations were 'on the house'; and 'the house' was the Treasury of the United Kingdom. This was a grievance that made permanent and temporary Foreign Office clerks conscious of their solidarity with each other as United Kingdom taxpayers. Kipling had chanted to us: 'If blood be the price of admiralty, Lord God, we have paid in full.' That might pass; but, if drinks were the price of empire, this surcharge was the last straw. It was an intimation that playing 'the mother-country' was a luxury that our heavily-laden country might soon have to drop.

Though I left Paris earlier than Will left, we had had time to see enough of each other at the peace conference to make friends. From that time onwards we kept in touch with each other by correspondence, but we did not meet again till 1925, when I paid the first of my visits to the United States. By that time, Will had exchanged his chair at the University of Wisconsin for one at Columbia University, New York, which he continued to hold till he reached retiring age; and, when he heard from me that I was going to be in New York for a few days, *en route* for Williamstown, Massachusetts, he invited me, with characteristic American hospitality, to be his and his wife's guest, and told me that he would be meeting me at the dock.

As the saucy tugs nudged the ship towards the quayside, I saw two figures standing there; they were Will and his brother;

and, when they waved to me, I was doubly glad. I was going to
see an old friend of mine again, and I was going to make my
first contact with New York under his protection. It was a Sunday afternoon in August; and I could not, I suppose, have chosen
a quieter moment for making my first acquaintance with this
overwhelming city; yet, even before we had docked, the scale
of the buildings and the roar of the traffic had intimidated me.
The Westermann brothers 'ran me in' by taking me for a tour
down-town and ending up with mint-juleps in the Bronx. Before
dark, I had acquired an outline-sketch of New York which I
could fill in afterwards for myself.

Outline-sketches were Will's brother's business. Will described
to me, later, what his brother's business was. He was apologetic
about this, but not from snobbery. Will was American in being
without a trace of that, but he was still German enough to feel
that an unintellectual profession was unworthy of an educated
person.

Will's brother's profession was a novel one to me. In 1925 the
car-age in the United States was still in its infancy, and about
half the population was then still living on the farm or in small
country towns. These rural Americans' range of movement was
narrow. Mentally, they were living on in the horse-and-buggy
age. They were not within reach of large-scale general stores in
which they would have been able to inspect personally the various
makes of the multifarious articles that they needed to buy. This
shopping problem of rural America's had been solved for her by
mail-order houses, which did their business by producing huge
illustrated catalogues. The illustrations were so elaborate that they
were a tolerable substitute for a direct sight of the objects that the
mail-order houses had on sale. In this business the attractiveness,
as well as the accuracy, of the catalogue-illustrations was all-
important, and this was the point at which Will's brother had
found his opening. He had built up a business concern of his own
for supplying the mail-order firms with the illustrations that they
required, and his paying innovation had been to carry the division
of labour to unprecedented lengths. He was employing a staff of
draftsmen who were all ultra-specialists. One would draw the

back curve of a woman's stocking; another would draw the shin; one would draw the flounce of a skirt; another would draw its waist; and the most highly specialized craftsman of them all was the one who assembled these standardized parts, as his opposite numbers in Henry Ford's works had been learning to assemble the standardized parts of a car.

Will's description of the way in which his brother was making his living fascinated me. Here was a specifically American craft that had previously been quite unknown to me, and the organization involved in it seemed to me to be as clever in its own way as Will's accomplishment of deciphering papyri or as mine of composing Greek verses. Will did not dispute his brother's cleverness; he merely deprecated his having put it to this unintellectual though profitable use.

Will himself remained faithful to papyrology, and in this he developed a special line of his own. Papyri have added greatly to our information about the institutional aspects of Greek and Roman slavery, and Will Westermann shares with Joseph Vogt of Tübingen the distinction of being one of the two leading authorities on this subject in their generation. Will had the good fortune to live just long enough to finish writing his comprehensive and conclusive work on the subject that he had made his own. He did not live to give the book its final touches and to see it published, but what of that? A scholar writes, not for himself, but for his readers.

16

Charles R. Crane

LIKE my friendship with Will Westermann, my acquaintance with Charles R. Crane was a windfall from a barren peace conference. I first met Mr. Crane, too, at Paris in 1919.

The peace conference had reached a deadlock in its deliberations about the future of Syria. It had failed to resolve the conflict between Franco-British promises to the Arabs and French demands. In the hope of making progress, and perhaps also of ascertaining the truth about the pertinent facts, the American delegation had proposed that a joint Franco-Anglo-American commission of inquiry should be sent to Syria to report back to Paris. The French had agreed reluctantly, and the British without enthusiasm. All the same, they had both agreed; so the machinery was set up, and I found myself appointed secretary to the Commission's British section, of which Sir Henry McMahon had been appointed the head. My American opposite number was Professor Lybyer of the University of Illinois, and, one day in Paris, he took me with him to introduce me to the two joint heads of the American section, President King and Mr. Charles R. Crane.

President King was a college president—a fair sample of his profession, as I came to realize later, after I had visited a number of American colleges and universities. Obviously President King was fully adequate for his present temporary assignment; but obviously, too, he was not unique. Not so Mr. Crane; his uniqueness hit one in the eye as soon as one saw him. He looked like a parrot, and his quizzical air suggested that he might be speculating whether the humans who might be laughing at him suspected that he was finding them far more funny than they were finding him. It struck me that he would have made a first-class jester if he had happened to live before that sly profession had gone out of vogue. The simpleton cast of his countenance might well be a mask for shrewdness.

These first impressions of mine were confirmed on further acquaintance, and they were borne out by the legend of what had passed between Charles R. Crane and his brother when they had jointly inherited the Crane family business. Charles R. was said to have asked his brother how large a share of the family fortune the brother would be prepared to concede to Charles R. if Charles R. would consent to waive his legal right to be an active partner in the business from which the family fortune flowed. According to the story, the brother, who was a born businessman, immediately named a very high figure (the family fortune was big), and the bargain was closed on these terms. This transaction had sufficed to set up Charles R. Crane for life as a millionaire at large. Charles R. Crane's brother's motive for buying Charles R. out at this high cost had not been any doubt of Charles R.'s ability; what his brother had doubted was how Charles R. would have dealt with the family business if he had had a free hand to play with it. Charles R. Crane might have made the Crane business hum, but perhaps not in a remunerative way. For him, the business might have been an instrument for indulging his intellectual curiosity by making curious, but perhaps ruinous, experiments with it. For both brothers their bargain worked out satisfactorily. Charles R. was now well enough endowed to be able to satisfy no end of curiosity in other fields; and his brother, now that he had the management of the family business to himself, could make it yield a handsome living wage for him after it had provided Charles R.'s princely income. I repeat this story as it was told to me, without vouching for its truth.

My fleeting first glimpse of Charles R. Crane in Paris turned out to be all that I was going to see of him for some time. A few days later, I left Paris for London with Sir Henry McMahon to make preparations in Whitehall for our expedition. I had been thrilled to meet Sir Henry in the flesh after he had become so familiar a figure to me on paper. I had become familiar, long ago, in that second-hand way, with other historic European negotiators of agreements with Middle Eastern powers—with Callias, for instance, and with Antalcidas—but these Ancient Greeks were long since dead past recall, whereas this British counterpart of theirs was alive and was now my chief. During the weeks for which I worked for Sir Henry McMahon, I spent a greater number of hours in a greater number of London clubs than I have ever spent since then. If I remember right, Sir Henry had six clubs and, for convenience, he got me made a temporary member of one or two of these. This was not merely convenient; it was necessary; for Sir Henry transacted his business in the course of making his daily round of his clubs; and I had to take my instructions, which, naturally, were numerous, in holes and corners of club smoking-rooms.

One of Sir Henry's instructions to me was to induce the Ministry of Shipping to put a whole ship at the Syria Commission's disposal for the unpredictable duration of its labours. I failed, though—or perhaps because—the official with whom I had to deal happened to be a schoolfellow and friend of mine. I am not ashamed of this failure; for my mission was a forlorn hope. At a time when British shipping losses from the German submarine campaign had not yet begun to be made good, our request was bound to stay at the bottom of the Ministry's long list of priorities; and, supposing that we had won our ship, I never could make out how we could have come back from Syria to that ship each night to sleep on board, as Lord Cardigan used to come back to his yacht from the cavalry lines at Balaclava.

This last phase of my first tour of service as a temporary Foreign Office clerk was enjoyable, but it was almost as strenuous as my last six weeks before Armistice Day had been. My work for Sir Henry McMahon was ended for me abruptly by my doctor ordering me to go to bed, and I was ruefully handing over my job to a successor when the job itself evaporated together with Sir Henry McMahon's. At the last moment, the French Government had pressed the British Government hard to join it in withdrawing from participation in the commission, and the British Government, for their part, had been glad to yield to their ally's pressure. However, this reduction of the original trinitarian commission to a unitarian one did not bring the commission to an end, as no doubt the French had hoped that it would. King and Crane went ahead, with their hands now free to observe and report the whole truth and nothing but it, without being embarrassed by having colleagues who might have tried to needle them into making diplomatic concessions to objectionable French and British desiderata.

King and Crane correctly reported that the Syrian and Palestinian Arabs wanted independence without any strings. They had just been relieved of a Turkish domination that had been weighing upon them for the last four hundred years; they did not want to see one obnoxious foreign régime replaced by others. King and Crane looked into the Syrian and Palestinian Arabs' reaction to the proposal for the imposition on them of 'mandates' to be exercised by foreign powers. Their finding was that this proposal was unacceptable to the Arabs, whoever the mandatory power or powers imposed on them might be. The least objectionable mandatory power, from the Arabs' point of view, would be the United States. The Arabs were totally unwilling to be mandated either to Britain or to France.

I was not taken by surprise either by the British Government's going back on its agreement to be represented on the commission or by King's and Crane's findings in their report, when this was eventually published. I had been prepared for both things by previous episodes that I had witnessed in Paris.

One day I had had to hand some papers to Lloyd George just after the close of some meeting on Middle Eastern affairs. I had frequently seen Lloyd George and heard him speak, but this was the only occasion on which I had ever met him, and this encounter of mine with him had lasted for no longer than a minute or two, but it had been unexpectedly revealing; for, when he had taken the papers and started to scan them, Lloyd George, to my delight, had forgotten my presence and had begun to think aloud. 'Mesopotamia . . . yes . . . oil . . . irrigation . . . we must have Mesopotamia; Palestine . . . yes . . . the Holy Land . . .

Zionism . . . we must have Palestine; Syria . . . h'm . . . what is there in Syria? Let the French have that.' Lloyd George's unconscious soliloquy had revealed a shrewd awareness of the Ottoman Arab countries' economic and political assets; but there had been no audible mention of the human factor that was to be the subject of King's and Crane's investigation and report. In counting up the Arab countries' 'points', Lloyd George had left out the rights and wishes of the Arabs themselves.

The truth about these that was reported to the peace conference by King and Crane had been known already by the members of the conference before they had agreed to send out a commission to ascertain it. They knew, for instance, that, within the few hours' interval that had elapsed between the defeated Turkish army's evacuation of Northern Palestine, the Lebanon, and Syria and the occupation of these evacuated territories by Allenby's victorious troops, the Arab flag had been hoisted everywhere to proclaim the Arabs' political aspirations while they were free to declare them. After that, the Council of Ten had already given a hearing, in Paris, to the President of the American University of Beirut, Dr. Howard Bliss; and Dr. Bliss's testimony had anticipated the subsequent findings of Dr. King and Mr. Crane. The exactness of the agreement between their findings and Dr. Bliss's previous statement was not surprising. All three observers were honest and disinterested; all three were telling the truth; and truth, unlike falsehood, is necessarily self-consistent.

The session of the Council of Ten at which Dr. Bliss gave his testimony was the strangest, and also the most moving, of any of the sessions at which I was present. Here was a man speaking with authority. He was the head of an old-established and distinguished educational institution whose students were drawn from all over the Near and Middle East, and in greatest numbers from the ex-Ottoman Arab region in which the University itself was located. Dr. Bliss was the scion of a dynasty of missionary-educators that had founded the university and had continued to be associated with it ever since. There can have been few, if any, other neutral first-hand observers who were so well qualified as Dr. Bliss was to appreciate what the ex-Ottoman Arabs' political wishes were. Besides, Dr. Bliss was obviously a noble character, and, as obviously, he was a sick man too. When he stood up to give his testimony, his physical weakness bowed him down, and he had to lean heavily on the back of the chair in front of him. He knew that his days were numbered. (I suppose his death was hastened by the fatigue of the journey to Paris from Beirut.) He was determined, at whatever cost to himself, to tell the truth to the conference before being called to render his account to his Maker. (Dr. Bliss was a believing Presbyterian Christian.)

As Dr. Bliss talked, I could see that he was putting the Ten out of countenance—or at any rate nine of them, perhaps excluding his fellow-Presbyterian, President Wilson. This was perhaps the first time, during the Ten's proceedings, that they had been confronted with a witness who had no axe to grind and whose sole concern was to tell the truth and to see justice done in the light of it. They did not like this; they did not know how to take it; and they were unable to conceal their embarrassment. Comedy and tragedy were jostling each other in a Shakespearean discord —the comedy of the Nine's manifest disarray; the tragedy that was impending over Dr. Bliss and over the Arabs, with whose destiny he was so much more concerned than he was with his own prospects of life. Dr. Bliss's testimony was, in effect, an advance copy of the subsequent King-Crane report.

My next meeting with Charles R. Crane after my first one in Paris was not till some time later, and, this time, it was in London. By now, Mr. Crane had resumed his normal peace-time occupation of seeing the world. Mr. Crane was, before all else, a traveller, but he had nothing in common with a globe-trotting tourist. His expeditions were carefully prepared beforehand, and some of them were such as perhaps only he could have carried out successfully.

Mr. Crane's visits to London followed a pattern that was unusual but unvarying. He always stayed at the Curzon Hotel, and, the morning after his arrival, 'his' taxi always drew up at the entrance to the hotel and waited for Mr. Crane to appear and to take his seat in it. That taxi can properly be called Mr. Crane's, though he neither owned it nor chartered it nor even notified the driver, in advance, of the date of his impending arrival. The driver had his own intelligence service for ascertaining that. This service never failed; and, indeed, the driver could afford to maintain a first-rate intelligence service out of his profits from Mr. Crane's intermittent and usually brief visits to Britain; for, in Britain, Mr. Crane rode in that taxi wherever he went. Today his itinerary might take him just round the block; tomorrow it might take him to John-o'-Groat's or to Land's End; but, within the shores of the island, the taxi was Mr. Crane's exclusive means of conveyance.

In Britain, Mr. Crane also had a staff-officer, Mrs. George Young (Lady Young), who happened also to be a friend of mine. I do not think Mrs. Young had taken shares in the taximan's intelligence service. I think she used to learn that Mr. Crane was coming by the ordinary prosaic means—a cablegram, probably. Transatlantic telephone-calls were, in Mr. Crane's travelling days, still unreliable. If they had already been up to their present standard, Mr. Crane's use of them might have increased Bell Telephone's profits substantially. In any case, whenever Mrs. Young had word, through whatever channel, she put her own household chores aside and was at Mr. Crane's disposal for the duration of his stay.

Mr. Crane had the art of making his friends and acquaintances wish to do things for him without any thought of reward; but the pattern of Mr. Crane's visits to London did include a standard reward for Mrs. Young. It was a double reward, and it was receivable, not in London, but in Paris. At the end of each of his visits to London, Mr. Crane would take Mrs. Young to Paris with him as his guest, to give her the opportunity of obtaining a French hat and of dining with Mr. Crane in a French restaurant. The hat-reward was always satisfying. Mrs. Young was at liberty to spend all the daylight hours viewing every hat on sale in Paris. She herself made the eventual choice; Mr. Crane simply paid the bill, whatever it might amount to. The dinner-reward, however, was always an anticlimax; for here the choices were Mr. Crane's. He did always choose one of the best restaurants in Paris; but this only made the sequel the more disappointing; for he kept the ordering of the dinner in his own hands, and his order was always for boiled chicken and rice pudding. Parisian restaurants of the quality of those that Mr. Crane patronized make it a point of honour to meet their clients' most exotic requests. After some delay and at a fancy price, the boiled chicken and rice pudding would duly appear on the table. If Mr. Crane had asked for a lamb roasted whole in a pit or for a dish of Australian witchetty grubs, that, too, would have been forthcoming. Mr. Crane's tastes happened to be plain, and this was sad for Mrs. Young. She could have found just as good boiled chicken and rice pudding in England anywhere and any day.

On the particular visit of Mr. Crane's to London in which I came to be involved, I think it was Mrs. Young who arranged with me for me to meet him. (This would, of course, have been part of her official duties.) When I waited on Mr. Crane at the hotel, I found him full of an approaching visit to India. He explained to me that this expedition would be the ripe fruit of long preparations. For years, he had been placing friends of his in key observation-posts in the Sub-continent—a Y.M.C.A. officer here, a U.S. consul there, and so on. By now he had allowed them all time enough to learn the ropes, so that their first-hand experience of India would be worth having. All was ready—all but one thing, and this thing had to be done in England here and now. Before finally setting out for India, Mr. Crane needed to meet the author of *A Passage to India*. Did I know Mr. E. M. Forster? Could I tell Mr. Crane where he lived? Could I give Mr. Crane an introduction to him?

I happened to know where Mr. Forster lived, because the place was the home-town of the archaeologist F. W. Hasluck, who had been the librarian of the British School at Athens when I had been a student there in 1911–12. Hasluck used to tell us, with amusement, how little the neighbours had suspected what Mr. Forster was up to. Mr. Forster had lain low while he was taking his mental notes of life in his native community. (It was a dormitory town, inhabited all round the clock only by the wives and children of the commuters.) The town had suffered a shock when the first of Mr. Forster's novels had exploded.

I told Mr. Crane where Mr. Forster lived. 'Where about is that?' 'Well, it is on the south side of London.' 'Why, that will just fit,' said Mr. Crane. 'This afternoon, I am going down in my taxi to Brighton to play with some children there. I can call on Mr. Forster on the way, if I may have that introduction to him from you.' Hoping to avoid the issue, I explained to Mr. Crane that Mr. Forster's home really was not on the way from London to Brighton; but this failed to put Mr. Crane off. Detours did not repel Mr. Crane; they attracted him. (Mr. Crane was un-American on this point or perhaps he was simply archaic.) Any-way, a journey from London to Brighton via Mr. Forster in his taxi would be child's play compared to some of the journeys that he had already negotiated.

I was not going to be able to get out of it; I was going to have to write that letter of introduction; and this was most embarrassing; for I was not on terms with Mr. Forster that would justify my taking this liberty with him. I had met him casually once or twice; that was all. When Mr. Forster read my signature, it was improbable that this would ring a bell. However, I found myself writing to Mr. Forster. Mr. Crane had something about him that made his requests impossible to refuse. As soon as the letter was in his hands, Mr. Crane boarded his taxi and set off, leaving me wondering unhappily how Mr. Forster would take my impertinence; but, contrary to my expectations, the incident turned out fortunately for me. When, next morning, I asked Mr. Crane how his South-of-England taxi-expedition had gone off, he told me that his taxi-man had tracked down Mr. Forster's house, but that they had not found Mr. Forster at home. I was surprised and was selfishly relieved. I had felt sure that Charles R. Crane would run Mr. Forster to earth that afternoon. Fortune usually guided Mr. Crane's wildest shots right to their target.

Charles R. Crane's prowess as a purposeful traveller is illus-trated by two exploits of his. I know of them, not from Mr. Crane himself, but only at second hand, so I cannot vouch for these two stories. However, I believe them to be true, and at least they can claim verisimilitude; for they are thoroughly in character.

At the time of the American presidential election of 1920,

Mr. Crane was American ambassador in China. He had been appointed by President Wilson, and, when he received the news of the Republican Party's sweeping victory at the polls, he foresaw that, on the day on which the Administration at Washington changed hands, he would receive a cablegram informing him that he had been relieved of his post. March 4 1921 arrived, and the expected cablegram arrived with it; but the dismissed ambassador was not downcast. Ever since the Democratic Party's defeat, Mr. Crane had been making his preparations for an exit from China that promised to be still more interesting than his official sojourn there had been.

Charles R. Crane was soon going to have to go home from China to the United States. Which of the several alternative possible routes would be likely to be the most interesting? Charles R. Crane chose the route that James Bryce had chosen eight years back, when, at the expiry of his term of office as British Ambassador in Washington, he had had to make his way home from the United States to Britain. Like Bryce before him, Crane chose to return home via Siberia. The route was the same, but everything else was different; for, in Russia between 1913 and 1921, the deluge had descended; and, in Eastern Siberia, the waters that had covered the Earth had not begun to recede till one month before the presidential election in the United States which had served a three-months' notice to quit on Charles R. Crane at Peking. The condition of Russia had not, however, deterred the lame-duck ambassador from working out his arrangements for traversing the Russian chaos.

In 1913, travelling by Trans-Siberian had been so comfortable that Lord Bryce had had to abandon the main line and take to a branch line and then to the road in order to find a touch of the testing hardship of which he was in search. In 1921, the Trans-Siberian traveller would not have to go out of his way to look for hardship; he could count on hardship's rushing to meet him. Mr. Crane's problem was not how to find hardship; it was how to find media of payment. There was, in fact, no Russian money-currency in 1921 that you could find abroad or could use inside Russia if you could have found it. After one thousand years of a money-currency, Russia had now relapsed into barter. If Charles R. Crane was to traverse Russia-in-Asia and Russia-in-Europe, he must carry with him some commodity that would be in brisk enough demand to induce people to give him food in exchange for it. What commodity? After thinking it over, Mr. Crane decided upon nails. He reckoned that human beings must always be using nails, whatever their ideology; so, while President-Elect Harding was preparing for his inauguration, Ambassador-under-sentence Crane was employing the same period of grace in Peking in buying up nails—big nails, little nails, iron nails, brass nails, nails of all shapes and sizes. At the same time he bought two railway-waggons, one to hold his nails and the other to hold himself. (He made this second waggon over into an amateur *wagon-lit*.)

At this point there is a hiatus in the story as it was told to me. The story does not name this railway-caravan's starting-point. It cannot have been Peking, for the pair of trucks must have been broad-gauge, and in 1921 the nearest broad-gauge rail-head to Peking was somewhere on the far side of Mukden—at Chang-chun, perhaps, or farther afield, beyond the railway-bridge over the Sungari River. Anyway, the ex-ambassador did set off on his westward ramble across Russia from wherever his starting-point may have been; and he not only started; he came through. Weeks grew into months; the migrating trucks were hitched on to one decrepit train after another; sometimes they were side-tracked for days; but, in the end, imagination and perseverance triumphed. One day, the two trucks turned up at the broad-gauge rail-head on the Russo-Polish frontier. The last days had been anxious; the passengers had been scraping the bottom of their nail-truck; yet, on the day on which they at last left barter-land behind them, they still had enough nails in hand to have won them a few more meals.

Charles R. Crane's emergence from the Soviet Union into Poland in 1921 cannot have startled the Polish frontier-authorities more than the British frontier-authorities were startled, some years later, by his emergence from the Yaman into the Aden Protectorate. This time, Charles R. and his party could not come riding on railway waggons; in Southern Arabia there are still no railways of any gauge, broad or narrow. This time they came riding on camels; and Charles R.'s performance as a cameleer must be accounted more remarkable than T. E. Lawrence's; for, by the date when Charles R. Crane did the Queen of Sheba's journey in reverse, he was already well on in years.

How had Charles R. managed it? If one of those British officials had put his foot across the frontier on to the Imam's side of the line, he would have been a dead man within two seconds. Yet this American dilettante had just traversed the Yaman highlands unscathed. My guess is that he had managed it in the way in which he managed the passage to India which he had been preparing when he had conscripted me to give him that introduction to Mr. Forster. Like his passage to India, Charles R.'s transit of Arabia was, no doubt, the ripe fruit of years of preparatory work. Give Charles R. Crane time to prepare the ground, and you can be sure that, when he is ready, no obstacle is going to stop him. If he had been alive in 1966 and had taken it into his head to repeat his Arabian trip, his first step would have been to bring off an Arab summit conference between President 'Abd-al-Nâsir of the United Arab Republic and King Faysal of Sa'ûdî Arabia. Their agenda would have been the provision of a joint safe-conduct for Mr. Crane, and, with this in hand, Charles R. would have ridden his camel through no-man's-land, between two rows of grounded arms, as safely as the Children of Israel once marched between two walls of Red-Sea water.

My last sight of Charles R. Crane was in his house in his native city of Chicago. I was breaking a journey in Chicago, and I took the opportunity to call on my old acquaintance to pay my respects. In the room in which he received me, my eye was caught by two large landscape-paintings. The scenery and the buildings had a Central Asian look. 'Do those pictures interest you?' said Mr. Crane. 'I am glad, because they were painted by my artist. Let me tell you his story. In Bokhara I once came across a boy who looked as if he were starving, so I took him along with me, and found that he had quite an artistic gift. After discovering that, I sent him to Paris to be properly trained. I had him paint those two pictures for me to remind me of the trip on which I had picked him up. I generally take him along with me nowadays when I am going on one of my travels.'

When I said good-bye, Mr. Crane begged me to come back next afternoon. I would find the house full of Chinese students, he told me. He had just acquired a collection of records of Chinese Buddhist hymns, and he was going to play them over to the students to observe their reactions. He had invited all the Chinese students that were to be found in Cook County. Of course I came again, and it was all as Mr. Crane had foretold. The hymns were droning; the students were crowding round to listen. When I bade my final farewell to Mr. Crane, he put into my hand a handsome Chinese jar, filled with exquisite China tea, as a present for my wife in England. Graceful courtesies like this one came natural to him.

Charles R. Crane was a successful man, and a happy one. He did what he had wanted to do. He satisfied his curiosity. My guess is that he felt that his life had been well spent, and, if he did feel that, I declare that I agree with him.

17
The Meyendorffs

I HAVE introduced Baron Meyendorff already in recording a crushing comment of his on a discourse of Sidney Webb's. Those severe words had been drawn from Meyendorff by his grief and indignation over the fate of dead Russian friends of his who had been victims of the Bolshevik Revolution. I never heard Meyendorff complain of his own fate. He and his wife had escaped with their lives to live in exile; and this is one of the severest tests of character that Fortune can impose. An exile is in danger of becoming either embittered or dispirited. Meyendorff took the fate that Fortune had brought on him with dignity and sweetness. (Even his reproof to Webb had been uttered in a gentle tone.) The pre-revolutionary Russian world in which Meyendorff had occupied a distinguished position had foundered. He was a castaway in England in straitened circumstances. Yet he did not lose his hold on life. He found a new interest in the unfamiliar academic work by which he was now earning his and Baroness Meyendorff's daily bread; and, being what they were, they both made English friends. The Meyendorffs in exile were as admirable as two other exile friends of mine, Adnan Adivar and the Baroness's countryman Ra'ûf Orbay. Adnan Adivar and Baron Meyendorff are the only men whom I have known who, to my mind, could compare, in gentleness and sweetness of character, with another of my friends, Lawrence Hammond.

The Meyendorffs had lost their country, but they still had each other. Theirs was a happy marriage, and it was Russia that had brought them together, though neither of them was a Russian by descent. Both had become Russians by adoption, and their

union on Russian ground gave impressive testimony to the assimi-
lative power of the Russian way of life in their generation. The
Meyendorffs had come from two utterly different worlds, sundered geographically by the whole length of Russia between the
Black Sea and the Baltic. The Meyendorffs had started worlds
away from each other, and this in the cultural as well as in the
geographical sense; but the intervening Russian culture had proved,
in their case, to be not an insulating but a conductive medium.

Ra'ûf Orbay used to remark that he would have been one of
Baroness Meyendorff's subjects if her family had not been deported,
and if his had not been evicted, from the country that was their common homeland. This country was Abkhazia, the narrow strip of
land between the north-east coast of the Black Sea and the crest
of the north-westernmost section of the Caucasus Range. Today
Abkhazia is a bathing-resort for summer visitors from the cities
of the Soviet Union; but, at the date of Baroness Meyendorff's
birth, it was still as wild as the Highlands of Scotland were till
after 1745.

The Baroness's father had been an important highland chief.
(Hence, Ra'ûf Orbay's joke. Ra'ûf's own family's social position
in their native Abkhazia had been less highly exalted.) This was
the generation in which the Russians were 'pacifying' the Caucasus: the process that had been applied to the Scottish Highlands,
and that was to be applied to the High Atlas by General Lyautey.
The method by which the Baroness's family, in particular, had
been 'pacified' had been high-handed yet elegant in its characteristically Russian way. One day, when the whole family were out
hunting, the Russians had taken the opportunity to round up the
entire party—chieftain and chieftainess, son and daughter, horses,
hawks, and hounds—and they had then carried them off to be
parked in a Russian gilded cage. The future Baroness had been
perhaps about ten years old when she and her family were overtaken by this surprising change of circumstances. She had been
placed in an academy for educating Russian girls of noble birth to
become ladies-in-waiting at the Imperial Court; and this was
indeed the social background that one would have attributed to
her, when one met her in exile, if one had had to guess. Baroness

Meyendorff gave the impression of being, as in fact she was, a highly-bred Victorian lady for whom it was more difficult than it was for her husband the Baron to adjust to bourgeois British life. What one could never have guessed was the Baroness's barbaric origin; the impress of Russian culture had obliterated that completely.

That was a bewildering social and cultural metamorphosis to undergo in a single lifetime. Yet I suppose there must have been Scottish Highland chieftains' daughters, born in 1735, who lived to find themselves at home in Jane Austen's world. Baroness Meyendorff had manifestly come to be at home in the aristocratic world of the classical nineteenth-century Russian novelists. It was this vivid Russian world, not the dim and distant world of her native Abkhazian highlands, that kept a hold upon the Baroness when she was uprooted for the second (but not the last) time in her life.

Nineteenth-century Russian high society had been the milieu in which the Baroness and the Baron had met. Baron Meyendorff himself was a Baltic German nobleman from Estland. Presumably he was descended from one of those previously celibate German Knights of the Sword who founded families in the sixteenth century after they had turned Lutheran.

The Baltic provinces of the Russian Empire had been an integral, though outlying, part of the Western World since the thirteenth century, when the Teutonic Knights had conquered them and had forcibly converted the surviving pagan natives. Estland and Livland had been conquered from Sweden for Russia by Peter the Great in the Great Northern War; Courland had been acquired by Russia in the third partition of Poland. The Baltic provinces were the only portion of the nineteenth-century Russian Empire in which the Western civilization was indigenous, if we leave out of account the autonomous Grand Duchy of Finland, which had been united to Russia only by a personal union. (The Grand Duke of Finland was the Tsar.) In contrast to the nineteenth-century Russian nobility and bourgeoisie, whose Westernization was then still rather superficial, the Baltic German nobility and bourgeoisie were Westerners through and through; and the

Western civilization of these provinces was not only thorough at
the upper levels of society; it had also percolated down to the
peasantry. In the inter-war period the percentage of literacy in
the Russian Empire's short-lived Baltic successor-states Estonia
and Latvia was one of the highest in the world; and this twentieth-
century Baltic cultural achievement had a nineteenth-century
background that is illustrated by an amusing experience recounted
to Baron Meyendorff by his father.

Baron Meyendorff's father was once bringing some Russian
friends of his home with him to Estland out of Russia Proper.
At the border they changed carriages—not railway-carriages, but
horse-carriages; this was in the Russian Empire's pre-railway
age. As the party was climbing into the Estlandish carriage, the
coachman took out his handkerchief and blew his nose. At this
spectacle, the Russian visitors held up their hands in admiration.
'Yes, this is Europe,' they exclaimed. 'This is civilization! Why,
in this country, even the coachmen have handkerchiefs.'

The Western culture of which these Baltic handkerchiefs were
visible symbols had a rarity value in nineteenth-century Russia;
and, for the Baltic barons, this opened up avenues to employment
in high official positions out of proportion to their numbers. That
made them unpopular, to some extent, with their Russian fellow-
aristocrats; but their superior level of education also made the
employment of them indispensable for the efficient working of
the Imperial Russian administrative machine; and their unpopu-
larity was mitigated by their semi-assimilation to the Russian way
of life. The attractiveness of the native Russian culture for these
Westerners was a more remarkable testimony to its charm than
its attractiveness for Caucasian highlanders was; and Baron Meyendorff himself was a living case in point.

If it had not been for his name, one might have mistaken
Meyendorff for a Russian who had become thoroughly Westernized without having ceased to retain the Russian attitude to life.
Except, perhaps, for the thoroughness of his intellectual culture,
Meyendorff displayed none of those traits that are characteristic
of a German in the conventional non-German Western picture—
or caricature—of what a German is like. There was no trace in

Meyendorff of the overbearingness and the obtuseness that are associated with the Germans in the, possibly prejudiced, Western image of them. Meyendorff never lapsed into a Germanic hectoring manner; the mere thought of lapsing into that would have set his teeth on edge. Meyendorff exhibited, in a high degree, the sensitive Russian perceptiveness and its corollary, the fine Russian sense of irony. By the time when Meyendorff was starting his education, the Baltic provinces had become Russified enough to have abolished the barbarous Western practice of inflicting corporal punishment on schoolboys. Meyendorff once told me what a shock he received when his father sent him to finish his schooling at Stuttgart. When he saw boys being beaten by the masters, he could not convince himself that Europe was the heart of the civilized world.

When I think of my German-Russian friend Baron Meyendorff, and compare him with my German-American friends Will Westermann and Reinhold Niebuhr, I am led to the conclusion that the German variety of the Western culture, which is capable of producing regrettable effects when taken neat, can be warranted to produce excellent results when it is taken as one ingredient in a mixture.

Now that I have sketched in the cultural background of both the Meyendorffs, I find myself searching for some imaginary British parallel that might bring home to British readers the extraordinariness of the *tour de force* that the Russian way of life had performed in educating a Baltic baron and a Caucasian princess to become fitting helpmates for each other. Imagine the daughter of a Pathan chieftain and the son of a Protestant Irish landowner both going to the university (non-red-brick) in England and so meeting there and marrying. That is the nearest British potential parallel that I can think of.

When Meyendorff reached retirement-age at the London School of Economics, he had been benefiting by the London University pension scheme for far too short a time to have become entitled to a pension on which he and his wife could continue to live in England. Accordingly the Meyendorffs clubbed together with some other Russian exiles to buy a seaside villa in Finland, on the Karelian Isthmus. This location was a natural choice; for it was familiar ground for Russians who had played a part in public life before the Revolution. In the pre-revolutionary age, when Finland had been associated with the Russian Empire, the south-eastern extremity of the Karelian Isthmus had been virtually part of the suburban environs of St. Petersburg.

The Meyendorffs and their friends duly migrated from England to the Karelian Isthmus with their goods and chattels, and they had just settled into their villa when Munich Week came and went. It went, and the Meyendorffs went with it. Meyendorff now announced to his fellow-householders in the villa that he was going to take his wife and property back to England. Why on earth? Because Meyendorff's conclusion from the events of Munich Week was that the Karelian Isthmus was not a safe place to live in. 'Why, you are mad,' his friends protested. 'What has just happened in Munich Week means that Britain is soon going to be at war with Germany. Why return to that future war-zone when you have been lucky enough to have moved, in good time, to a neutral country?' Meyendorff was not shaken by these apparently rational representations. He carried out his decision. He took his wife and property back to England, while his friends stayed where they were. Within a year from the date of his departure, these same friends of his were acknowledging his prescience and were regretting that they had not followed his example. When the Soviet Union attacked Finland, the Karelian Isthmus became the war-zone, and the Meyendorffs' improvident friends had to evacuate their villa helter-skelter.

In returning from Finland to England on the eve of the Second World War, Meyendorff had deliberately chosen the lesser evil. His prognostications had proved correct, but life was now doubly difficult for him and the Baroness in war-time England. They were old, and their means of subsistence were inadequate. Their English friends were much concerned, and they did what they could to be friends in need; but the Meyendorffs were not easy to help in material ways. They presented at least three obstacles: they were uncomplaining, they were proud, and they were saintly. Baulked of assisting them with money, their friends fell back upon trying to assist them in kind. They took to sending them food-parcels; but they found themselves frustrated once again. The Meyendorffs, Tawney-like, just gave the food away to English neighbours whose need was probably not so great as theirs was.

After his wife's death, Meyendorff's plight in post-war England was forlorn; but his hard life, borne for so long with such stoicism and such good humour, took a happier turn in its very last phase. He found a haven in the home of kind and congenial friends; and at my last meeting with him, which was in their house, I found him serene. He had stood up triumphantly to the last of Fortune's searching tests.

18

C. P. Scott

ONE day during the First World War, when I came
to pay one of my periodical calls at Lord Bryce's
flat to report progress in the compilation of the
Blue Book on the treatment of the Armenians, I
found another visitor already waiting in the study. He was an
elderly and obviously distinguished man, with a kindly but
determined countenance and with very bright eyes. When I came
into the room he turned to me genially, and he quickly put me
at my ease with him by starting to talk. I cannot now recall
what phase of the war we were talking about; I only remember
that we were standing together at a window looking across
Buckingham Gate towards an archway at the corner of Buckingham Palace. When Lord Bryce came in, my fellow-visitor did
his business with him, and left; and, when he had gone, Lord
Bryce asked me if I knew who that had been. I did not; and he
told me that his visitor was the Editor of the *Manchester Guardian*,
C. P. Scott. This interested me greatly, and I was glad to have had
this accidental opportunity of meeting him. C. P. Scott was a
celebrated public figure, and I had also often heard Lawrence
Hammond talk about him. I have mentioned already that Lawrence worked for Scott for many years, and that there was a close
personal friendship between them.

My next meeting with Mr. Scott was in 1920, and this time
it was on professional business. After taking up my appointment
to the newly-founded Koraïs Chair of Byzantine and Modern
Greek Studies in the University of London, I had obtained leave
of absence for the summer term of the academic year 1920–1 in

order to visit Greece and the Graeco-Turkish war-zone, and Mr. Scott had commissioned me to serve, during my stay in the Levant, as the *Guardian*'s special correspondent. This commission had a double value for me; it was going to help finance my expedition to the Levant and it also promised to help me to get an inside view of what was happening there. People would be readier to talk to the representative of a famous newspaper than they would have been to pay attention to a young don if he had been representing no one but himself. The agreement between the *Guardian* and me had been concluded, and the Editor had invited me to stay with him for a week-end in his house in Fallowfield to have a talk with him about my job for him before I set off for Greece.

I found Mr. Scott as affable as he had been at our first meeting, and this time I learnt that the look of determination on his countenance was matched by a physical spartanism that reminded me of my Uncle Harry. The English tradition of hardiness had not died with Uncle Harry's generation after all; in Mr. Scott it was still alive, as I discovered when, as his guest, I took my bath the first morning before breakfast. One whole side of the bathroom yawned open to the winter skies, and both of the bath taps ran cold. Mr. Scott himself, no doubt, could take this; probably he had never missed a morning of it since he was a boy, so he was inured to it. Ashamed to be less hardy than a man who was so much my senior, I plunged in, while the humid Lancashire wind whistled round my shoulders. I had saved my self-respect, but this at the cost of going down with a chill after getting back to London. However, I was in high spirits. My liking for Mr. Scott, which I had felt, at first sight, five years before, had now been amply confirmed on further acquaintance; and I realized that I had taken service under a man who was as stalwart as he was strong-minded.

In the field, I found Mr. Scott a generous employer and, what was still more important, an unyieldingly upright and courageous one. I experienced Mr. Scott's generosity after the second battle of Inönü. At this battle, which proved to have been a turning-point in the Graeco-Turkish war of 1919-22, I had been the only newspaper correspondent present, and my telegram to the *Guardian* was the first news of the battle to be published in any European or American newspaper. Mr. Scott wrote me a personal letter, telling me that he was giving me a bonus of twenty pounds. His probity and courage came into play when he began to receive from me telegrams describing atrocities that were being committed by the Greek Army against the Turkish population in territories along the Asiatic shores of the Sea of Marmara that the Greeks were evacuating.

The *Manchester Guardian* was the leading Liberal newspaper in Britain; it was an exponent of the Gladstonian tradition; and its reputation for an impeccable Gladstonian orthodoxy was one of the features for which it was particularly prized by a number of its readers. Some influential readers of this school now wrote (so I learnt later) to Mr. Scott, charging him with betraying their principles and his own in publishing dispatches that were sympathetic to 'the unspeakable Turk'; but these critics received an uncompromising answer. Mr. Scott told them that he had confidence in his correspondent; that he believed that he was reporting the truth; and that he was therefore going to continue to publish his correspondent's reports. Mr. Scott was as good as his word. He supported me in my reporting of facts that were unwelcome news, not only in British Liberal circles, but in the Western World as a whole, in which the traditional 'Christian' prejudice against Muslims had survived in many minds that had repudiated Christianity itself. In supporting me, Mr. Scott was being true to a tradition of the *Guardian*'s that was still dearer to it than its Gladstonianism, and that therefore prevailed now that the two traditions were in conflict. The *Manchester Guardian* stood, above all else, for publishing the truth, as it saw it, without fear or favour. In my brief term of temporary service on the *Guardian*'s staff, I had the paper's high standard of probity borne in on me by finding myself one of its beneficiaries. I came through this experience with lasting feelings of gratitude and admiration for the *Guardian* and for its chivalrous editor, C. P. Scott.

19
Some Turkish Friends

I WAS fortunate in my friendship with Adnan and Halidé Adivar, and this good fortune of mine sprang from their misfortune. I had met them first in Istanbul in 1923, but I did not come to know them well till they, like the Meyendorffs, had become exiles in England.

Adnan's forebears had been hereditary superiors of a *tekke* of one of the dervish orders, and, from father to son, they had transmitted a gift for faith-healing. Adnan himself was a physician, but not of his ancestral school nor, again, of the Graeco-Arabian school that is still followed in some of the more backward parts of the Islamic World. Adnan was a modern physician of the school that, in the West, had superseded the Graeco-Arabian school since the seventeenth century. He was not only a modern physician; he was also a modern man, and this for good only, and not for evil. His modernity was of the humane and not the demonic kind. In Adnan Adivar's lifetime, these two antithetical strains in the modern Western spirit were contending for the mastery of Western souls. In Adnan's Westernized soul, human feelings had no demonic antagonist to overcome. Adnan's nature was incapable of harbouring any of the seven devils.

When I first met Adnan, he was in politics. He was acting as the Turkish Nationalist Government's administrator of the City of Istanbul during the interval between the signing of the Mudanya armistice and the conclusion of the Lausanne peace-treaty. Since 1919, Adnan and Halidé had been playing an active and distinguished part in the Turkish resistance movement; but politics was not the natural element of either of them. Turkey after the First

World War, like France in the Second World War, met with a crisis in which her very existence was at stake; and, in both countries, on these respective occasions, this supreme emergency drew into active public life a number of high-minded men and women whose temperaments would probably have kept them remote from politics in quieter times. Adnan and Halidé paid for their patriotism by being driven into exile—not by their country's adversaries at the time when Turkey had her back to the wall. They were exiled, after the national crisis was over, by the national leader who had saved Turkey with the aid of comrades of the Adivars' disinterested kind. When Atatürk's death made it possible for the Adivars to come back home, they resumed their natural vocations, which were scholarly. Halidé had made her name early as a novelist and she now became professor of English at the University of Istanbul, while Adnan took a leading part in the production of the Turkish version of *The Encyclopaedia of Islam*: a new edition that became virtually a new work.

Halidé's marriage with Adnan was, for Halidé, calm after storm. She had been married before, but her first marriage had ended in a battle; for her first husband, unlike Adnan, had been a modern man only within the limits of his profession. He had been a mathematician but also a reactionary. After Halidé had borne two children, he had announced his intention of taking a second wife; Halidé had told him that she would leave him if he did; he persisted in his course; and Halidé did as she had said. Her refusal to become a party to polygamy required high courage; for, at that date, the institution of marriage was still governed, in Turkey, by the Islamic religious law, under which it is legitimate for a Muslim man to have four wives simultaneously. (It was not till 17 February 1926 that polygamy was made illegal in Turkey by the enactment of the Swiss Civil Code, translated into Turkish, as the law of the land.) In parting from her first husband, Halidé had been fighting a battle for a vital human right in the teeth of the law that was then in force, and she had not been fighting simply for her own hand. It had been a battle for all the women of Turkey and, indirectly, for all the women of the rest of the Islamic World as well. For Halidé, this personal crisis had

9(a) Lawrence and Barbara Hammond, and the dog with the iron shoe, between the wars

(b) Lawrence Hammond with horses, between the wars

10   Sidney and Beatrice Webb, between the wars

been as severe as the public crisis of 1919–23 was for her country. Her reward was her meeting and marriage with a man who saw eye to eye with her on moral issues and who captivated her fiercer spirit by his gentler one.

When Halidé's first husband insisted on exercising his legal right to take a second wife, the clash between the two irreconcilable principles of polygamy and monogamy was tragic because the parties to the conflict were sophisticated and were therefore aware of the full import of the issue. In the course of my own experience in Turkey, however, I was the witness of another quarrel over the same issue in which the parties were unsophisticated and in which the *mésintelligence* was a comedy with a happy ending.

In 1921 my wife and I were guests of the American College for Girls at Arna'ûtköi on the Bosphorus, and one of the key members of the College's staff was a major-domo whom I will call Ahmed, as I do not remember what his name actually was. Ahmed was indispensable to the American faculty, because he served them as their dragoman for all communications with the Turkish world outside their gates. One day, Ahmed's wife said to him: 'My dear, we are both getting old and I am beginning to find the housework too much for me; but fortunately these Americans pay a very generous salary; so we can afford a second wife for you —a young one, to help me. She can do the rough work and the plain cooking, and I promise you that I will still cook your favourite dishes for you myself.' This proposal made such obvious good sense that it was no sooner said than done. The young wife was installed and the old wife was opportunely relieved of her heavier domestic chores.

At that moment, however, a new American professor and his wife arrived on the campus. They came from 'the Bible Belt'; and, when the wife heard of Ahmed's second marriage, she said that this was immorality on the campus, and that, unless it was stopped, she and her husband would not stay. When Ahmed heard what the newly-arrived professor's wife had been saying about his second marriage, he said that, if she stayed on the campus, he, for his part, was going to leave. In point of respectability,

Ahmed and the newly-arrived professor's wife were on a par. Both were utterly respectable from head to toes; so both were utterly outraged. Put yourself in Ahmed's position. Even now, Ahmed had only two wives, and the holy law of the True Faith allowed him four. He had two vacancies still in hand; yet this unbeliever had had the effrontery to accuse him of immorality and to suggest that his dear first wife should be deprived of the domestic help that he had just procured for her.

This quarrel put the faculty in a fix. They could not afford to lose Ahmed, but they could not afford to lose their new professor of mathematics either. The whole faculty had to drop all other work in order to concentrate on the herculean task of persuading Ahmed and the 'Bible-Belt' lady respectively that the lady and he were, after all, each behaving respectably according to his and her own peculiar lights.

Here were two Turkish wives taking diametrically opposite views about the Islamic institution of polygamy. Ahmed's wife's view was traditional and matter-of-fact; Halidé's view was revolutionary and idealistic. The major-domo's wife was perhaps not more than half a generation older than the authoress was. The extreme difference between their respective views was a result, not so much of their difference in age, as of their difference in up-bringing and consequent outlook. Halidé Hanum had had a Western education at the college at which Ahmed was employed, and her break with the Islamic tradition was a sample of a change that, in her generation, was overtaking the Turkish intelligentsia but that, so far, had hardly begun to affect other strata of Turkish society.

This onset of Westernization was challenging many traditional Islamic institutions besides the Islamic marriage law. Every civilization has its own distinctive code of behaviour. The Islamic code is lax about sex but strict about drink; the Christian code is lax about drink but strict about sex. (I am stating here merely what the codes enjoin; no rules of conduct are ever fully obeyed in practice.) One effect of Westernization on Muslims is therefore to make them take a stricter line about marriage but a laxer line about alcohol.

The consequences of Westernization in the matter of drink are illustrated by Atatürk's life—and death. Atatürk became a gargantuan consumer of hard liquor. One evening in 1923, when I was his guest for dinner at Ankara, I watched what happened when a very large brass tray, loaded to the rim with neat whiskeys, was placed in front of him. The glasses were emptied as quickly as if the whiskeys had been mutton chops and the dictator had been a great dane. Atatürk did his drinking ostentatiously, as a gesture to signify that he had emancipated himself from all traditional Islamic tabus, but he also drank recklessly, because this Western vice was congenial to his nature. Atatürk's nature was demonic, and, like some contemporary American men of action, he used alcohol as his stimulant for maintaining the superhuman 'drive' that he put into everything that he did. Atatürk accomplished more than most people achieve within a human lifetime, and alcohol was one of the generators of his energy; but alcohol was also responsible for his premature death; and this demonic ex-Muslim's failure to cope with this Western poison suggests that, after all, the Prophet Muhammad's tabu on drinking alcohol may have been salutary—may, in fact, be an Islamic tradition that the West might do well to adopt.

The prohibition of alcohol is not the only Islamic tabu in the field of food and drink. Muslims are also forbidden to eat swine's flesh. I once witnessed an intriguing violation of this particular Islamic tabu on the opposite fringe of the far-flung Islamic World.

In China in 1929, just after the Kuomintang had at last got the upper hand over the northern war-lords, I was invited by President and Madame Chiang Kai-shek to dine with them in Nanking. When I presented myself, Madame Chiang said to me: 'I hope you will not mind our giving you some rather peculiar food this evening. Our other guest is General Ma. He has recently come over to our side, so we want to be careful to treat him with particular courtesy; but he is a Muslim, and Muslims have peculiar ideas about food, you know.' I assured Madame Chiang that I did know. I had spent some time in Turkey, and I had liked the food that I had been given there. Everything seemed to be now in order; but, when General Ma arrived and the dinner arrived, I had two surprises. The main dish was pork, and General Ma ate it, not only without wincing, but with apparent relish.

How were these surprising facts to be interpreted? Was the Chiangs' cook a snake in the grass? Had he served pork this evening deliberately and maliciously, in order to defeat his employers' intentions? Had he designed to make General Ma believe that his hosts were going out of their way to insult him? Had the cook calculated that this apparent insult would offend the General deeply enough to make him change sides again to the Kuomintang's detriment? And how was one to explain General Ma's sedate behaviour? Was he capable of such self-command that he could make himself swallow that unclean food and could also conceal his disgust and indignation till he could find his opportunity for taking his revenge?

General Ma's serenity had puzzled me because I knew that one's automatic aversion from a forbidden food is apt to outlive one's belief that the tabu is binding. Harold Laski had once told me, as a curious piece of self-observation, that the sight of bacon still gave him a feeling of nausea, though, at the conscious level, he was entirely emancipated from his Jewish traditional background. I knew, too, from my own experience, that English people with a Christian background had a feeling of nausea at the sight of horse-flesh, and I was aware of the reason for that. In the pre-Christian stage of English history, our pagan ancestors used to feast on the flesh of horses that they had offered as sacrifices to their gods; so the Christian missionaries who had converted them had placed a tabu on an article of diet that was associated with the religion that was now banned. (My French and Walloon contemporaries can eat horse-flesh with gusto today because the Teutonic horse-sacrifice was not included in their pre-Christian religious ritual, so that, for them, no tabu on eating horse-flesh was needed as a precaution against the risk that they might relapse into their ancestral paganism.) How, then, had General Ma managed to swallow that pork without even an involuntary shudder?

After pondering over my problem, I finally came to the conclusion that the simplest explanation was the most likely to hit the truth. I concluded that all concerned had been acting in good faith because they had all been acting in ignorance. When Madame Chiang had given her orders to her cook, she and he had simply got things the wrong way round. The ideas of Islam and of pork were vaguely associated in their minds, so they had assumed that, if you were entertaining a Muslim, pork would be the right, not the wrong, thing to give him. As for General Ma, I now believe that he either did not know that the meat on his plate was pork or else did not know that pork was tabu for Muslims.

General Ma may not have been aware of this Islamic tabu; for, in China, Islam has gone farther than in any other part of the world within my knowledge in coming to terms with local practice. In 1929, I visited the mosque in a Muslim Chinese village within riding-distance of Peking. The Arabic inscriptions had been turned, through an angle of ninety degrees, to run vertically instead of horizontally, like the Manchu and Mongol inscriptions in the Syriac alphabet on the Temple of Heaven. Worse than that, the gables of that Chinese village mosque were crowned by rows of guardian genii, posted there to ward off evil influences, that would have been in place if the building had been a pagan temple, instead of its being dedicated, as it was, to the worship of a jealous god who had prohibited graven images.

Atatürk's ex-comrades whom he had driven into exile were no more unfortunate than my Russian refugee friends were in point of material circumstances, but they had a psychological problem to wrestle with which the Russian refugees had been spared. The Russian refugees had no call to show any consideration for the reigning Communist régime in Russia. They were members of a class on which the Communists had made war to the knife, and they had been lucky to escape with their lives. The Turkish exiles' relation to the reigning dictator of Turkey was more complex.

These former comrades of Atatürk's had followed him as their leader in their country's supreme crisis. They had followed him to victory—a victory in which they too had played their part—and they would have liked nothing better than to go on working with him for the regeneration of their country's life. In driving them into exile, Atatürk had committed a major crime both against the exiles personally and against his and their common country too. At a time when Turkey needed every public-spirited and honest and able citizen whom she could muster, Atatürk had deprived her of almost all of these except himself, and, in the act, he had convicted himself of lacking the public spirit that his victims had shown. These had been eager to go on working for the country under his leadership; Atatürk had responded by driving them out; and their offence in his eyes had been the inadmissible one that they too were personalities with opinions of their own and that, so long as these other eminent Turkish men and women were working with him, he could not be the lone star in the Turkish firmament. Atatürk had succumbed to a dictator's occupational infirmity of being unable to co-operate with his equals, and the exiles were paying the price for this. Each of them had as good a right as Dante had had to sign himself *exul immeritus*. But would it be warrantable for them to assume Dante's posture of implacable aggrievedness? Atatürk was flagrantly at fault, but he was still the saviour of his and his victims' country. The exiles still approved of Atatürk's past acts, and they also continued to approve of much of his current policy. What line were they to take about Atatürk, both among themselves and in the presence of sympathetic foreign friends?

In this difficult moral situation, my Turkish friends in exile showed good judgement and admirable generosity. Their comments on Atatürk's acts were frank but discriminating and objective. No note of personal bitterness ever crept into what they said; and Ra'ûf Orbay, in particular, invariably accompanied any critical comment that he might have made by adding that, in spite of all, Atatürk was a great man; that his vision and will-power had saved Turkey; and that every patriotic Turk owed him admiration and gratitude for what he had done for the country, irrespective of Atatürk's behaviour to individuals. Adnan and Ra'ûf were men of different temperaments and gifts. Adnan was primarily a scholar; Ra'ûf was primarily a man of action; but, in nobility of character, they were kindred spirits.

Besides being conspicuously frank and honourable, Ra'ûf was romantic. I have already mentioned his Abkhazian origin.

(In religion the Abkhazians were divided between Eastern Orthodox Christianity, which was Baroness Meyendorff's ancestral religion, and Sunni Islam, which was Ra'ûf Orbay's.) By profession,
Ra'ûf was a naval officer. In the First Balkan War he had commanded the cruiser *Hamidié* and had sallied out in her from the
Dardanelles into the Aegean, running the gauntlet of the Greek
naval blockade. He had then managed to do some commerce-
raiding without being caught, though the Greek navy commanded the sea in which he was operating. After Turkey's intervention
in the First World War, Ra'ûf had made an equally daring land-
raid on the Anglo-Iranian Oil Company's pipeline between its
oilfields and its refinery on Abâdân Island. If he had succeeded in
this enterprise, he might have brought the British Navy to a
standstill. When I first met Ra'ûf, which was at Ankara in 1923,
he was Prime Minister in the Nationalist Government. He lived
to return from exile and to serve as Turkish Ambassador in London during the Second World War. In private life, he was a
friend whose constancy was never in doubt.

Those of my Turkish friends who were in exile during the
later years of Atatürk's régime were the ones whom I had the
opportunity of seeing the most often and getting to know the
best. But I had, and have, others as well. One of these was Fethî
Bey Okyar, a comrade of Atatürk's whom Atatürk did not choose
to evict—though he came near to quarrelling with him at least
once. Fethî was able to continue to serve his country without any
loss of personal integrity and honour. Fethî's son Osman is one of
my most valued friends of any nationality in the next generation
to his father's and mine. My first meeting with Osman was in
1923, in his parents' house at Ankara. He was hardly out of his
cradle; he grew up to become a distinguished economist, and he
is now Rector of the recently-established University of Erzerum.
In my own generation, one of my Turkish friends is Şerif Remzi
Bey, the star pupil of my old Canadian friend Dr. MacLachlan,
the President of the former International College at Izmir. In an
older generation than mine, I had Turkish friends who did not
all share my Nationalist friends' political views. (One advantage
of being a foreigner is that one's friendships need not be confined

to any one political camp.) There was the lovable 'Inglîz' Rif'at, an Anglophil Turk of the old school to whom I was introduced by Aubrey Herbert and who became my friend too. There was the Platonist philosopher Rizâ Tevfîk, who had made himself *persona non grata* to the Nationalists to a degree at which it was no longer prudent for him to remain at large. When I first met him, he had taken sanctuary within the bounds of the American College for Girls at Arna'ûtköi. He was afterwards given a permanent asylum in Transjordan by the Amir 'Abdallah.

It will be seen that I have had many Turkish friends, and some of them close friends. How did I come to enter into these personal relations with Turks? The ultimate origin of these Turkish friendships of mine lies in the work that I did for Lord Bryce in compiling the United Kingdom Blue Book on the treatment of the Armenians in the Ottoman Empire in 1915. The study of genocide set me moving along a road that led to my making friends with fellow-countrymen of the criminals by whom the genocide had been committed. This may sound like a *non sequitur*, so I will trace the steps that carried me from the starting-point to the end of this voyage of exploration. It was a mental voyage and, as I see it now in retrospect, a spiritual one too; for, in essence, it was an inquiry into the mystery of human nature.

The collection and collation of the evidence from which the Blue Book was compiled had occupied most of my working time for a number of months; and, after the Blue Book had been published, I could not dismiss its contents from my mind. I was not only haunted by the victims' sufferings and by the criminals' deeds; I was exercised by the question how it could be possible for human beings to do what those perpetrators of genocide had done. There were features of the story that were enlightening. It was evident that the criminals had not been the Armenians' local Turkish neighbours. For the most part, these had looked on passively. (Of course, that was bad enough.) In a few cases there was evidence that the local Turks had done what they could to protect and help their Armenian friends. The deportations had been carried out by orders from the Government at Istanbul, and the orders had been executed by gendarmes and soldiers who had no personal connexion with the localities. These facts suggested that human beings were not inclined to commit atrocities on fellow human beings with whom they were personally acquainted. If one is going to behave atrociously to other human beings, one's relation with one's victims has to be impersonal. For instance, in Britain we had had to de-humanize our mental picture of the Germans by labelling them 'Huns' in order to make our minds easy about killing 'Huns' *en masse*. In the genocide of the Armenians the criminals had been members of the Committee of Union and Progress—above all, perhaps, Tal'at, the most intelligent of the ruling triumvirs. But how had those three men brought themselves to commit their fearful crime? Only eight years before, the Committee of Union and Progress had overthrown Sultan 'Abd-al-Hamîd II's autocratic rule with the programme of transforming the Turkish Empire into a democratic commonwealth in which all the component religions and nationalities were henceforward to enjoy equal rights. The revolution of 1908 in Turkey had caught my attention at the time, and it had appealed to my imagination. In fact, it was the event that had led me to take an interest in current international affairs. In the course of the eight years 1908–15, the leaders of the C.U.P. had apparently degenerated from being idealists into becoming ogres. How was one to account for this sinister metamorphosis?

A pertinent point here was that the triumvirate's motives in setting out to exterminate the Ottoman Armenians had been not only impersonal but political. Since the Russo-Turkish War of 1877–8, the Armenian diaspora in the north-eastern territories of the Ottoman Empire had been nursing political ambitions. Like the Greek diaspora farther to the west in Anatolia, the Armenians had been hoping to be able, one day, to carve out a successor-state of the Ottoman Empire for themselves. These Greek and Armenian political aspirations had not been legitimate; for the diasporas were minorities scattered among a Turkish majority. Their aspirations did not merely threaten to break up the Turkish Empire; they could not be fulfilled without doing grave injustice to the Turkish people itself. For Turkey, the Armenian question had come to a head after Turkey's intervention in the First World

War, when the Russians had defeated an abortive Turkish invasion of Russian Transcaucasia and had successfully invaded North-Eastern Turkey. The Turkish authorities now found that the local Armenian diaspora might serve the Russian invaders as what we have since learnt to call a 'fifth column'. They therefore decided to deport the Armenians from the war-zone, and this, in itself, might pass for a legitimate security-measure. In similar circumstances, other governments have taken similar action. The United States Government, for instance, deported the Japanese-American diaspora from the Pacific slope to the Mississippi basin after Japan had attacked the American fleet at Pearl Harbor; and, in that deportation too, misdemeanours were committed. The Japanese-American deportees were cheated and robbed on a large scale. In Turkey, however, in 1915, the Ottoman Armenian deportees were not only robbed; the deportations were deliberately conducted with a brutality that was calculated to take the maximum toll of lives *en route*. This was the C.U.P.'s crime; and my study of it left an impression on my mind that was not effaced by the still more cold-blooded genocide, on a far larger scale, that was committed during the Second World War by the Nazi.

Any great crime—private or public, personal or impersonal —raises a question that transcends national limits; the question goes to the heart of human nature itself. My study of the genocide that had been committed in Turkey in 1915 brought home to me the reality of Original Sin. Human nature has in it an inherent vein of abominable wickedness; but then it also has in it an inherent vein of lovable goodness too. Every human soul is a battlefield on which these two irreconcilable spiritual forces are perpetually contending for the mastery. The moral inconsistency of human nature is a mystery that each of us must try to probe—and this not just to satisfy an intellectual curiosity, but in order to grapple with Original Sin with intent to subdue it. One must probe human nature in oneself; one must probe it in one's neighbours; and, among my own neighbours, I, in my case, must begin with my Turkish neighbours. The Turkish criminals—Tal'at, Jemâl, Enver, and their agents—were only a minority of the Turkish people; yet this was the people from which those criminals had sprung. I must not, however, rest content with a study of the Turkish people in the mass. I must not forget the dehumanizing effect of collective labels. If I was to get to know human nature in Turkish embodiments of it, I must get to know live Turkish men and women individually, and I must meet each of them as one of my fellow human beings, of like passions with myself. I held on to this resolve till my release from war-work gave me time to begin putting my intention into effect.

My first step was to start to learn the Turkish language. One cannot get very far in making contact with people whose language is a different one from one's own unless one can communicate with them, however haltingly, in at least a smattering of their mother tongue. So, as soon as I had a don's margin of leisure once again in the Koraïs Chair at the University of London, I enrolled myself as a student of Turkish at the London School of Oriental and African Studies; and this brought me my first Turkish friend, the School's lecturer in Turkish, 'Alî Rizâ Bey.

Long afterwards, I heard from the Director of the School, Sir Denison Ross, what 'Alî Rizâ's first reaction had been when he had found my name on the list of his next batch of students. 'Alî Rizâ had gone straight to the Director and had told him that he was unwilling to accept as a pupil a man who had been a party to producing a book that showed him to be an enemy of 'Alî Rizâ's country. The Director's reply had been: 'If you do refuse to teach Professor Toynbee Turkish, you will be showing a lack of faith in your country. If you truly believe in your country, as I am sure you do, you will be confident that someone who seems to you to be prejudiced against your country will change his mind on better acquaintance with it. In being asked to teach Professor Toynbee Turkish, you are being offered an opportunity of helping him to change his mind. A language is the door to an understanding of the people who speak it. In seeking to learn Turkish, isn't Professor Toynbee showing a wish to become better acquainted with the Turks?' 'Alî Rizâ had seen the force of Sir Denison Ross's argument. He had waived his objection; and, when I turned up, he gave no sign of the hostility that he had felt towards me before meeting me. He must soon have realized that my wish to make closer acquaintance with Turks was sincere. Our work together resulted in a lasting friendship.

Sir Denison Ross's advice to 'Alî Rizâ had obviously been wise in itself. It had also been based on a first-hand acquaintance with me. Sir Denison's mother had lived in Upper Westbourne Terrace, only a few doors off from Uncle Harry and my parents; and, when I was a boy, I had seen something of Denison during his tours of home leave from India. (He had been appointed to the headship of a madrasa by the Viceroy, Lord Curzon, who had a high opinion of his abilities.) Denison Ross had sometimes let me help him to sort out his books and papers; and I had learnt a great deal from these, and still more from casual conversations with him. He had the gift of tongues, and he also had a lively intellectual curiosity, especially about anything to do with Asia.

My lessons in Turkish with 'Alî Rizâ were part of my preparations for my second step, which was to visit the Graeco-Turkish war-zone as the *Manchester Guardian*'s correspondent. I planned, as a matter of course, to see things in the Levant from both sides. This would be my professional duty towards the *Guardian*, and it would anyway have been my own impulse. I had taken to heart, long since, the precept *Audi alteram partem*; and I had interpreted the words *alteram partem*, not as meaning just 'the other party's case', but as meaning particularly the case that, of the two, was the more in danger of not being given a fair hearing. I had already taken the measure of the propaganda advantage that is gained by a party that captures a monopoly of the telling of the tale. I had realized that we saw the Persians through the Greeks' eyes, the Spartans and Boeotians through the Athenians' eyes, the Philistines and Phoenicians through the Israelites' eyes. If one was to see straight, one must also see things from the mute party's point of view; one must not let the vocal party have the last word as well as the first. In the present conflict and controversy between Greeks and Turks, the Greeks were the vocal party once again. The Greeks had the ear of the West, and the West was in the ascendant in the world. I was familiar with the Greeks' case; I felt that it could take care of itself; the Turks' case was the one that I must take pains to understand. So, after I had looked at the

Graeco-Turkish war from the Greek side of the front, I went to Turkey to look at it from the Turkish side in turn.

In Turkey I ran up against the barrier that I should have met with in 'Alî Rizâ if, in his case, Sir Denison Ross had not lowered the barrier for me in advance. I found that the Turks whom I now approached regarded me with hostility and suspicion. I had worked for Lord Bryce on that Blue Book, and, to Turkish minds, 'Bryce' was almost as bad a name as 'Gladstone'. I was a professor of Modern Greek studies. I had just come from a visit to the Greek army that was trespassing on Turkish soil. Worst of all, I was the representative of that Gladstonian English newspaper the *Manchester Guardian*. I had a number of unprofitable interviews with the director of the Istanbul Red Crescent, Hâmid Bey. (This attractive but formidable man's head was as huge and square as Namier's and Ehrlich's.) One day, Hâmid Bey suddenly challenged me to board, that very evening, a Red Crescent ship that was going to Yalova, on the Marmara coast of Anatolia, to evacuate Turkish refugees. Yalova was under Greek military occupation, and there had been a massacre of the local Turkish population by local Greeks and Armenians. Hâmid Bey was surprised when I jumped at this opportunity of seeing things from the Turkish side; he was more surprised when, after returning to Istanbul, I showed him the text of the telegram, reporting what I had seen, that I had sent to the *Manchester Guardian*; he was most surprised of all when he received a copy of the issue of the *Guardian* in which my dispatch was printed. I can still see the scene in the Red Crescent's office: big Hâmid Bey with the English newspaper in his hands, and his colleagues crowding round, with radiant faces. Their case was being put in Britain at last.

I had convinced the Turks of my good faith, and I had won a number of Turkish friends in the process. In the act, I had forfeited the good opinion of the Greeks. In their eyes, I was now a traitor; and, no doubt, if some British Islamic scholar—say, Sir Thomas Arnold—had visited the Graeco-Turkish war-zone and had come to the conclusion that the Greeks were in the right, the Turks would have reacted against him as the Greeks reacted against me. To convince the Greeks of my good faith would hardly be possible. It was going to be a hard enough task, when I came home, to persuade my countrymen to give a fair hearing to my presentation of the Turkish case.

I realized this in advance, because I remembered the atmosphere of animosity against Islam and against the Turks in which I had grown up. My parents were not partial to Roman Catholicism; but, after Uncle Harry had declared, at tea-time one day, that Muhammad had not been so bad as the Pope, my parents advised me privately afterwards that the Pope was really not so bad as all that. I remembered also how one day my father had come home from his work full of an interview that he had had with an Armenian refugee. My father was an officer of the Charity Organization Society; his job was to superintend the Society's district offices in South London; and the Armenian had applied to the C.O.S. for financial assistance. This was in 1897, and this Armenian was one of those who had escaped from the massacre of Armenians that had just been perpetrated by Sultan 'Abd-al-Hamîd II. Afterwards, I had asked my mother about those Turks who had persecuted the Armenian whom Daddy had been helping, and my inquiry had drawn from her a denunciation of the Turks that went farther than Gladstone's denunciation of them by a whole continent. When Gladstone had called for the expulsion of the Turks from Europe, 'bag and baggage', he had been willing to 'let them go—to Asia where they belong'. Thus Gladstone, (though I did not know this yet) had abandoned to the Turks the largest of the continents, 'Bible lands' and all. But, twenty years later than the date of Gladstone's celebrated speech, my mother told me that Asia Minor was much too good a country for the Turks to have. At that time, all that I knew about the relations between Dâr-al-Islâm and Christendom was the story of the Crusades. Unlike Monsieur Clemenceau in 1919, I did already know in 1897 that, in the Crusades, the Christians had eventually been defeated. 'I suppose the Christians are not powerful enough to turn the Turks out of Asia Minor,' I said. 'Yes, they are,' said my mother, 'they could turn them out any day if they wanted to. What keeps the Turks where they ought not to be is the Christian countries' selfish rivalry with each other.' This incidental censure of my mother's was my first introduction to the cynical and senseless international power-game that was to be the death of half my school and college friends and of millions more of my contemporaries. When, in Paris in 1919 and again in 1946, I was seeing, at close quarters, how the game was played, I found that my mother's severe words had been an inadequate description of the reality.

When, in 1921, I had returned to London from my tour in the Levant, I asked Headlam-Morley whether he could arrange for me to be invited to be the speaker at one of the autumn meetings at Chatham House, in order that I might have an opportunity of describing my experiences to the members of the Institute and of putting before them the case for the Turks. The meeting was held on 22 November 1921; Sir Arthur Evans took the chair for me; and he asked me to have dinner with him first. This was hospitable, but I was unhappy when, over the soup, he told me what he was going to say when he was introducing me to my audience. He was going to say that we and the Modern Greeks were co-heirs of the Ancient Greek civilization, and that we Western heirs of Ancient Greece ought to support people who shared this heritage with us against people who did not. I put it to him that the right criterion for passing judgement on a dispute was not one's respective degrees of affinity with the disputants but was the rights and wrongs of the case; but Sir Arthur had made up his mind. When he opened the meeting he said just what he had told me that he was going to say, and his thesis drew loud applause. The chairman at a meeting on a controversial subject is expected to refrain from throwing his weight into either scale; but my chairman at this meeting had given Sisyphus's stone a kick-off that had sent it rolling down from the top of the mountain right to the bottom, and I had to start rolling my stone up again on a steep adverse gradient of hostile prejudice. This was indeed uphill work.

Sir Arthur's thesis was vulnerable both intellectually and morally. An Islamic scholar would have reminded Sir Arthur that the Muslims, too, were heirs of the Ancient Greek civilization. Where in the world in 1921 would one have found Aristotle's authority still unchallenged and Hippocratic medicine still being practised? Not in Modern Greece and not in the West, but in Dâr-al-Islâm. And why had Sir Arthur failed to remind my audience that the Modern Greeks and we were co-heirs of a Jewish heritage besides our Ancient Greek one, and that the Muslims were co-heirs with us of this Jewish heritage too? Western Christians, Eastern Orthodox Christians, and Muslims are all worshippers of a god whom the Jews, not the Ancient Greeks, made known to them. Christians and Muslims agree with Jews in regarding the Ancient Greeks as 'pagans', however much they may admire these 'pagans'' intellectual and artistic achievements. In Modern Greek, the word for 'pagan' is 'Hellene'—i.e. the name by which the Ancient Greeks had called themselves. These facts are damning for Sir Arthur's thesis intellectually; but the intellectual untenability of the thesis is a secondary consideration; its primary fault is a moral one. The contention that one should support the party with whom one considers oneself to have the greatest cultural affinity can be seen, when analysed, to be a refined version of Stephen Decatur's doctrine 'our country, right or wrong', and, when this is translated into more emotional terms, it becomes Hitler's doctrine of 'blood and soil'. In any form, refined or crude, the sacrifice of the claims of justice to ties of kinship is immoral. Hitler's way of putting his and Sir Arthur's common doctrine shows the doctrine up.

However, at the Chatham House meeting in the autumn of 1921, my talk was seriously prejudiced by Sir Arthur's prelude to it. In putting the Turkish case in Britain, I had two formidable difficulties to contend with. The first was the traditional Christian prejudice against Muslims and Turks; the second was that, for all but a very small minority of my countrymen, the Turks were anonymous ogres. Like 'the Huns' and 'the Boers', the 'unspeakable' Turks had a pejorative collective label but no human personal names or countenances. Few people in Britain had any Ra'ûfs or Adnans or Halidés among their friends. In my experience the solvent of traditional prejudice has been personal acquaintance. When one becomes personally acquainted with a fellow human being, of whatever religion, nationality, or race, one cannot fail

11 Lord Bryce, during the First World War

12   Sir James Headlam-Morley

to recognize that he is human like oneself; but it would take time
to weave a network of Turco-British personal friendships that
would knit the two peoples together.

In all my dealings with or about the Turks, personal relations
had been, for me, the key; and this thought was uppermost in my
mind on the evening in the spring of 1923 on which I was
Atatürk's guest for dinner at Ankara. In this encounter with
Atatürk, as in my encounter with Hitler thirteen years later,
I had the opportunity of making only a single point; so, in speaking to Atatürk, I tried out on him my conviction of the paramount
importance of personal relations in all fields, public as well as
private. When Atatürk disagreed with what someone had said,
he intimidated the other person visually, before opening his
mouth, with a frown that brought the whole of his forehead
down, like a thunder-cloud, upon his brows; and I was confronted
by this lowering face while he was telling me that I was entirely
wrong. Personal relations, he said to me, were of little importance;
they produced no appreciable effect. Impersonal public relations
were what mattered.

Our exchange of ideas was brief, but it told me that I was in
the presence of a mind that was powerful but was also 'monadic'
in the Leibnizian sense. Atatürk's mind had, I knew, conceived at
least one idea that was a stroke of genius. Atatürk had realized
that, for the Turkish people, national salvation lay in renouncing
their imperial role in order to concentrate all their energies on the
cultivation of their own long-neglected garden. The weakness of
this vigorous and imaginative mind was that, when it had conceived an idea of its own, it closed like a clam, and so debarred
itself from the possibility of having second thoughts; for the most
fruitful source of second thoughts is an exchange of ideas between
one's own mind and others. This clam-like closure of Atatürk's
mind was, I suppose, the price of his demonic will-power.
Atatürk's will-power had saved his country, but his obstinacy
was a high price for the country to pay now that he had become
her dictator.

In raising with Atatürk the issue of personal versus impersonal
relations, I had been guided by my own experience and not by an

appreciation of Atatürk's character; but, as it happened, I had hit a blind spot in him. Atatürk did in truth have no use for personal relations; and he had no use for them because the quality that was lacking in him was love. Atatürk had both intelligence and will-power in a high degree, but the faculty that makes a human being human had been denied to him. If Atatürk can be said to have loved anything at all, what he loved was an abstraction. He loved Turkey (if love is the right word in this connexion), but he did not really love any Turks; and this was unnatural; for, in the heroic resistance movement in which he had taken the lead, he had had a number of human-hearted comrades—among them, my friends Adnan and Ra'ûf. These comrades of Atatürk's in a great common experience and common achievement had given him their loyalty, and they would have given him their affection too if there had been any answering feeling in him to give their own feelings access to him. Unhappily, Atatürk's relations with his comrades had left him cold. When the national crisis was over, Atatürk saw in his former companions merely so many objects that were getting in his light; and he dealt with this nuisance by driving into exile fellow-patriots who were nobler-minded than himself. By the time of Atatürk's death, only two leading figures of his own stature had escaped this fate. One of the two was Fethî Bey Okyar; the other was Ismet Inönü.

Well, I do not agree with Atatürk. For me, personal relations are the most precious thing in life. So, in thinking of my Turkish friends, my thoughts run back to the Adivars, with whom my friendship was the closest of all. My last sight of my old friend Halidé Hanum Adivar was in Istanbul on 19 November 1962. She was still living in the quarter between the Conqueror's Mosque and the shore of the Marmara in which she and Adnan had settled after their return home from exile. (In choosing to live in the heart of Istanbul Proper, the Adivars had been ignoring the Turkish intelligentsia's current fashion, which was to migrate to Pera, the Frankish suburb of Istanbul 'beyond' the Golden Horn.) In 1962, Halidé was still where I had found her before, but now she was alone and lonely. Adnan had met the same death as Lawrence Hammond, of whom he had reminded me so strongly. Heart-failure had carried off Adnan Adivar too, and Halidé was left grieving, as Barbara had been. Halidé's grief, too, was sad to see; yet it had brought out a side of her character which had been latent while Adnan had been alive. When I had seen Halidé and Adnan together, I had been conscious of an impetuosity in her that had been tempered, but not entirely over-come, by Adnan's influence. Now, when Adnan was no longer there, the old impetuosity had given way to tenderness. Adnan's widow was living in her love for him. I could not wish her to go on living a life that was so sad; and, when the news of her death reached me, I felt that this had been, for her, a happy release. Halidé's life had ended sadly, but she had not lived in vain. As a writer, as a patriot, as a woman, and, above all, as a human being who had loved and been loved, Halidé had lived to the full.

20

Professor Lutosławski

'IS it your habit to eat?' Professor Lutosławski had shot this
question at my wife and me in a tone which seemed to
imply that this habit was both unusual and discreditable. If
he had been addressing us in Latin—a language with which
he will have been familiar both as a Pole and as a classical scholar—
his question to us would certainly have opened with a *num*, not
with a *nonne*. If we were to retain Professor Lutosławski's respect,
we should have had to shake our heads; but human frailty made
us confess, shamefacedly, to being addicts. The question had come
up towards the end of the sixth hour of our séance with the professor in his apartment in the city of Wilno on some day in the year
1928; and he had already announced his intention of taking us
along with him to see a Polish play which threatened to last at
least as long again, since its plot, he told us, covered the whole
history of human civilization. Even if our spirit had been willing,
our flesh would have been too weak to hold out for another six
hours without refreshment.

It takes a Slav to get right down to the roots of things. I had
thought of my English friend Harry Tawney as being a radical;
but Harry Tawney had not put Professor Lutosławski's primor-
dial question to his schoolfellow William Temple when the
archbishop had been spending the night with him. He had betrayed his British intellectual slovenliness by taking the answer
to Professor Lutosławski's question for granted, and, what is
more, he had arbitrarily assumed that the answer would be in the
affirmative. Plunging *in medias res*, Harry had gone straight to
asking William whether he would like to have supper now. For

Harry, nothing but the timing had been in question; the habit of eating had not been in doubt.

Professor Lutosławski's intellectual discipline was more rigorous, and he also lived up to his own principles. In the restaurant in which my wife and I were now taking a hasty meal, he did not break his fast, and he had not broken it when, long afterwards, at the end of the prolix world-history play, we said goodnight to each other in the small hours of the following morning.

Professor Lutosławski not only practised on himself the habit of not eating which he preached; he maintained that he had once come within an ace of practising it successfully on others. He had offered his services to the directors of a mining company as an adviser on scientific management, and the nature of his advice had made these businessmen take his offer seriously, in spite of the apparent irrelevance of his field of academic study. (This was Greek.) Professor Lutosławski had reported to these mine-owners that their miners were the worse for eating, and he had advised that the men would do much better if this bad habit of theirs could be reduced to vanishing-point. He had offered to take charge of the reducing process, and, at this, the directors had pricked up their ears. No food, no family budget; no family budget, no wages; if Professor Lutosławski's project came off, they might be able to get the work done for love; and then the miners' no longer necessary wages could be diverted to increase the profits of the shareholders. The directors gladly gave the professor a free hand; and, according to his story, he had trained the miners to subsist on one lettuce each *per diem* when the experiment inexplicably broke down. The miners now struck and relapsed into eating their habitual corned beef and potatoes.

At Wilno in 1928, Professor Lutosławski had tolerated my wife's and my habit of eating, but he had allowed us so little time to indulge it that we did not reach the theatre till after the play had begun. We were still able to buy tickets, but, when we went in, we saw that every seat in the auditorium was occupied. 'Follow me,' said the professor, and he led us straight to the middle of the front row of the dress circle. He then whispered in three people's ears, whereupon the three jumped up, ceded their seats to us, and withdrew, to stand at the back for the next five and a half hours. My wife and I felt some compunction. 'Please, what did you say to them?' we asked. 'What I said', the professor answered, 'was: "I, as you know, am Lutosławski and these are two English friends of mine. It is in the interests of the resurrected Polish people that foreigners should see and appreciate our cultural achievements, so I would like to have your two good seats for them and one for me too, since they will not be able to follow the play without my sitting with them to interpret for them." Of course', he added, 'they were delighted to be able to perform this service for their country.'

This incident revealed to us that Professor Lutosławski was a power in the land—or at least, a power among the Polish minority of the population of the city of Wilno. The majority of the population of this much-disputed city consisted of White Russians and Jews; but these two nationalities were not the rival claimants to sovereignty. The sovereignty over Wilno was in dispute between Poland and Lithuania. The city had been seized for Poland, after the close of the First World War, by the high-handed action of a Polish soldier, General Zeligowski. The general had successfully defied the Paris peace conference when it had ordered him to withdraw his troops and to respect the peace conference's right to decide Wilno's political destiny. This lawless Polish act had been one of the earliest indications that mankind had not yet been cured of its habit of resorting to violence and that therefore the First World War would probably not be the last. Meanwhile, the Polish Government had condoned the ostensibly free-lance Polish general's *fait accompli* by taking advantage of it. Poland had annexed Wilno in the teeth of opposition from the Soviet Union and from Lithuania.

Against the Soviet Union the Polish Government had recklessly used *force majeure* when in 1921 it was enjoying a military superiority that could only be ephemeral. Poland had imposed on the Soviet Union a peace-treaty that gave to Poland a belt of Ukrainian and White Russian territory in which Wilno was included; but Poland's hold on Wilno had remained precarious; for, in the Wilno sector, the belt of annexed non-Polish territory narrowed to a ribbon which barely insulated the Soviet Union from Lithuania by reaching up to touch Latvia on the River Dvina. As for Lithuania, she had refused to conclude a peace-treaty with Poland, and she remained implacable; for Wilno had been the capital of Lithuania at a time, now some six hundred years ago, when Lithuania had extended from the Baltic to the Black Sea. The Polono-Lithuanian armistice-line remained closed to traffic; in order to reach Kovno, Lithuania's provisional capital during the inter-war years, my wife and I had to travel up into Latvia and then down into Lithuania from this neutral stepping-stone; and at Kovno the Lithuanians' obsession with their lost historical capital kept thrusting itself on our attention at every turn. An example was the behaviour of the cash-register-machine in the Kovno railway-station restaurant. We had arrived in Kovno at Eastertide; though Lithuania is a Roman Catholic country, osmosis from Eastern Orthodox Christendom has keyed up the severity of the pre-Easter fast in Catholic Lithuania to a near-Orthodox pitch; from the eve of Good Friday to midday on Easter Sunday, 1928, no food or drink was served in the city, and we had to resort to the pagan railway-restaurant to get a cup of black coffee and a rusk. There, each time that the waitress pressed the keys of the cash-register-machine to make the price of our rusk and coffee bob up, the slogan 'Remember Vilnius' used to bob up side by side with the figures.

It will be seen that, in order to hold Wilno, Poland needed a valiant garrison; and Professor Lutosławski was a notable part of this. He was a host in himself; for, when he had moved in, Polish culture had moved in bodily in his person. His patriotic gesture was appreciated highly by his compatriots, and the three of them who had vacated seats for us in the theatre were paying their tribute to the patriot scholar. They must, of course, have been Poles. Had they been Lithuanians, they would not have budged. Moreover, Lithuanian residents in Wilno would not have countenanced the Polish occupation of the city by going to see a Polish play there.

Wincenty Lutosławski was a cultural asset to Poland because, in the world of Greek scholarship, he was world-famous. He had

been a pioneer in the search for an objective procedure for determining the chronological order of Plato's dialogues. Light on
this would bring with it an important advance in the understanding of Plato's philosophy; but Lutosławski's predecessors
had been baffled by the scantiness of the surviving information
on the subject. Lutosławski had been the first Platonic scholar to
hit upon the brilliant idea of looking at the 'internal' evidence. He
had made a minute examination of the whole corpus of Plato's
extant works from the stylistic standpoint. He had noted recurrent
mannerisms and tricks of style; had counted up the number of
occurrences of each and the number of times that any one of them
was associated with any other; and had calculated the respective
frequencies of each of these items in each of the dialogues. He
believed that his scrutiny had brought to light the successive
stages in the development of Plato's literary style; on the strength
of these indications, he had proposed a tentative chronological
order for the dialogues; and, though his findings could not claim
to be definitive, they had been received by his fellow Platonic
scholars with appreciation and gratitude.

Nowadays a man with a computer would be able to follow
up Lutosławski's pioneer work by tracing out a vastly greater
number of combinations and permutations of points of Plato's
style. He would just have to 'programme' the machine ('just' is
here the equivocal word), and this electronic Briarieus would do
the rest. Lutosławski, in his day, had to serve as his own computer,
and, in this kind of work, the 'do it yourself' method is laborious.
Foreign scholars who knew Lutosławski only through his publications are likely to have formed an erroneous mental picture of
what this painstaking Polish scholar was like. Probably they will
have pictured Lutosławski as being a dry-as-dust *Gelehrter* of a
German type, raised to the nth degree. The mistake would have
been natural, but, if Lutosławski had become aware that he was
being thought of as being Germanic, he would have been furious;
for Lutosławski was the most militant Germanophobe whom I
have ever met.

I once had an embarrassing first-hand experience of this phobia
of his. He was in London and had been having dinner with my

wife and me when an English friend of ours, Charles Siepmann, happened to look in. I introduced Siepmann to Lutosławski, and, at the German name, the Polish scholar's eyes flashed and he instantly opened fire: 'You Germans are boasting that you are going to get back the Polish territories that we re-took from you in the last war. Yes, indeed, there are going to be many more wars between you and us, and we Poles are going to suffer again each time, but each time in the end we shall take back more territory from you.' I tried to intervene, but I could not get a word in edge-wise. I could not make Lutosławski understand that he was firing his tirade at the wrong target. Charles Siepmann was as English as I was, and a further transfer of territory from Germany to Poland would not be his funeral any more than it would be mine—except, of course, in the not improbable event of another German-Polish war's rankling into another world war that might blow the rest of us, too, sky-high.

Every country in Europe has good citizens with foreign surnames, and these indicate that the bearer's family is of foreign origin, recent or remote. For instance, inter-war Poland's citizen Marshal Edward Smigly-Rydz bore a surname that appears to betray an English origin if one keeps the Polish pronunciation and uses the same Latin alphabet but spells the name with the letters that have the equivalent phonetic values in English that the spelling in Polish has. This reduces Smigly-Rydz to an ancestral Smiley-Ridge, but it does not make Smigly-Rydz any less of a Pole for that; and, if Smigly-Rydz had been told by Hitler that Germany was going to wipe out England, Smigly-Rydz would not have felt that his country's goose was being cooked, any more than the astonished Charles Siepmann felt that he had a stake in Germany's destiny. All this must really have been patent to Lutosławski while he was delivering his broadside; but he was not going to let himself be cheated out of this opportunity for indulging his Germanophobia by recognizing that Charles Siepmann was an Englishman after all.

Lutosławski was not merely a Germanophobe; he was a Polish messianist. He interpreted Deutero-Isaiah's 'suffering servant' as being a nation, not a human being; and he cast the Polish nation instead of Israel for this tragic collective role. In Lutosławski's apocalyptic vision the Polish nation had been destined to suffer for the sake of all mankind. This destiny gave the Poles the key-role in world-history. However much suffering that might cost them, Lutosławski was prepared to see them pay the price.

In this point, Lutosławski may have been an accurate exponent of his countrymen's outlook. At least, this is suggested by an experience of Lawrence Hammond's when he was in Paris in 1919 as the *Manchester Guardian*'s special correspondent for the peace conference. During the conference, Lawrence had a number of meetings with the Polish delegates to ascertain their aims and to discuss these with them. The Poles and Lawrence did not always see eye to eye; and, after a time, one of the delegates said to him: 'The fact is, Mr. Hammond, that you and we look at things quite differently. We have now realized that, for you, the paramount concern is to make a peace-settlement that will not sow the seeds of another war. For you, this last war has been a catastrophe, and you want, above all else, to preclude a repetition of it. But we Poles do not look at things like that at all. For us, war is just one of the permanent facts of life; so our paramount concern is not the avoidance of future wars; we assume that there will be as many wars in the future as there have been in the past. Our paramount concern is to get as much as we can for our country now, whatever the future may hold in store.' I feel sure that Professor Lutosławski would have endorsed this exposition of the Polish attitude if he had been present.

I have mentioned that, on the day on which I first met Professor Lutosławski, he practised what he preached. On that occasion, he was practising the doctrine that it is better not to eat. There was also an occasion on which he made a move to apply to himself his doctrine of Polish messianism; but in this case he was foiled by Gilbert Murray. On Murray's part, this was an act of legitimate self-defence; for Lutosławski's design required that Murray should become involved in it. As I heard the story from Murray himself, he once received a letter from Lutosławski that threatened to put Murray in a quandary. Everyone, Lutosławski wrote, needs to be crucified once in his lifetime; he, Lutosławski, was now feeling that his time for being crucified had arrived; he had just read the announcement that the chair of Greek in one of the northern English universities (which he named) had fallen vacant; he believed that this post would be the appropriate crucifixion for him; so he would be obliged if Murray would kindly write a letter of recommendation to the university authorities in support of his, Lutosławski's, candidature. After reflection, Murray wrote back that, in his opinion, the crucifixion that would be afforded by this post would not come up to Lutosławski's specifications. (Murray could say this with his hand on his heart; for the university in question was a distinguished one.) Murray therefore advised Lutosławski to give up the idea of standing for this particular chair and to look for a more adequate crucifixion in some other quarter. To Murray's relief, Lutosławski desisted.

The chair which Lutosławski had held before the liberation and re-unification of Poland had been in what was then Austrian territory. I have no record of the exact place. This may have been Cracow, but, if it was Lvov, that would have been more in character; for Lutosławski liked to garrison Poland's outposts, as his subsequent settlement at Wilno shows. Wherever his professorial chair under Austrian rule may have been located, his Polish patriotism got him into political trouble at this stage of his career. In a course of lectures that he was giving on Dante, the Polish question would keep breaking in. Time and again, Lutosławski would start his lecture with the intention of talking about Dante and would then find himself talking about the Polish question before he had reached the end of his academic hour; and, each time, the change of subject would come at an earlier point. After this had happened to Lutosławski several times, he noticed that his audience had been reinforced by three newcomers. These were conspicuous, because they sat together in the front row; they were all wearing top-hats; and they were taking notes diligently. Their identity was soon revealed. They were alienists, and they had been commissioned by a paternal Austrian Government to verify a rumour that the gifted professor's mind was wandering alarmingly. Lutosławski's genius was a precious asset to the world, and the authorities' conscience would not allow them to stand idly by when the genius was in evident danger of suffering an eclipse. The alienists now considerately removed the professor from his lecture-room to an asylum in order to give him a long course of remedial treatment. The story does not tell how Lutosławski managed to extricate himself. We may perhaps guess that the alienists were eventually able to report to the Austrian authorities that he was unlikely to confuse Dante with the Polish question again if he were to be liberated.

This was an elegant way of choking off the public expression of national aspirations that were incompatible with the integrity of the bundle of kingdoms and lands that were represented in the Reichsrath at Vienna; but then the professor's way of promoting Polish nationalism had been elegant likewise. In this case, the conflict between the Habsburg Monarchy and a restive nationality was conducted on both sides by the soft-handed technique of Chinese boxing. The Monarchy's methods of maintaining its authority were not always so gentle. The Lombard city of Brescia has not forgotten her *Dieci Giornate* of desperate resistance to being re-subjugated; and at Schönbrünn in 1937 the walls of the palace's state-rooms were still covered with bloodthirsty pictures of the repression of the Magyars' abortive war of independence in 1848–9. I asked whether these pictures had not made Magyar magnates bristle when, after the conclusion of the *Ausgleich* of 1867, they had taken to calling at Schönbrünn to pay their respects to the King-Emperor. The answer was that these tactless reminders of an unhappy past passage of Austro-Hungarian history had indeed given considerable offence, but that Franz-Josef had refused to spare his Magyar visitors' susceptibilities. He had had those lurid pictures painted specially for his delectation, and he was entirely unwilling to part with them.

Professor Lutosławski was much in my thoughts after the outbreak of the Second World War, when inter-war Poland's three hostile neighbours paid off old scores at last by partitioning Poland again—the fifth partition that Poland had undergone so far. Wilno now became Lithuania's capital again. The Russians occupied Wilno and handed it over to the Lithuanians, but the Russians did not lose hold of Wilno in effect, since they annexed

Lithuania itself to the Soviet Union. A son of Professor Luto-sławski's was in England at the time, but he knew no more than I knew about his father's fate. There are, however, two things of which one can be sure. As a Polish messianist, Professor Luto-sławski will not have been surprised at seeing Poland once again suffer martyrdom. He will not have been surprised, nor will he have been dismayed. His faith in Poland's messianic destiny was invincible.

21
Bonn in Nazi-time

BY the year 1930 my son Tony seemed to have come to a dead end in his classical division at Winchester. Unfortunately for him and for the other men in the division, their 'div don' was a 'dug-out'. After having already retired before the outbreak of war in August 1914, he had come back to hold the fort for a younger don who had gone to the war, and he had then stayed on into the post-war years. (Too many of the Winchester dons had been killed to allow their 'dug-out' *remplaçants* to be dispensed with yet.) I had pointed out to the higher authorities that Tony's dug-out div don was sickening him of the classics; but I had received no satisfaction. 'Mr. X', was the answer, 'has sickened many boys of the classics before your son, and, no doubt, he will sicken many more before he retires for the second time; and that is that.'

Not reconciling myself to seeing Tony's intellectual promise finally blighted, I now suggested to the authorities that they should transfer him to the parallel modern-side division. 'Happy thought,' the authorities replied, to my relief. 'We will do that.' They did transfer Tony, and it turned out better than I could have hoped. Tony's new div don, Mr. Donald McLachlan, was still young, and he was, and is, a live wire. At the time, he was commuting between Winchester and Germany, sandwiching tours of teaching German at Winchester between tours in Germany as special correspondent of *The Times*. He was as good a teacher as he was a journalist, and he quickly brought Tony back to intellectual life again. Tony was a born linguist, and, now that he was getting first-rate teaching in a living language, he was responding with zest and with credit. However, he could not stay in Mr. McLachlan's division till his time at Winchester ran out, and I did not care to risk his falling into the hands of a dug-out again; so I decided to bank on his now proven gift and appetite for German, and to give him an immediate opportunity for following this up.

To take a boy away from an English public school a year before he is due to leave is a serious decision. It means switching him off the rails of a conventional English middle-class higher education, with the likelihood that he will not be able to find his way back on to them. I must not do that without having found, for Tony, an equally good alternative. I now remembered Tony's great-great-uncle George Toynbee, who, in 1833, had gone from the farm in the Lincolnshire fens to the University of Bonn. George Toynbee's experiences at Bonn were familiar to me, since my sister possessed a copy of the journal that he had written while he had been a student there. George Toynbee had found the University of Bonn stimulating, and his judgement was good evidence; he was an uncommonly able man. What about Bonn for George Toynbee's great-great-nephew? Tony liked the idea, and we acted on it. Tony went first to Weber, an Englishman in Bonn who gave intensive coaching in German to English boys. He then went on to the university. So, after an interval of just a century, a Toynbee was enrolled as a student at Bonn once again; and, for Tony too, the experiment turned out well. At Bonn Tony's linguistic gift broke into flower. His command of German became almost perfect. It used to please him when Rhinelanders asked him what district of Germany he came from; and he thought it perceptive if he was told that he spoke German with a Russian accent; for he was also an eager student of Slavonic languages. Before his short life ended, he was teaching himself Mongol and had made a beginning with the Chinese characters.

The University of Bonn had been founded in the seventeen-eighties by one of the last in the series of prince-bishop electors of Cologne. The founder had been exceptional in his public-spirited concern for higher education. The Electorate of Cologne had come to be a preserve for younger sons, or members of cadet

branches, of the Bavarian ducal dynasty; and most of them seem
to have treated their office as a personal perquisite. Their record
as princes had not been any more edifying than their record as
prelates. Bonn had been their seat, though Cologne was their see.
They had moved from Cologne to Bonn long ago. Cologne,
with its aspirations to civic self-government, had been uncongenial
to its prince-bishops. On occasions it had even been too hot to
hold them. The prince who founded the University of Bonn had
installed it in a large palace of his there. (This sounds more generous than it perhaps really was. The Elector of Cologne had
palaces to spare. If he had alienated or forfeited all the rest, he
could still have lived in luxury in his palace at Brühl, on the
Rhine between Bonn and Cologne. The palace at Brühl is small,
but it is a gem. Pay a visit to it if you are curious to see the lengths
to which the rococo style can be carried.)

The Bavarian founder of the University of Bonn had been
'working for the King of Prussia' without knowing it. In the
European peace-settlement of 1814-15, the myriad statelets of
the Rhineland and Westphalia had been consolidated into a Prussian new dominion. The previous mosaic had been easy for
French invaders of Germany to break through; the new block of
Prussian granite might perhaps prove a more effective barrier.
As things turned out, this granite's grain was never put to the
test; for, in 1870, the invaders were not the French but the Prussians. Yet the memories of French aggression died hard. I have
inherited from my great-uncle Harry a copy of the war-map
published by *The Times* when the Franco-Prussian War of 1870–
1871 broke out. On this map, which is printed mostly in black,
the region presumed by the compiler to be the coming war-zone
is picked out in flaming red. This conspicuous red patch does not
include Sédan or Paris or, indeed, a single square yard of French
territory. It coincides with the boundaries of the Prussian Rhineland, which, in this war, was to see no fighting.

When the Prussians had acquired the Rhineland in 1814–15,
they had taken over the University of Bonn with the rest of the
territory's public property and institutions. They had taken the
University over and had developed it—and this both academically

and politically. Academically, they had raised it to the high level of intellectual distinction at which it stood in George Toynbee's time, and in Tony Toynbee's too. Politically, they had made this Catholic prince-bishop's foundation into a stronghold for a Protestant ascendancy. The University of Bonn had become a fashionable resort for Prussian aristocrats, and the aristocratic Korps there (Korps were more or less equivalent to the American universities' fraternity houses) were among the most sought-after, and the most exclusive, of all university Korps in Germany. (Tony, who had taken to rowing at Winchester, joined, at the university, a rowing-club, the *Rhenus*.)

At the University of Bonn, the Nazi did at least one good deed after they had come into power. They organized new, unsnobbish, fraternities for that large majority of the students who had hitherto been left out in the cold. (The members of the Korps had taken care to make these outsiders feel that they were second-class citizens.) These new democratic fraternity houses at Bonn were the only places in the Rhineland in which I ever came across any enthusiasm for National Socialism. The Nazi's recognition of the ordinary students' human rights had been shrewd, as well as genuinely humane. The newly enfranchised students were heartily grateful to the first régime in Germany's history that had thought of doing something for them.

In 1933, when Tony became a student at the University, the barbaric ritual of duelling was still being kept up there. It was confined to a small group of students—those who, besides being aristocrats, were Protestants. For Catholic students, duelling was banned by their ecclesiastical authorities. It was the Protestants who were the barbarians; but, in the Rhineland and Westphalia since 1815, the Protestants had been top dog. The relation between the two communities reminded me of the relation between them in Eire before the liquidation of the Protestant ascendancy there. There was a Protestant ascendancy in the Rhineland and Westphalia too, though, measured by Irish standards, the régime in these two Prussian provinces was mild. All the same, at Bonn, the tension between Protestants and Catholics lasted on into the Nazi Era.

At some date after Hitler had come into power, I found myself in Bonn on Corpus Christi Day. I stood watching the long procession that issued from the Domkirche and eventually returned to it after parading through the town. A man standing next to me, noticing that I was a foreigner and was therefore presumably not a Nazi spy, ventured to whisper to me that these were the Catholic religious fraternities, and that, though officially they had been *gleichgeschaltet*, they were marching (of course, without their emblems) nevertheless. Later, that day, I mentioned this conversation, as a point of interest, to a Protestant resident in Bonn who was an acquaintance of mine. As I knew that he was a strong anti-Nazi, I had expected him to approve of the Catholic fraternities for being irrepressible. But, no, for him, even in the Nazi Era, the Catholic community was still his enemy Number One. 'On this day', he said coldly, 'we Protestants in Bonn stay at home behind closed doors.' Happily the leaders of the German Protestant churches were not so fanatical as this particular member of their flock. By that time, the Protestant and Catholic ecclesiastical authorities, finding themselves with their backs to the same wall, were already beginning to co-operate in trying to uphold, against Nazi neo-paganism, the traditional principles of their common Christianity.

The Nazi régime clamped down on Germany before the end of Tony's first year as a student at Bonn. Meanwhile, I, as well as he, had got to know a number of the professors, and we now watched, with sympathy and awe, their behaviour under an ordeal that, in England, we had not had to face—at any rate, not since 'the Glorious Revolution' of 1688.

The professors whom I got to know best were Fritz Kern (modern history), von Beckerath (economics), Ernst Robert Curtius (a world-famous scholar in medieval European literature), Hübener (English), Levison (the leading Germanist of his time), and Kahle (oriental studies). From the first moment of the Nazi Era, all professors, in all German universities, found themselves under pressure. The Nazi hated intellectuals, and they persecuted them with the vindictiveness that Senator McCarthy afterwards displayed in his persecution of American 'egg-heads'. Like

McCarthy, the Nazi suspected, not without some reason, that intellectual prowess was apt to breed liberal opinions.

One of the first defence-measures that the Bonn professors took was to secure the appointment of a Rektor who would be qualified, so far as any man could be, for coping with the appalling new situation that they suddenly had to face. In Prussia, when Prussia was still on the map, the Rektor of a university was not the elected representative of the professors; he was appointed by the Prussian Ministry of Education as the Ministry's representative at the university. In practice, however, the appointment of a Rektor was made in consultation with the professors of the university in question; and, in the Nazi emergency, the Bonn professors secured the appointment of a Rektor who, in his political views, was far enough to the right not to be in danger of being *persona non grata* to the new régime, yet whose paramount loyalty was to the University, irrespective of the political opinions of his colleagues.

I am sure that the new Rektor loyally did his best, but no one could save the professors now from being led a dog's life. They were humiliated by being required to give the Nazi salute at the beginning and the end of a lecture; they were made ridiculous by being compelled to perform Nazi antics; and they were in constant danger of losing their jobs to ambitious Privatdozenten— some of whom, to their shame, would make a show of zeal for the Party in the hope that, one day, they would be rewarded by being given the chair of some professor who had made a false step.

The only one of my friends at Bonn who managed to hold his ground till after the Nazi régime had been liquidated was Curtius; and Curtius was already a marked man by the time when Hitler came into power. Only the year before, he had published a book with the title *Deutsche Geist in Gefahr*. His opinion of the Nazi was thus on record; and he continued, from first to last, to say openly exactly what he thought. Why did the Nazi leave Curtius alone? Perhaps for the reason for which Tolstoy was left alone by the Russian régime of Tolstoy's day. The most tyrannous régimes sometimes forgo the satisfaction of making martyrs of opponents who have a world-wide reputation, on the ground that this self-indulgence would not be worth its price in odium. Yet the Nazi did not hesitate to get rid of Einstein, and Einstein, whom pre-Nazi Germany had treated with honour, was a still more eminent public figure than Curtius was. Einstein was, of course, a Jew, and Curtius was not. Anyway, Curtius's survival gives ground for the Spartans' belief that, in battle, courage is the most effective of all life-preservers.

When Einstein had had to leave the country that had once invited him to make it his home (Einstein's original home had been, not Germany, but Switzerland), he had found a temporary home at Christ Church, Oxford, before he moved on to his final home at the Institute for Advanced Study in Princeton, New Jersey. Gilbert Murray, too, was at home in Christ Church. As Regius Professor of Greek, he was attached to Christ Church *ex officio*. Entering Tom Quad one day, Murray caught sight of Einstein sitting there with a far-away look on his face. The far-away thought behind that far-away look was evidently a happy one, for, at that moment, the exile's countenance was serene and smiling. 'Dr. Einstein, do tell me what you are thinking,' Murray said. 'I am thinking', Einstein answered, 'that, after all, this is a very small star.' All the Universe's eggs were not in this basket that was now infested by the Nazi; and, for a cosmogoner, this thought was convincingly consoling.

Levison received two official letters by the same post one day. The first was a personal letter from Hitler, thanking him for his life-long service to German scholarship; the second was a letter from the Ministry, dismissing him from his chair for being a Jew. Levison was as popular as he was learned, and this shameful treatment of him nearly provoked a riot among his students.

Von Beckerath, too, had no use for the Nazi. He was a Rhineland Mennonite. He relieved his feelings by trailing his coat. For instance, when he said 'good-bye' at the end of a telephone conversation, he made a point of always adding: 'And good-bye to you, too, Mr. Spy, who have been listening in.' No doubt this stock sally of von Beckerath's was promptly reported each time to the local Nazi control, to aggravate the count against him. Prudently, von Beckerath did not wait for the reckoning. When, rather to his surprise, he received sanction for accepting an invitation, from one of the distinguished universities of North Carolina, to spend a semester on its campus, he went and never came back. They appointed him to a permanent chair, and he married an American wife.

Germany's loss of von Beckerath was America's gain—one of the many gains of refugee scholars that America had been making since she had opened her arms to the White Russian scholars after the Bolsheviks had seized power in Russia in 1917. America has not only been charitable and hospitable to refugee foreign scholars; she has been generous to them. American university faculties have appointed refugees, over their own heads, to the highest academic posts. It is all very well to say that these appointments were no more than a fitting recognition of the refugee's intellectual eminence. In making the appointments, the native-born American academic community was showing self-denial and public spirit. The only parallel that I know of is the appointment of refugee republican Spanish scholars to a number of chairs in the University of Mexico. I do know, though, of one case in which Senator McCarthy has given a European university an opportunity to reciprocate. An old friend of mine, who had been one of McCarthy's victims, had been vindicated without ceasing to be made to suffer socially from the effects of the outrageous 'smear' on his reputation. He has now been made a happy man again thanks to his having been appointed to a chair in a British university in the field in which he has made his name.

Like von Beckerath, Hübener got away before it was too late. He found a new post in the Maritime Provinces of Canada—no equivalent of Bonn academically, but in Canada he could once again breathe free air. Hübener's assistant at Bonn, a New Zealander, went to Canada with him, and they married there.

Kern reacted to Nazidom by playing a more dangerous game. He had a streak of waywardness and mischief in him. He organized an anti-Nazi secret society—'the Bridge Club'. Tony belonged (as a foreign student, he could compromise himself without much danger). So did Tony's bosom friend at the University, Markov; and, for Markov, the risk was much greater. Markov

was a Slovene by origin, but he enjoyed the status of an Auslands-
deutscher, and he was drawing a government scholarship on the
strength of this. When (this did not happen till after Tony had
left Bonn) 'the Bridge Club' was detected, Kern got away to
Switzerland, but Markov landed in prison. We could do nothing
for him, and we gave him up for lost. Indeed, my other German
friends who found their way into Nazi prisons were all eventually
done to death. Bernstorff, an ex-member of the German foreign
service, and Kuenzer, at one time editor of *Germania*, were both
shot, out of spite, in the last days of the Second World War, when
the Nazi knew that they themselves were doomed. Markov,
however, did survive, 'red' though he was. The next time that I
met him was at Rome in 1955, at a meeting of the International
Congress of the Historical Sciences. By that time, Markov was
in a high position in the administration of the universities of
Eastern Germany. He has lived to be a married man and the father
of a family. His survival is a greater miracle than Curtius's
survival was.

Kuenzer, like Kern, was rash. He went boldly to meet trouble
rather more than half way. So long as he lived, he never once gave
the Nazi salute, and, if one was having dinner with him and his
wife in their house in Berlin, he would entertain his guests with a
perilous practical joke. Towards the end of the meal, one was
startled suddenly to see Hitler glide across the far end of the room
giving a dozen Nazi salutes as he went by. This was a servant of
Kuenzer's who was the image of Hitler when he put on an Hitlerian false moustache. The performance was amusing, but it was
unwise, even though one could be sure that the guests at the
Kuenzers' table were anti-Hitlerites to a man.

Anti-Hitlerites, yes; but that did not necessarily mean that
they were democrats, humanitarians, and anti-militarists. At one
of Kuenzer's dinner-parties, we were discussing whether, if Hitler
were to make a second world war, Germany would have any
chance of winning it. We had agreed that she would not, when
one old man broke in: 'Of course, if I thought that Germany did
have a chance of winning, I would give a son.' 'Oh, yes, of course,
so would I,' said another. Give a son! They meant: give a son's

life. A citizen of a defeated France or Britain or United States might perhaps have said: 'I would risk my skin.' If he had contemplated giving a life, it would have been his own, not someone else's, and it would have been unthinkable that he should offer up his child. Human sacrifice! Moloch! Mesha slaying his son on the city-wall, and Manasseh passing his son through the fire! A great gulf yawned open between me and those hitherto apparently *bien pensant* guests of Kuenzer's.

My last meeting with Kuenzer was in June 1939. He had come to England, and up to Yorkshire, where I was living at the time, to beg me to induce Mr. Chamberlain and Lord Halifax to talk to Hitler rudely. 'I know the English,' Kuenzer said, 'so I know that, when they say a little, they mean a lot. But the Nazi do not know the English; so, when your English statesmen speak the muted language of English gentlemen, the Nazi infer that these soft-spoken fellows do not really mean business. If your leaders do go on talking like gentlemen, the last chance of deterring Hitler from going to war will vanish. Do please put the point to the Prime Minister and the Foreign Secretary.' The point was a pertinent one, but what could I do? I did not have the *entrée* to Downing Street; and, even if I had succeeded in intruding on Halifax and Chamberlain and in convincing them, they would have been psychologically incapable of acting on Kuenzer's good advice. When they had opened their mouths with intent to talk Billingsgate, nothing but the same old gentlemanly under-statements would, or could, have passed their lips. This was the only language that they knew how to speak. Like Lord Grey and Lloyd George, they were no linguists.

Poor Kuenzer: this last mission of his was a forlorn hope. Besides world peace, Kuenzer's own life was at stake in this throw; and Kuenzer lost.

Kahle's reaction to Nazidom was the most remarkable. When I had met him first a few months before Hitler's take-over, Kahle had reminded me of Carlyle's Professor Teufelsdröckh in *Sartor Resartus*. Intellectually omnivorous, he was utterly absorbed in whatever he might be working on at the moment, and he appeared to be a replica in real life of the legendary German professor. You would have judged him to be totally oblivious of politics.

For instance, in the early months of 1933, when the Nazi hurricane was fast brewing up, Professor Kahle could think and talk of nothing but a recently discovered Turkish copy of what will have been one of the earliest Spanish maps of the New World. (The Spanish original must have been captured by the Turks and have been lost, and this was what made the Turkish copy so interesting.) This map did indeed suggest some intriguing reflections. The Turks had taken the trouble, not only to copy the map, but to transliterate the names on it into the Arabic alphabet. This indicated a Turkish interest, unsuspected hitherto, in Columbus's Transatlantic discoveries. Well, suppose that the Turks had occupied Algeria in 1490 instead of in 1525. By 1490 it was already well within their power to do what they did, in fact, do thirty-five years later. In that event, the Muslim Kingdom of Granada might not have been conquered and annexed by the recently united Christian kingdoms of Castile and Aragon; instead, it might have become an Ottoman protectorate, as the Tatar Khanate of Krim did; and, then—who knows?—Andalucía, too, might have been reconquered for Islam, and the Ottoman flag might have flown over Palos, the port from which, as things actually turned out, Columbus sailed on the voyage that carried him to Hispaniola. In this hypothetical constellation of international affairs in the Western basin of the Mediterranean, would Columbus ever have addressed himself to their Catholic Majesties? Would not the obvious patron for him to cultivate have been the Padishah? And then, if Columbus had sailed for the Indies under Ottoman auspices, would not the New World be a Muslim world at the present day?

Plunged deep in exciting thought about this suggestive early sixteenth-century Turkish map, Professor Kahle was taken off his guard by the major event of the year 1933. But the new régime in Germany quickly made him aware of politics and drove him, in self-defence, to become a politician himself. He proved to have a talent for this art too.

While Kahle had been keeping one eye on his Turkish map,

his other eye had been trained on a definitive edition of the Hebrew text of the Torah, which he was preparing with the help of a first-rate Hebrew scholar who happened, not surprisingly, to be a Jew. Before Kahle knew where he was, the Nazi had dismissed his Jewish assistant and had substituted an Aryan one who, according to Kahle, was good for nothing beyond tying up brown-paper parcels. I found Kahle in a gloomy mood. His darling edition of the Torah was now in jeopardy; and this stirred him to take action. He made an expedition to the Ministry in Berlin and represented that it was essential, for Germany's prestige, that the definitive edition of the Torah should be a German one. Now that the Nazi had dismissed Kahle's assistant, the Americans would get in first, and then Germany's prestige would slump. The official to whom Kahle was telling the tale wrung his hands. 'You are right,' he said; 'it is dreadful. But what can I do?' 'I will tell you exactly what you can do,' Kahle replied. 'You can send the money that you have been paying for my assistant's salary to the Stuttgart Bible Society, and ask no further questions.' On my next visit to Bonn, Kahle's unwanted Aryan assistant had faded away; his former Jewish assistant was back again on the job; and he was drawing his previous salary by a sure, though circuitous, route. The Bonn edition of the Hebrew Torah was now almost ready to be printed off, so it was time for Kahle to visit the Ministry in Berlin again. 'The prestige of Germany', he lectured them, 'requires that the edition of this monument of German scholarship shall be a very large one.' The Ministry gave him two truck-loads of the best paper.

As a match for the Nazi, Kahle might have been unique if he had not been surpassed by the youngest of his five sons. (All five boys were remarkable, but the fifth of them was one in a thousand.) At about this time, the Kahles moved house in Bonn, and, among the junk left in the attic by the previous occupants, the boys found four signed photographs of the ex-Kaiser. Naturally the four eldest boys each claimed one; there was none left over for their little brother; and he took this hard. Accordingly, one day at breakfast, not long afterwards, a parcel appeared on his place, and this, on being opened, was found to have a signed photograph of the Kaiser in it. 'Goodness gracious, child,' his parents exclaimed, 'whatever did you do?' 'Do? Why, I wrote to the Kaiser at Doorn. I wrote: "We have just moved house and, in our new house, we found four signed photographs of you, and my four elder brothers got the four, and there wasn't one left over for me. Wasn't that hard? Won't you send me one for myself?" Well, you see, the Kaiser has sent it.' 'Well, anyway,' the parents admonished him rather lamely, 'be sure never to do anything like that again.' However, a few weeks later (this is a true story), another parcel arrived for the Kahles' youngest son and another signed photograph emerged from it. This time it was a photograph of Göring, and the parents were horrified. 'What *did* you do?' 'Why, this time it was quite simple. I just wrote to Göring: "The Kaiser has sent me a signed photograph of himself. Won't you send me one too?" You see, it worked.'

It was not long before the Kahle parents had reason to be thankful for the sharpness of their youngest son's wits. A Jewish professor (it may have been Levison) had just been dismissed, and Frau Kahle had called on the dismissed professor's wife to condole with her. After that, she and her husband had to make tracks for the Belgian frontier *quam celerrime*. They dared not wait to collect the boys from school. Their promptness in getting away had saved them, but the boys were stranded. How could the family manage to reunite? The British consul in Cologne tried to get the boys exit-visas, but he got nowhere, and then the youngest boy took command. He bluffed himself and his brothers through all the Nazi frontier controls and piloted them into Belgium without a hitch. (It strikes me now that, at this point, the signed photograph of Göring might have come in handy, but this is just a guess; I have no information.)

The boy was worthy of his father. Though the professor had reached England alive, he was deprived of all his books and papers, which, for a scholar, is even worse than being penniless. He rose magnificently to this desperate occasion.

The Kahle family's story had a relatively happy ending, but the University of Bonn in Nazi-time also had its tragedies. My last visit to Bonn before the Second World War was in 1937.

Knowing what was coming, I wanted to see—it might be for the last time—those of my friends who were still there. Rather to my surprise, each of them in turn made a point of telling me that I must be sure to meet the professor of geography. I was puzzled, because this particular professor was not one of my old acquaintances. However, these quickly arranged a tea-party; the professor of geography was there, and he gave me a copy of his latest book. After the party had broken up and the professor of geography had left the room, the reason for his having been introduced to me was revealed. 'You see,' they said to me, 'he is a very unfortunate man. His wife is Jewish; he has been given the choice between divorcing her and losing his chair; and he is not going to divorce her.' What they were conveying was : 'Please do what you can for him if he and his wife turn up in England.' (In the event, they made their way to America.) The Nazi surely broke mankind's previous record for meanness.

22

A Lecture by Hitler

I HAD been invited to give a talk to the Nazi Law Society at its next meeting, which was to be held in Berlin in February 1936. I had accepted this invitation, and had been reproached for this by my old friend Charles Webster. In accepting, I was condoning the Nazi's atrocities, he had said. I had defended my acceptance by pointing out that to study the Nazi was an important part of my job at Chatham House. How could I study them without meeting them? And I could not meet them without entering into human relations with them to some extent. Anyway, I had accepted and I kept the engagement.

Of course, on this visit to Berlin, I was not intending to meet the Nazi exclusively. When one is studying a house that is divided against itself, as Germany was at the time, *Audi alteram partem* is a binding precept. Accordingly, I arrived in Berlin— *incognito*, so I supposed—a week before the date at which my official visit was to start; and I spent this preliminary week on meeting members of the anti-Nazi opposition: the Catholic bishop of Berlin, for instance, and my old friend Kuenzer. After that, on the appointed day, I presented myself, as if I had just come off the train, at the office of Fritz Berber, the assistant of Ribbentrop's who had originally conveyed the Law Society's invitation to me, and with whom I had been in correspondence about it since. Before I had had time to utter a word, Berber said to me quietly: 'Herr von Ribbentrop knows exactly whom you have been seeing during this last week, and he is not at all pleased.' After a pause, Berber added, still more softly: 'Though you did not arrive in Berlin this morning, I did. I had guessed what you might be going to do, so I took care to be away in Hamburg till now.'

Berber was something of a mystery man for me. He was (and continued to be) a Quaker. (He had been converted, after the First World War, by British members of the Society of Friends who had been doing post-war relief-work in Germany.) At the time of Hitler's take-over, Berber had been secretary of the Berlin *Hochschule für Politik*. This had been a German counter-part of the Paris *École Libre des Sciences Politiques* and of the London School of Economics and Political Science. Like these sister-insti-tutions, the *Hochschule* had been a stronghold of liberalism, and, as such, it had been marked out for destruction by the Nazi. As soon as they had come into power, they had turned their batteries on the *Hochschule*. All the members of the teaching staff had been dismissed; some of them had had to flee the country. Berber alone had survived. By February 1936 he had not only become Ribben-trop's draftsman for writing Ribbentrop's speeches for him. He had also become head of an institute for the study of inter-national affairs in the Thurn und Taxis building in Hamburg. During the Weimar régime, the director of this Hamburg In-stitute had been Mendelssohn-Bartholdy. Now the Hamburg In-stitute had been Nazified; the ex-director was in exile; and Berber had succeeded him. Thus Berber was holding down two impor-tant jobs in the Nazi régime. 'Holding down' is the right word. Berber once told me that, when he had to lecture at Hamburg on controversial current affairs, he managed it by constructing his lectures entirely out of a cento of quotations from Hitler's books and speeches. Broken up and re-combined, Hitler's words might be made to render different meanings from those that they had borne in their original context. Never mind. Berber's use—or misuse—of the Führer's utterances could never be criticized by Nazi who doubted Berber's loyalty or who merely coveted his job. To challenge *Führerwörter*, even out of context, would be a risk that no one in Germany would care, at that time, to take. Berber had foreseen this, and he had calculated on it.

Berber was sly, and he was double-faced; for, in talking with me, he would pass judgements on Hitler and on National Socialism that were identical with mine. These strictures must, I think, have represented Berber's real views and feelings, for he had nothing to gain by communicating them to me, and, though he could be virtually sure that I would not give him away to the Nazi, it was strange that so circumspect a player of so hazardous a game should take even the slightest additional risk unnecessarily. What were the motives that led Berber to act as he did in his respective relations with his Nazi employers, to whom he was making himself so useful, and with me? Logic might convict him of being a time-server and a hypocrite. Yet I believe that he was sincere, though I am unable to guarantee that he was not self-deceived to some extent, since I am unable to explain how he can have justified his ambiguous behaviour to his own mind, which was a highly intelligent mind, and, still more, to his own conscience, which was, or had been, a Quaker one.

On the morning on which Berber had told me of Ribbentrop's cognizance of my meetings with members of the opposition to the Nazi régime, he had a far greater surprise for me up his sleeve. After another pause, he said to me, in the same flat voice as before: 'You are going to see Hitler.' This was news indeed, and it excited me. I was now going to have an unexpected chance of studying the National Socialist movement at its source. I was also puzzled. What use could Hitler have imagined it to be to him to spend time on seeing me? Why did he think this worth while? And this after I had just been incurring his henchman Ribbentrop's disapproval? Berber kept a poker-face and left me guessing. He was not going to give me the explanation till after the interview was over.

I was to have my audience with Hitler in the Chancery in the Wilhelmstrasse. (The date was just a week before Hitler's military re-occupation of the Rhineland.) I arrived with Berber at the appointed hour and we were shown upstairs into a room in which we found Ribbentrop, Neurath, Dieckhoff, and Hitler's interpreter, Schmidt, already assembled. The first three were the principal foreign affairs authorities in Hitler's set-up at the time. Hans Dieckhoff was a civil servant. He was now permanent undersecretary of state at the Aussenamt. Neurath (a respectable conservative) was Hitler's foreign minister. Ribbentrop was Hitler's ambassador at large. Dieckhoff was an old friend of mine; and I had met Ribbentrop, too, a number of times already. (Dieckhoff's and Ribbentrop's wives were sisters; they were Swiss.) The presence of these three men indicated that the occasion was being taken seriously.

Hitler entered promptly after Berber and me, made the Hitler salute, but then held out his hand for me to shake so quickly that I had no time to be embarrassed by not knowing what the proper reply was to a Hitler salute from Hitler himself. This gesture of Hitler's was tactful, and, from the start, it was clear to me that Hitler was taking pains to make an agreeable impression on me. Why?

Should I be needing Dr. Schmidt's services? I declined them. A translation would halve the effective time of the conversation (if it was to be a conversation), and it would set up a psychological barrier. By this time I could understand and speak German just well enough to venture to take a chance on talking with Hitler direct. As it turned out, understanding German (which is the easier part of the mastery of a foreign language) was a good deal more important than speaking it (which is more difficult).

Hitler then led off. 'Why are you so friendly with Russia?' ('You': he addressed me, throughout, as if I were either His Britannic Majesty's Government or an epitome of the electorate of the United Kingdom.) Hitler did not expect me to try to answer this question of his. He was going to answer it himself. 'I know why. It is because you are afraid of Japan. But, if you need a friend to help you against Japan, why should your friend be Russia? Why should not I be the friend that you need? Of course, if I was to be your friend in need, you would have to give me back my colonies. But, if you had given me back my colonies, and you then had trouble with Japan, I would give you six divisions and some warships at Singapore.' (The preciseness of the figure 'six' made a mark on my memory; and, when Singapore fell in 1941, I noticed, with interest, that the Japanese army that had captured the base was reported to have been six divisions strong. Was this recurrence of Hitler's figure just a coincidence? I think not. I guess that Hitler had ascertained from his military advisers what was the maximum number of divisions that could operate simultaneously at the tip of the Malay Peninsula.)

This headlong plunge into a question of contemporary power politics proved to be only a preamble. What followed was a lecture on an historical topic: Germany's role, through the ages, as the guardian of the eastern gate of the Western World against the Yellow Peril. Hitler began in the sixth century with the repelling of the Avars by the Merovingians. The Avars may, perhaps, have been yellow; they had issued out of the depths of Central Asia; but it soon became apparent that, in Hitler's résumé of world-history, the protagonist in the 'yellow' role was to be Russia. The Communist régime in Russia might not, perhaps, have repudiated the part for which Hitler was casting Russia. Had it not been Lenin's declared policy to bring Communism and anti-colonialism together into a world-wide united front against the capitalist and imperialist West? And did not this require Russia to assume the leadership of the yellow, brown, and black majority of the human race? Stalin might have acquiesced in the colour that Hitler was painting him. But what would Mao have said? And what would Mao say today, when he is stripping his Russian colleagues of their war-paint in order to reveal the tell-tale Americanoid white skin hidden underneath?

Beginning in the sixth century, Hitler's lecture rolled on till it arrived at the present day. (Here he pulled up short, without, of course, giving me an inkling of the sensational piece of history that he was going to make within a week.) Ostensibly the lecture was comprehensive, but I noticed that Hitler contrived never to mention Italy once. Hitler was, of course, then angling for Italy, who, by this date, had fallen out with Britain over her invasion of Ethiopia and was now in process of subjugating her African victim while Britain and the other states members of the League of Nations were flinching from the imposition on Italy of the oil sanction. In February 1936, Italy was too delicate a subject for Hitler to mention, and his avoidance of mentioning her was skilful. So, indeed, was the lecture as a whole. It lasted for two hours and a quarter, minus five minutes or so that were taken up,

at the end, by the one question that I was able to put, and by
Hitler's reply to it. For those two hours and a quarter, Hitler developed his theme with masterly coherence and lucidity. I cannot
think of any academic lecturer to whom I have ever listened who
could have spoken continuously for that length of time without
ever losing the thread of his argument. 'We did not know that
he knew all that' was the listening pundits' comment when, after
the audience was over, Hitler had again made the Nazi salute, and
had again quickly followed it up by a handshake, as he was
leaving the room. During the proceedings, I had been watching
the five German members of the audience out of the corner
of my eye. They had all been sitting demurely, with their
legs uncrossed and with their hands on their knees, like well-drilled
schoolboys listening to a lesson being delivered by a formidable master.

Most of the time, my eyes were following Hitler's hands. He
had beautiful hands. He used them to accompany his words; and
his gestures were eloquent, as well as graceful. His voice, too,
was, unexpectedly to me, agreeably human in its pitch and cadence
—human, that is, so long as he was not talking about Russia.
Whenever the word 'Russia' issued from Hitler's mouth, his
voice became raucous and its pitch rose to a hoarse shriek—the
shriek that had made one shudder when one had been listening
to him, on the wireless, delivering one of his inflammatory dema-
gogic speeches. I am sure that this was involuntary. The last thing
that Hitler will have wanted to do on this occasion will have been
to cancel the pleasant effect that he was making on me by re-
minding me of his other role. I believe that, whenever he thought
and spoke about Russia (and he could never keep off this torment-
ing subject for long), he genuinely went crazy. The intermittent
outbreaks of Russophobe raucousness that punctuated his lecture
to me reminded me of the reaction of a monkey who, in my
childhood, had been one of the entertainments at the London zoo.
Normally this monkey was placid; but, if you uttered the word
'policeman' in his hearing, he would immediately fly into a rage,
in which he would scream and gibber. The sore spot that had been
touched in that monkey's psyche by the word 'policeman' was

evidently the same that was now being touched in Hitler's psyche by the word 'Russia'.

When Hitler's 130-minute-long lecture had come to a close, he asked me whether there was any point that I would like to raise. I then said that what made us, in the countries to the west of Germany, anxious was the possibility that Hitler might be going to go to war with Russia. In a duel between Germany and Russia, I went on, we expected that Germany would be the winner. Indeed, we expected her victory to be so decisive that it would enable her to annex the Ukraine and the Urals, with their vast agricultural and mineral resources. In that event, Germany would shoot up to the stature of a super-power on the scale of the United States; and then we, Germany's western neighbours, would be overshadowed and dwarfed by this vastly expanded Third German Reich. We might find ourselves at its mercy, and this was a prospect that we did not relish.

Hitler's riposte was adroit. He began by saying that he appreciated the compliment that I had just paid him when I had assumed that Germany would be the victor in a Russo-German war. Would he want, as I had suggested that he might, to exploit a German victory over Russia by annexing the Ukraine and the Urals? 'Well, in the first place,' he said, 'I should not want to include these inferior people (*diese minderwertigen Leute*) in my Reich, and, in the second place, if I did annex the Ukraine and the Urals, I should have to keep six hundred thousand young Germans permanently in garrison there; and I have better uses than that for German youth. Anyway, if you do not like the prospect that you have outlined, won't you make some alternative suggestions about what Germany's future should be?'

Hitler had parried my question neatly. I had been trying to probe his ambitions, and I believed—and still believe—that my probe had been in the right direction. My suggestion that Hitler's ulterior objectives were the Ukraine and the Urals seems to me to have been confirmed by his assault on the Soviet Union in 1940—a wanton act that was to have so disastrous a sequel for Hitler and for Germany. At the time of my interview with Hitler, however, we were only in February 1936, and the date was still a week short of his reoccupation of the Rhineland. At this stage, Hitler had no intention of showing his hand; and, though his response to my challenge had not allayed my suspicions, it had also cleverly avoided giving me any additional grounds for them.

'Now,' said Berber to me, when, after my audience with Hitler was over, we had walked back to Berber's office—'now I am going to tell you why it was that Hitler saw you'; and, as he spoke, Berber pulled down from a shelf a copy of the Chatham House *Survey of International Affairs for 1934*, which was the latest volume in the series to have been published up to date. Opening it at a page that had a marker in it (it was p. 325), he pointed to a passage that ran as follows:

> The shockingness of these events of the 29th-30th June, 1934, in West-European eyes was indeed manifold. It was shocking to see the head of a state—even when he was the leader of a recently victorious revolutionary movement—shooting down his own former henchmen in the style of an American 'gangster'. . . .

Yes, now that Berber had reminded me, of course I remembered. That was what I had written about Hitler's savage liquidation of the S.A.; and, if, at the time, I had been writing the *Survey for 1934*, and not the *Survey for 1935*, as I then already was, I should not have had a word to alter in that denunciatory passage.

'Well, now,' Berber went on, 'I always buy the volumes of your *Survey* as they come out.' (As he spoke he pointed to a row of them.) 'It is part of my business to follow what is being written abroad about Germany under the present régime. Well, after I had conveyed the Law Society's invitation to you, and had had your acceptance of it, this volume of yours came off the press. Do you remember the publication date?' (I had forgotten that too, as well as the denunciatory passage.) 'Well, when I ran through the book and came to this page, I had a shock. The arrangements for your lecture were in my charge. I had already agreed the date with you, and it had been publicly announced. It was too late now to call the lecture off without creating an incident. I was in a dangerous position. I was the officer directly responsible for your having been invited, and now you had published this about Hitler. What

should I do? Should I go to my superiors and make a clean breast
of it? Or should I keep silence, in the hope that this offensive
passage would not come to the attention of anyone in the régime
except myself? I decided to say nothing. So far as I was aware, I
was the only person in the régime who studied your *Survey*
regularly. If I keep quiet, I said to myself, it is a thousand chances
to one that Toynbee's sally against Hitler will be overlooked by
everybody who might want to have my blood, on account of it,
if the passage became known to anyone else in the régime.'

'Well, I was unlucky,' Berber went on. 'As it happened, the
Swiss Government had been having trouble with our Government over criticisms of our régime that had been appearing in
the Swiss press. The Swiss authorities had been anxious to ease
the friction that had arisen over this between them and us; so
they had secured the passage of a law forbidding the Swiss press,
for the future, to publish provocative criticisms of foreign governments. The Swiss newspapermen had been furious at being
muzzled; they had scrutinized the law under a microscope in
search of loopholes in it; and they had found that the draftsman
had forgotten to stipulate that they must not quote provocative
criticisms that had appeared in print abroad. They had therefore
started to make use of this freedom, of which they had not been
deprived, to criticize the Nazi by proxy; and, of course, when
your volume appeared, this passage in it was grist to their mill.
They translated it *verbatim*, with acrid comments. "Look," they
wrote, "even in that flunkeyish old monarchy England people are
free to publish things like this about Hitler; and now, in our free
democratic republic, we have been forbidden to. Isn't this
scandalous?" '

I verified Berber's account of the Swiss press's use of my
volume when I got back to Chatham House. There was a clutch
of cuttings, under this head, in our press archives. Berber had
received a corresponding clutch from his own press-cutting
organization, and, when he had glanced through it, he had been
horrified; for he knew that, though he might be the only person
in the régime who read my *Survey*, there were a number who read
the Swiss press; and, sure enough, within the next few hours, he

was rung up, on the telephone, by an enraged Nazi potentate. 'You have invited this Englishman to speak here,' the potentate shouted at Berber on the line, 'and now just listen to what this Englishman has published about the Führer.'

At this Berber had thought that he was sunk, but he had one last resource. He was one of the few employees of the régime who were entitled to ask Hitler to grant them a personal interview. Berber had immediately asked for one, had obtained an appointment, and had come to Hitler with my volume in his hand. 'Mein Führer,' he had said, 'I have a confession to make to you and your pardon to ask. I have invited an Englishman to give a lecture here, and, since this was fixed, he has published something unpleasant about you. I couldn't know beforehand that he was going to do that, but I am most heartily sorry that this should have happened.' 'Translate what the Englishman has written about me,' Hitler had said, and Berber had translated the offending passage. 'That isn't fair,' Hitler had commented. 'The American gangsters do it for money, and I did not do it for money. Arrange for me to see the Englishman when he arrives.' Berber had escaped with his life, and I had been rewarded for my denunciation of Hitler by now being booked for an interview with him.

How had Hitler's mind worked? The key, I think, is the flair that he had for public relations—a gift of his that comes out in Hans Dieckhoff's story, recounted later in the present chapter. 'This Englishman,' I think Hitler had rapidly reflected, 'this Englishman produces a *Survey of International Affairs* every year. It is not at present in my power to stop him. Before I am in a position to stop him by putting pressure on his Government, he may have produced half a dozen more of these volumes, and it is possible that they may have some effect on public opinion in the English-speaking countries. It is important, if my policy is to work out according to plan, that the British and the Americans should not become more hostile to me than can be helped. Perhaps, if this Englishman meets me, I shall be able to change his picture of me; and then perhaps he will not write about me so offensively again. Yes, it will be worth my while to give him two hours and a quarter of my time on the chance of that.'

The day following the date of my audience with Hitler was the appointed date for my lecture to the Nazi Law Society. I delivered the lecture to them. (I spoke in English, with one passage in German to take them by surprise. The Aussenamt had circulated a German translation of the whole lecture in advance.) Afterwards, I had lunch with my audience in the Berlin Rathaus. In my lecture I had gone out of my way to tease the audience by quoting St. Paul. (The Nazi had no use for any of the Christian worthies, and I knew that St. Paul was the apostle whom they detested the most.) In the banqueting hall at the Rathaus, high up above the welter of Nazi uniforms, armlets, and flags, I spied, still hanging there, a large picture of Bismarck springing forward, with hands held out in a welcoming gesture, to greet Disraeli on Dizzy's arrival at the Berlin Conference of 1878. It was a period piece of the Second German Reich. 'What an unexpected oversight,' I said to my Nazi table-companions. 'You have left that picture of a Jew in this conspicuous public place.' The Nazi were abashed. 'And do you remember what Bismarck said about Disraeli?' I asked. 'No, we don't.' 'Well, what he said was: "*Der alte Jüde, das ist der Mann.*" . . . Yes, I did say "Bismarck"; you did not mis-hear me; those words are his.' Bismarck could not now be made to suffer for his tribute to Disraeli; but I wonder how long the picture in the Rathaus survived my exposure of its flamboyant philojudaism.

That evening, I was to have supper with a high-up Nazi propaganda official (I forget, now, which of them it was) in order to be shown a film of the latest Nüremberg rally. The film took three hours to reel off; for those three hours it made me bristle; the propaganda man would have been rueful if he had known what high-powered anti-Nazi propaganda treatment he was unintentionally inflicting on me; but I do not think he had any suspicion that his propaganda-engine had gone into reverse. As I was leaving, my host said: 'I hear that you saw the Führer yesterday.' 'Yes, he was good enough to see me,' I answered. 'And who else was there?' 'Oh! Herr von Ribbentrop and Baron Neurath and Herr Dieckhoff and, of course, Dr. Schmidt—oh yes, and Herr Berber too'; and with that I left, without realizing, at the time, that this conversation had any significance.

Meanwhile, between lunchtime and suppertime on that same day, Fritz Berber had been making an apology to me. 'I didn't attend your lecture yesterday,' he said. 'This was not my fault. It was the doing of that man with whom you are going to have supper tonight. When that man heard that you were going to have an audience with Hitler, he concluded that the sponsoring of your lecture was an asset, so he snatched the arrangements out of my hands (he is much more powerful than I am), and then he sent me a third-class ticket for the gallery. If I had used that ticket, I should have been publicly humiliated—which was, no doubt, what that man intended.' 'Forget about it,' I had answered, 'we can be friends without having to attend each other's lectures.'

Next day, when I called on Berber in his office, he said to me: 'This morning an extraordinary thing happened, which I can't explain. Before I was out of bed, I was called upon by a very tall man in a very grand uniform, carrying a great bouquet of flowers and a letter from that man with whom you had supper last night—he was the man, you remember, who had snatched the sponsorship of your lecture away from me. The letter was in the man's own hand. "By a most inexplicable and unfortunate mistake", the letter said, "my office sent you a third-class ticket for Herr Toynbee's lecture. We had, of course, reserved a first-class seat for you, in the front row. Do please accept this letter as my most sincere apology, and accept these flowers too, as a token that you bear me no ill-will for a slip which must have seemed to you like a deliberate slight." I can't make it out,' Berber said. 'This just doesn't fit with that man's previous behaviour.'

I burst out laughing. 'Now, for once, the tables are turned,' I said. 'There is something that puzzles you which I can explain. As I was leaving that man's house last night, he asked me who had been present at my interview with Hitler, and I told him— mentioning your name with the rest, of course. Evidently this gave our man a shock. "Berber there! So he is in the inner circle! He is one of those who stand next to the throne! Suppose that, next time he is at the Führer's elbow, he were to ask the

Führer for my head on a charger. Perhaps the Führer would give
the word, and then my head would fall. I must do what I can to
appease Berber before he has time to get to his office tomorrow
morning. If once he gets to work on ruining me, I may be lost." '
Berber agreed that I had cleared up that morning's mystery
completely. We were both laughing now.

Hans Dieckhoff—one of the five German dignitaries who had
been present at my interview with Hitler—was one of my German
friends for whom I felt a particular esteem and affection. On each
of my visits to Berlin, I used to have a talk with him at his office,
and he and his wife used to invite me to their house in Dahlem.

Hans Dieckhoff was a shrewd judge of international affairs.
For example, during this visit of mine in February 1936 he had
told me (making his point as courteously as he could) that he
thought that the British people had found a psychologically
adequate vent for their indignation at Italy's attack on Ethiopia
when they had compelled their government to reject the Hoare-
Laval plan and had forced Sir Samuel Hoare himself to resign.
'Now that they have found their scapegoat in Hoare,' Dieckhoff
said to me, 'I think we shall find that they will take no further
action. Ethiopia's fate is going to be something far worse than the
Hoare-Laval proposals that raised such a storm in Britain. If those
proposals had been submitted to Mussolini and had been accepted
by him, Ethiopia would have got off with the loss of some slices
of her territory. This loss would have been painful, since the
severed slices would have been large; but, at this price, the rump
of Ethiopia would have survived as a nominally independent
state. As things are now, I think we are going to witness the total
conquest and annexation of Ethiopia by Mussolini, and I predict
that this is not going to arouse the British people to take any
further action. You have found a whipping-boy for Mussolini in
Hoare. Now that you have relieved your feelings at Hoare's
expense, you will not feel any impulse to save Ethiopia by having
a showdown with Mussolini.' Within the next few weeks the
miserable dénouement demonstrated that, if Dieckhoff had not
been a diplomatist, he could have been a psycho-analyst.

Like Berber, Dieckhoff was frank in talking to me about the

Nazi régime. At some date during the last phase of the inter-war period—it was after the German military reoccupation of the Rhineland—Dieckhoff told me the story of an experience of his in order to bring home to me the dangerousness of the situation that we had now reached.

During the weeks immediately following the reoccupation, Dieckhoff had been constantly travelling, with Ribbentrop, to and fro between Berlin and London, working—and this, in the end, successfully—to harvest for Germany the profits of Hitler's latest and, so far, his most risky, *coup* without bringing on, immediately, the war for which Hitler would not be ready till he had built the Siegfried Line, over against the Maginot Line, along the Franco-German frontier. At the most critical stage of these talks in London, it had been arranged that, on a certain day, Ribbentrop and Dieckhoff should fly, in the evening, from London to Bad Godesberg on the Rhine, to report to Hitler on the outcome of their crucial day's work in England. Bad Godesberg was to be the meeting-place, because Hitler's time-table was to bring him there that evening from Düsseldorf, where he was due to make a speech earlier in the day. The two negotiators and Hitler arrived in Bad Godesberg at the appointed time (this was just not too late for a late dinner), and they met each other there in a room in Hitler's favourite hotel. 'Now we shall be able to make our report to him,' Dieckhoff and Ribbentrop were thinking, 'and then we shall have dinner.' (Their day had been a particularly arduous and anxious one; they had not dined yet; and they were feeling the strain.)

Instead of inquiring about London, however, Hitler began to talk about Düsseldorf. He ought to have paid this visit to Düsseldorf long before, he said. He had weak-mindedly put the visit off, because he had been conscious that he was not completely in tune with local feeling; and, after he had screwed himself up, at last, to make the effort, he had still felt nervous. He had therefore arranged in advance that the ten front rows of seats in the auditorium should be filled exclusively with industrial workers, with whom he would be feeling the least ill at ease. All the same, he had been uneasy for the first ten minutes of his talk; but then he had perceived, from the look in the audience's eyes, that he was saying what they were feeling; and, after that, it had been all right. Hitler had gone minutely into technical details of a professional speaker's art. When he had finished at last, they thought: 'Well, now that he has got all that off his chest, he will ask us to tell him what happened today in London.' Just at that moment, however, the Director of the opera at Cologne was shown in. Hitler had made an appointment with him, too, to come to Bad Godesberg that evening to meet him. When the Director appeared, Hitler's face lighted up; he and the Director entered on an animated discussion with each other about ways and means of raising the standard of performance in the Cologne opera-house; this duologue took still more time than had been taken by Hitler's account of his own day's work at Düsseldorf.

Eventually, after Hitler and the Director had thrashed things out thoroughly, the Director took his leave; and then Hitler turned to Dieckhoff and Ribbentrop with an inquiring look. 'You have been somewhere abroad today, haven't you, on some foreign business?' 'Yes, we have.' 'Well, tell me about it.' They did, and their report naturally took some time too, though not so long as either of the first two acts of that evening's comedy. All the same, by the time they had finished, it was nearly 3.00 a.m. 'Have you had dinner yet?' Hitler then asked them paternally. 'No?' Thereupon Hitler rang the bell, and instantly there arrived a three-course dinner for them and, for Hitler, an apple and a glass of water. After they had eaten and drunk their respective portions, they all three went to bed.

'The point of this story', Dieckhoff wound up, 'is that it tells you what is Hitler's order of priorities. First and foremost, Hitler is a demagogue. His gift for moving audiences is the key to his power, so his relation with his public is his lifeline. That is why he had to tell us all about his speech at Düsseldorf before he could give his mind to any other business, and here you have his first priority. His second? Well, he is a demagogue with an artistic temperament; and, as he is an Austrian, an interest in art is in his cultural tradition. This gives him relaxation and refreshment too; so that is why he kept us waiting while he talked, first, to the

Director of the Cologne opera; and here you have his second priority. Foreign affairs? Third priority, and that is dangerous,' Dieckhoff concluded. He had made his point.

Poor Hans Dieckhoff! His career under the Nazi was a creeping tragedy. His ability was an asset for the régime which the Nazi did not want to lose; but Dieckhoff was an upright, honourable man; he was liberal-minded and humane-minded too; and his political shrewdness made him aware, far in advance, of the doom towards which Hitler was leading Germany—'with the unfalter-ingness of a sleep-walker', as Hitler himself once put it in an illu-minating flash of self-analysis. More than once, Dieckhoff dis-cussed with me—thinking aloud—whether the time might not be approaching when he had better resign; but, each time, the balance in his mind was tipped in favour of his hanging on by the thought that, if he did resign, the Nazis would be sure to give him a successor who would help to hurry Germany towards catastrophe still faster than Hitler's present pace. After all, the permanent-secretaryship of the Aussenamt was an important and responsible post; and the character of its occupant could not fail to make an appreciable difference to the way in which Germany's foreign relations would develop.

We are all of us less good at psycho-analysing ourselves than at practising the art on other people. I am sure that Dieckhoff sincerely believed that, in deciding, each time, to stay on, he was choosing the lesser evil; and the Nazi's handling of him made it difficult for him ever to meet the moment of truth. The Nazi handled Dieckhoff with a diabolically skilful finesse. They never let the situation arise in which his scruples would have come into headlong collision with their criminality. No issue that arose between him and them ever seemed big enough to warrant his breaking with them just over that; and, each time that he condoned some Nazi act of which he disapproved, he was com-promising himself a little more deeply, till, in the end, he was implicated inextricably. If you feel inclined to pass a censorious judgement on a good and able man who let himself be caught in this way, pause first to ask yourself two questions: Have you ever been in Dieckhoff's position yourself? And, if you have not, are

you sure that you yourself would have done better than Dieckhoff
did in wrestling with such an agonizing ethical problem?

The longer that Dieckhoff did stay on with the Nazi, the more
eager he and his wife naturally became to find grounds for thinking not so badly of the régime; and here chance played into the
Nazi's hands. The Dieckhoffs had an only child, to whom they
were devoted. Their reason for living at Dahlem was that there was
a school there which seemed to them to be just the right one for
her. The time then came when she would have to be enrolled in the
Hitler Mädels, and her parents approached this date with dread.
What kind of girls would their child meet in the local Hitler
Mädels troop, and what kind of woman would be in command
of them? They had been free to choose the child's school, but the
personnel of her Hitler Mädels troop was entirely beyond their
control. And then, when the child was enrolled, things all turned
out better than they had dared to hope. It was clearly doing their
daughter good to have to rub shoulders with other girls of all
kinds. It did for her something that her carefully selected school
had not done. It rubbed the corners off the characteristic idio-
syncrasies of an only child. Moreover, the child's troop-leader
turned out not to be a Nazi doctrinaire or fanatic. She was the
kind of person who would have been a success in a corresponding
post in the British or American Girl Guides. In their eagerness to
think well of the Nazi régime, the Dieckhoffs would have clutched
at a straw, and now chance had given them a life-belt. I believe
that their daughter's happy experience in the Hitler Mädels had a
decisive influence on their attitude to the régime as a whole, and,
if it did, that is not surprising; it is only human. Their child's
welfare was, for them, the most important thing in their lives, and,
contrary to expectation, the child's enrolment in the Hitler
Mädels had been the making of her. An irrational inference from
one child's stroke of good luck in her experience of the Hitler
Mädels to a blessing on the whole Hitlerian régime? A palpable
case of wishful thinking? Maybe; but, if you are moved to con-
demn the Dieckhoffs for this, can you swear that you are entitled to
cast the first stone?

Hans Dieckhoff's tragic story had its inevitable tragic ending.

At a date when the Second World War was fast looming up, he was appointed ambassador in Washington; and this was, I suppose, technically the culmination of his official career. At that time there could be no more important post for a German diplomat to hold. Some of Dieckhoff's dispatches from Washington are to be found in the collection of German diplomatic documents that was published, after the war, by the victorious Allied and Associated Powers. Dieckhoff's published dispatches testify that he warned his principals, frankly, that, if there were to be another world war, they must reckon with the likelihood that, sooner or later, the United States would intervene on the anti-German side, as she had done in 1917. This was a courageous fulfilment of an ambassador's professional duty. Presumably Ribbentrop paid no heed; and I should be surprised if Dieckhoff's dispatches ever came under Hitler's eye. Hitler did, however, pay attention when the pogrom perpetrated in the Third Reich in November 1938 provoked a wave of indignation in the United States. In Hitler's fantastic judgement, Dieckhoff ought to have prevented that; the ambassador had failed disgracefully to do his duty; so Hitler broke him—as if Dieckhoff could have cajoled the American people into putting up with the most outrageous exhibition, up to date, of Nazi anti-Semitism.

I am glad to be able to change to a lighter note. At Bonn in carnival-time, in one of the years between the reoccupation of the Rhineland and the outbreak of war, I was introduced to the Director of the Cologne opera whom Hitler had received, out of his turn in the queue, on that evening in 1936 on which Dieckhoff and Ribbentrop had been waiting on their master. 'I have a responsibility,' the Director said to me. I pricked up my ears. 'Well, not long after I had been appointed to my present post, a younger man asked me to give him a trial as a singer. After three weeks, I said to him: "Herr Göbbels, you will never make a success of this. My advice to you is: Go away and try your hand at being a journalist." Well, you see!'

The Nazi chapter of Germany's history is no less appalling in retrospect than it was when it was unfolding itself. From what depths in the human psyche did this lava-flow of utter evil erupt? And, when it had erupted, how did a band of wicked men succeed in capturing one of the great nations of the Western World—a nation which, by that time, had been professing Christianity for from eleven hundred to nearly fifteen hundred years, reckoning back, behind the forcible conversion of the continental Saxons, to the voluntary conversion of the Salian Franks? How did the Nazi succeed in mobilizing, to serve their criminal purposes, the whole of Germany's material and human resources? If the Christian German people could succumb to Hitler in the twentieth century of the Christian Era, what other people in the world—Christian, Muslim, Jewish, Buddhist, or Hindu—could now feel sure that it might not one day go this German way? The catastrophe that liquidated Hitler's 'Thousand-years' Reich' before the end of the twelfth year of its existence has not deterred fanatics in other countries from trying, since then, to start movements on the Nazi pattern. There must be a vein of Original Sin in human nature everywhere to which Hitlerism makes a strong appeal. The moral is that civilization is nowhere and never secure. It is a thin cake of custom overlying a molten mass of wickedness that is always boiling up for an opportunity to burst out. Civilization cannot ever be taken for granted. Its price is eternal vigilance and ceaseless spiritual effort.

Why did the German people lend themselves to Hitler so tamely? Why were they so pliant an instrument in his hands? Well, at all times and places, I suppose, a majority of the people flinches from taking the consequences of resisting militant evil. What can be said on the German people's behalf is that, under the Nazi yoke, they did produce, not a whole 'noble army' of martyrs, but at least a noble band of them. I think, for instance, of two friends of mine, Kuenzer and Bernstorff.

Hitler's take-over found Bernstorff posted at the German Embassy in London as counsellor there. Bernstorff never re-frained from saying in public what he felt about the Nazi régime, and he paid for his outspokenness by being dismissed, being imprisoned, and finally being put to death. The counsellor was not the only person on that embassy's staff in Nazi-time who had the courage to speak his mind. At some date at which Ribbentrop had not yet become German ambassador to the Court of St. James's, but was already Hitler's ambassador at large, I read in *The Times* one morning that he had just arrived in London. In Berlin, not long before, Ribbentrop had taken some trouble on my account, and he had also been hospitable to me. (The nurse-maids and perambulators in his suburban house outside Berlin had reminded me of scenes in my childhood in Kensington Gardens when I used to be wheeled there in my own pram towards the end of the Victorian Age. Ribbentrop's private domesticity was weirdly incongruous with the criminality of his public activities and with his eventual fate, which was, in my judgement, deserved.)

I wanted now to return Ribbentrop's courtesy; so, at lunchtime that day, I walked over from Chatham House to the German Embassy, which was then in Carlton House Terrace, in the first house to the west of the Duke of York's steps. I rang the bell; a grave-faced butler opened the door; and I offered him my card, saying: 'I should like, if I may, to leave this here for Herr von Ribbentrop.' 'We do not know anything about him here, sir,' the butler replied in an acid tone of voice. 'But I read in *The Times* this morning that he is in London as the Reichskanzler's envoy extraordinary.' 'I do not know anything about that, sir.' I must have looked non-plussed, and the butler must have been kind-hearted; for he now relented. 'Well, sir, you might perhaps try there'—and he pointed, up Lower Regent Street, towards the Carlton Hotel. I did try there, and it was impossible to miss. I found that Ribbentrop had taken an entire floor of the hotel for himself and his numerous itinerant staff. I should hardly think that the butler paid for his outspokenness with his life, as poor Bernstorff did. But I should also hardly think that he can have retained his job at the embassy for very long after Ribbentrop had installed himself there, as he did, not long afterwards. I do hope that the dauntless butler lived to be re-instated when, years afterwards, the present Republic of West Germany was constituted and there was a German embassy in London once again.

23
Sri Jawaharlal Nehru

My first meeting with Pandit Nehru was in London, at some date in the nineteen-thirties. He had just come out of prison in India (one of his many terms of imprisonment at the hands of the British authorities), and, characteristically, he had come to London for a short holiday before he would resume, in India, the non-violent non-co-operation with the British régime that was certain to result, before long, in his being sent to a British prison again. While Mr. Nehru was in London on this brief visit, my wife and I were asked to lunch, to meet him, by an English lady who was a friend of his and ours.

We arrived for lunch to find Mr. Nehru already there. He was discussing the Indian political situation with our hostess, and, as was to be expected, the line that he was taking was stiff—indeed, intransigent. After a minute or two the conversation was interrupted by the arrival of another guest. He was a British general, and, when he caught sight of Mr. Nehru, his jaw dropped and he halted on the threshold of the room as if he had half a mind to back out and beat a retreat. We learnt afterwards that this general had been involved, in some way, in sending Mr. Nehru to the British prison in India from which he had just been released; and our hostess's invitation to him to meet Mr. Nehru now presented the same kind of puzzle as Madame Chiang's cook's choice of pork as the dish to serve up to the Chinese Muslim General Ma. Had our hostess invited this British general out of mischief, to see what would happen when she re-confronted him with Mr. Nehru? Or had she just had a vague recollection that Mr. Nehru and the general had recently had something to do with each other? Had she light-heartedly assumed that their association had been a pleasant one and that they would be glad to meet each other again? We never discovered the answer to this question, but the answer to it is not material to the story. The interesting question is not whether our hostess's *gaffe* had been unintentional or deliberate; the interesting question at the moment was how Mr. Nehru was going to take it.

During those seconds for which the general was hesitating in the doorway, I was looking at Mr. Nehru's face. Was it going to turn grim? Was Mr. Nehru perhaps going to refuse to stay in the same room with a man who was obviously feeling that Mr. Nehru had some good cause for being angry with him? The interrupted conversation on the sore subject of Indian politics had left a slightly severe expression on Mr. Nehru's countenance. But, before the general had had time to pull himself together and to advance, Mr. Nehru's countenance relaxed and his eyes began to twinkle. It was clear now that his reaction to the situation that our hostess had created for him and the general was going to be amusement, not hostility. If anyone was going to be embarrassed, it would not be Mr. Nehru. When the general admitted previous acquaintance with his fellow-guest, his greeting to Mr. Nehru was ultra-polite, and Mr. Nehru swiftly exploited the comedy. His teasing reminders of the circumstances in which the general and he had last met drove the general to go to ever greater lengths of appeasement. Mr. Nehru had the general on the run. The general was not enjoying the encounter, but Mr. Nehru was.

This incident may sound trivial, but, to my mind, it was not. It was not just amusing; it was revealing too; and its revelation of Mr. Nehru's character made a deep impression on me. Here was a man who was fighting, with all his might, a political battle in a cause that he (and I too) believed to be just. He had recently been made to suffer personally for his political stand, and this not for the first time. Yet he had come out of his latest term of British imprisonment without any animus either against the British people collectively or against the particular representatives of the British régime in India who had been involved in the most recent of the penal measures that had been taken against him. In this drawing-room in a house in London, I was witnessing an exhibition of the Mahatma Gandhi's spirit. Here was non-violent non-co-operation in action. Resist foreign political domination with all your might, but resist it without bloodshed and also without animus. This was a directive that made an almost superhuman demand on human nature. Could any human being really live up to it? Well, I was in the presence of one who could and did.

My next meeting with Pandit Nehru was in very different circumstances. It was not in London; it was in Delhi. The date was the last week of February 1957; and Mr. Nehru was now not a recently-released prisoner; he was Prime Minister of India, and, by this time, he had been in office for little less than ten years. On this occasion it was my turn to be embarrassed at meeting him. I was on my way from the Ashoka Hotel via Shahjehanabad and the Old Civil Lines to the University, where I was to receive an honorary degree. I had been told, to my surprise and pleasure, that the Prime Minister was going to be present. I was now already very late for my appointment, and it was bad enough to be keeping the university authorities waiting; but I was keeping the Prime Minister waiting too; and prime ministers have no time to waste. The Ashoka Hotel and the University are at opposite extremities of the wide area over which the seven Delhis are spread. In most of the Delhis the traffic is as thick nowadays as it is in the world's other great cities. Ox-carts are more effective obstacles to progress than cars; and ox-carts abound in the narrow streets of Shah Jehan's walled city, which cannot be by-passed. I was getting later and later for my appointment. Could I hope that Mr. Nehru would treat me as leniently as he had treated that general, some twenty years back? Suddenly I saw a figure in white running towards our car and signalling to us the direction that we were to take. It was Mr. Nehru himself, and he was not angry this time either, but he had felt concerned to help us on our way, so he had slipped out of the university building, to the consternation of his security men, and he was now roaming the streets in search of us. So far from holding it against us that we had involuntarily kept him waiting, he asked us to dinner. It was a small family party in his home, which was, of course, particularly agreeable for us.

Once again, Mr. Nehru had impressed me; and, this time, what I had found particularly impressive in him was his immunity from a prime minister's occupational maladies. To be unsoured by imprisonment is, I imagine, less difficult than to be unspoiled by office. (I am guessing; I have had no personal experience of either of these two searching tests of character.) By now, Mr. Nehru had, as I have noted, been Prime Minister for nearly ten years; yet here he was, still human and still buoyant. A human spontaneity and a youthful buoyancy were the impressions of him that I carried away with me this time.

My third and last meeting with Mr. Nehru was in February, 1960. I was now back in New Delhi to give the second of the Maulânâ Azad memorial lectures, and, once again, Mr. Nehru found time to take part in an academic function. Maulânâ Azad, in whose memory the lectureship had been founded, had been a theologian, learned in the Islamic religious law. At the same time he had been an active and prominent Indian nationalist—active and prominent enough to see the inside of British prisons, like Pandit Nehru and the Mahatma Gandhi and large numbers of these leaders' comrades. When Mr. Jinnah had come out in favour of partition, Maulânâ Azad had opted for India, not for Pakistan. He had been independent India's first minister of education; and his Indian compatriots had valued and honoured him—primarily for what he was, but also for what he symbolized. Maulânâ Azad was an eminent personality, and, besides being that, he stood for Gandhi's and Nehru's ideal of a secular Indian state in which members of the Muslim minority were to have equal rights with their Hindu fellow-citizens.

Gandhi's and Nehru's India was a tolerant India. In a country in which the great majority of the population was Hindu, the first minister of education had been a Muslim. In a lectureship that had been founded in memory of an Indian nationalist leader, the second lecturer in the series was an Englishman. The inaugural course of Maulânâ Azad lectures had been given by Mr. Nehru himself. I started my first lecture in my following course by drawing attention to the remarkable facts. I was the second lecturer in a series founded in memory of an Indian whom my countrymen had put in prison; my predecessor in the series had also been put in prison by the British; yet here I was, speaking to this Indian audience by invitation from an Indian committee.

My last meeting with Mr. Nehru before this one had left me with a feeling that this man was invulnerable and invincible. By then, he had stood up already to ten years of unremitting political hard labour, with no more spells of enforced inactivity in prison to ease the strain. He appeared to have defeated time. His accumulating years of office had failed to weigh him down. Only three years had passed since then, but, this time, I found a sad change in him. What time had been unable to do to him had been done to him by China. I had not reckoned with China; and I believe Mr. Nehru had not reckoned with China either.

In February 1960 the conflict between India and China was not yet approaching its crisis, but already the Chinese screw was turning hard on India, and hardest on the man who was carrying, on a single pair of human shoulders, so much more of his country's burden than even prime ministers are usually required to bear. I had been notified that an appointment had been made for me to call on the Prime Minister in his office on the morning of 23 February, and I had deprecated this. Thanks to his presence on 21 February at the first of my lectures, I had already had the opportunity of exchanging a few words with him, then. The pressure on him was intolerable; I did not want to be responsible for increasing it by piling on an unnecessary extra chore. However, I was assured that my appointment with the Prime Minister had been made at his express wish; so I did not refuse this welcome opportunity of meeting him again; but I wanted to spare him as much as I could, so I had resolved not to say anything about China. I soon found that this was no good; Mr. Nehru could not talk of anything else. China had proved too much for him.

It is human to rebel against our human nature's limitations—against death, against defeat, and against weariness—and it is therefore human also to exult when one meets a human being who seems to have conquered Fate. The hero's victory is not his alone; it is a common victory for mankind. Alas! Our exultation is dearly bought. Its price is the tragic spectacle of seeing Fate triumph after all. 'There is no armour against Fate', and, early or late, all human beings have to stoop to their adversary. At this last meeting of mine with Mr. Nehru, I found his once buoyant spirit bowed down. Nehru, too, had been unable to defy Fate; his apparent victory had been an illusion; the adversary had only been biding his time for the delivery of one of his most telling strokes. When Fate overthrows, in the end, a man of more than ordinary spiritual stature, Fate is teaching us all a lesson and is calling us all to heel.

Since his death, Jawaharlal Nehru has been suffering the same treatment as T. E. Lawrence. The debunkers have been busy with him. Yet, after the vultures have finished their scavenging work, Nehru, too, will still be the great man that he was—great, though human; human, so lovable.

24
Lord Samuel

One morning in 1909 or 1910, I was looking out of my window in the front quad at Balliol when a man stepped out of the entrance of the next staircase, on which there was one of the college guest-rooms. His brisk step and his black hair together caught my attention, and I asked my scout, who was laying my breakfast, whether he could tell me who that was. 'Oh, that is Mr. Samuel,' was his answer, 'the Postmaster-General, you know. He is in college for that dinner that there was here last night. He is young, isn't he, to be in the Government. It is a distinction for the college.'

I could see that Mr. Samuel was young—young, at least, for a cabinet minister. He must then have been, I suppose, just under forty, and I myself was then just past the age at which all people over thirty-five look indistinguishably old. I did not get to know Lord Samuel well till after the beginning of the Second World War, when he was not far short of being as old as I am now. When I saw him, as I did fairly often, in the last stage of his unusually long life, I used to recall my glimpse, in Balliol, of the still young cabinet minister.

My first personal meeting with Lord Samuel was after the First World War. It was at an informal conference in his house in Porchester Terrace. He had been appointed High Commissioner for Palestine—the first British high commissioner under the mandate—and he had invited a group of people who had been concerned in one way or another with the Middle East to have a talk with him about the present situation there and about the prospects. Lord Samuel was open-minded, discerning, free from self-conceit, so he was willing and able to learn much from such consultations. I was struck by the way in which he handled this one, and I was not surprised to see him afterwards carry out his difficult mission successfully. In picking him out for the post, the Government had made an excellent choice. The appointment of a Jew was reassuring for the Zionists; the appointment of a just man was a guarantee for the Arabs. If anyone could have squared Palestine's Balfourian circle, it would, I think, have been Lord Samuel; and I should guess that it was largely thanks to the fair start that he did give to the mandatory régime in Palestine that Britain did not begin to run into serious trouble there till 1929, four years after the end of Lord Samuel's term of office, whereas France's serious troubles next door, in Syria, began as early as 1925.

Lord Samuel was perhaps the justest-minded man whom I have known. If I had been in search of an impartial arbitrator for a dispute to which I was a party, he would have been my first choice. I could have felt confident that, whether he decided in my favour or decided against me, his decision would be fair.

The salient feature in his character was his integrity; the next most striking feature was his common sense. The two factions of the fractured Liberal Party found in him a conciliator on whose rectitude and reasonableness both sides could rely.

Herbert Samuel's family were, I suppose, like Alfred Zimmern's, fairly recent arrivals in England from the Continent, but his roots in English soil had gone deep. After he had turned ninety, he once told me that, since he was six months old, he had always had a home in London within five minutes' walk of Kensington Gardens; and this struck an answering chord in me, since I had lived within ten minutes' walk of the Gardens at the perambulator stage and had been wheeled into them twice a day, and this sometimes down Porchester Terrace, which was Lord Samuel's all but lifelong street. In his last years, his legs could no longer carry him even that five minutes' walking-distance, and this was tantalizing for him. (The older one grows, the more one values one's earliest associations.) However, he provided himself with an improvised substitute. Round the corner from his house, within walking-distance for him still, there was a garage whose owner had just re-modelled it, and his new design had left a strip of unused space between the garage wall and the road. Lord Samuel persuaded the owner to let him turn this strip into a miniature public garden. He placed benches there and planted flowers, and he used to sit there among other old people who had also been attracted to this restful spot.

Balliol, where Lord Samuel had been an undergraduate and where I first saw him, had always meant a great deal to him. He had taken philosophy and Liberalism as much in earnest there as I had taken Greek and Latin. He was faithful to philosophy, as well as to Liberalism, for the rest of his life.

I have mentioned his fair-mindedness and his common sense. His third signal virtue was, I should say, his stoicism. This came out strongly in his old age, which was the stage of his life at which I saw the most of him and knew him the best. One of the trials of old age for a human being is that his various faculties may fall out of step with each other at different rates. Few people who live to a high old age are as fortunate as Lord Bryce, who kept both his mental and his physical vigour to the last. The most melancholy fate is to lose one's wits while remaining still physically alive (though this may be more painful for spectators than it is for the victim). Lord Samuel's mind, like Lord Bryce's, never lost its clarity, but Lord Samuel had to bear physical infirmities. His hearing began to fail, as well as his walking powers. But the worst loss of all, if one lives long without losing one's wits, is one's bereavement of other human beings whom one has outlived, but with whose lives one's own life is bound up. This most grievous loss of all overtook Lord Samuel at Lady Samuel's death. Lord Samuel was too clear-sighted and too straightforward-minded to be insensible to his troubles, or to wish to be, but he could, and did, bear his troubles with admirable fortitude. His spirit never closed in on itself. Till his death, he retained his lifelong interest in human affairs, and his lifelong concern for their betterment. If one ends like that, one has indeed done well.

Index